SANTA ANNA

The Napoleon of the West

BY

FRANK C. HANIGHEN

92 S

ILLUSTRATED

COWARD-McCANN, INC.

NEW YORK

PRINTED IN THE UNITED STATES OF AMERICA

ACKNOWLEDGMENTS

I wish to record my profound gratitude to Dr. Carlos E. Castañeda, Latin-American librarian of the University of Texas, whose help was indispensable in gathering material for this book ; to Professors Arthur W. Hackett, J. R. Spell, W. P. Webb and Dr. Hancock of the same institution for advice and guidance ; to Dr. E. W. Winkler, Mrs. Mattie Austin Hatcher, Miss Winnie Allen and Mr. Richard Burrell of the Library of the University of Texas, for their kind cooperation ; to Mrs. Lota Spell, Mr. Gilbert Doane, Miss Edith Tobitt, Mr. Frank Weitenkampf, Mr. Thomas Streeter, Mr. Robert McNeill Bland, Mrs. Gertrude Price, and Dr. Mariano Cuevas for assistance in my research.

To

My Parents

CONTENTS

LIST OF ILLUSTRATIONS

~~~~~~~~~~~~~~~~~~~~~~~~~~~~~~~~~~~

SANTA ANNA
The Napoleon of the West

PROLOGUE

40206

DESPICABLE YANQUIS

TEXAS is undeniably hot in summer and the heat
was particularly cruel that August day in 1813 as
the Spanish army plodded over the desolate and
sun-afflicted plains north of Laredo. There were no villages to give them rest and refreshment, not even a ranch ;
naught but dusty plain and harassing patches of chaparral.
Yet their leader, Arredondo, noted that they marched with
gusto and enthusiasm, that they displayed surprising confidence and fortitude in view of the weather and the battle
which they anticipated.

A few days before they had stopped at Cañada de
Caballos where they practised war-games and prepared
military stratagems to crush the enemy. There they were
joined by a small detachment of Spaniards who had retreated from San Antonio and who brought news about
the nature and strength of their opponents. A miserable
lot, it was learned, and spirits mounted as Arredondo described these adversaries as "perfidious enemies, headed by
vile assassins, ridiculously called generals and chiefs."

Perhaps these scornful phrases were to a certain extent
the proverbial whistling of soldiers before battle, but there

was indeed much truth in them. For the Spanish faced a polyglot band of rebels whose organization was far from intimidating. First of all, the largest element was composed of Mexicans who sought to overthrow the power of Spain in the New World ; groups of ignorant colonists whose leaders wrangled among themselves for the honor of being creole Washingtons and Bolivars. Then there were the inevitable Indian allies, the Cooshatties. And finally the "Anglo-Americans" as the Spanish somewhat inaccurately termed them.

The latter needed no hyphens — they were United States citizens who had a stake in the Southwest. A few were law-abiding settlers, the sort of sterling pioneers who later followed Stephen Austin into this new Canaan. But most of them were either adventurers recruited on the wharves of New Orleans — then invaded by the piratical ideas of Jean Lafitte — or simply border ruffians out for loot and quick riches. The latter came from the famous Neutral Ground.

After the Louisiana Purchase the United States and Spain had a controversy over the southwest boundary and compromised by creating the Neutral Ground — a strip of territory between the Arroyo Hondo and Sabine Rivers which neither nation occupied. It had no legal authority, no police system and a population consisting mainly of frontier riff-raff. The inhabitants throve on contraband trade and stoutly resisted the many punitive expeditions which the forces of the two nations sent against them. They were veritable two-gun warriors, each man carrying besides a rifle, two pistols and a long hunting knife, the latter characteristically grasped between the teeth. They went into battle with the cry—"We never surrender"—and well they might for they could expect no quarter.

It was a force consisting of about eight hundred and fifty of these men, together with about seventeen hundred Mexican rebels and six hundred Indian allies which Arredondo's scouts sighted near the Medina River on the 17th of August. It was more a horde than an army for, while one José Alvarez Toledo had the titular leadership, another Mexican Menchaca acknowledged it under protest; and the Americans recognized only their own chief, Captain Perry. Arredondo could well rejoice in his own carefully trained and officered troops.

While the latter numbered only about two thousand, they were well supported by good cavalry and artillery. One of their strongest units was the Vera Cruz regiment, recruited from the most loyal and conservative of Mexican provinces. A young officer of this regiment, Lieutenant Antonio Lopez de Santa Anna, had up till then been active only in skirmishes with guerrillas. Now he was approaching a genuine battle for the first time.

Arredondo with veteran deliberation disposed his troops. Near the river the chapparal was filled with many oak trees and there he placed his forces in a V-shaped ambush. An advance guard of several hundred men was sent ahead with strict orders to avoid battle, to skirmish, to retreat slowly and draw the enemy back with them.

The scheme worked only too well. Perceiving that their adversaries were falling back, the rebel allies swept confidently forward. A capture of two small Spanish cannon added to their eagerness and they ran blindly into the cul-de-sac. Too late Toledo saw the danger and called to his men to fall back; the Americans had transposed their slogan to "We never retreat," and led the rest in impetuous, foolhardy advance. They were soon caught in a withering cross-fire. A clumsy effort of Toledo to turn one of the flanks of the ambush was promptly smothered and the battle proceeded with the predictable smoothness of one of Arredondo's war-games. The Americans provided the backbone of the resistance, fighting with ragamuffin ferocity in a hopeless position. The Mexican allies ran away first, followed by the Indians, and finally as Arredondo's successful battalions counter-charged, properly inspired by the strains of a military band, the last group of Americans turned and fled. The Spanish cavalry pursued the fugitives and. butchered them so efficiently that only ninety-three Americans lived to bring the story back to the Neutral Ground.

This battle was indeed a crushing blow to the rebel cause in Texas. For many years in spite of desultory efforts to organize revolutions, the Texans remained under the sway of first Spain and then the Mexican republic. More important was this event as a decisive defeat of Americans by Spaniards and Latin-Americans. Disreputable as their members were, the Yankees nevertheless dominated the allied rebels and nothing seemed so clear after the battle as the superiority of Latins over Anglo-Saxons. This impression must have been very strong on the mind of Lieutenant Santa Anna who had been cited by Arredondo for valorous conduct and it was to be many years before his military education on this point was corrected.

Other matters, other lessons too for the impressionable young lieutenant. The cavalry scouring the plains captured a detachment of eighty insurgents. A ditch was dug, and the captives perched on timbers placed across it. Firing squads performed their task and engineers refilled the ditches. Indeed Arredondo seemed intent on proving that he was a notable practitioner in the age-old tradition of Spanish cruelty, a tradition which runs from the Duke of Alba down to the late General Weyler of Cuban fame.

Entering San Antonio, the center of rebel activity, he contrived to stuff three hundred of its citizens into a small improvised jail. Out of this "Black Hole," the next morning he dragged out, besides the eighteen who had died of suffocation, a sizable batch for his executioners. The merchandise, wealth and handsome women of the town were as usual legitimate loot. It was the old story of Spanish soldiery in the Southwest.

San Antonio was then a little city of small adobe houses clustering around two important buildings, two symbols of its history. The long, low-lying Palace of the Governors was the emblem of the constructive past, the last bastion of Latin administration in Texas. Some distance away on a knoll girdled by pretty streams stood the Alamo, bristling with battlements, a fort which had changed hands many times in the past few revolutionary years—an ominous portent of a war-like future.

One day during the Arredondo occupation, within sight of this very stronghold, an arrest was made. Lieutenant Santa Anna, celebrating his citation for valor in the recent battle, had joined the roystering of his brother officers who were staking their newly acquired riches at the gaming table. He lost, and then came the arrest on the charge that he had forged his commander's signature to a cheque for 300 pesos.   His defense was that he had merely helped out a fellow officer in distress, the honor of the regiment, etc.   A flimsy excuse, but after the expedition's surgeon came forward and covered the amount of the forgery, the affair was smoothed over and Santa Anna released.   The Spanish were too busy with their late enemies to expend their severity on one of their own men.

For during the following weeks, the truly Punic subjugation went on.   The belles of the town were the prey of the soldiers' fancy ; the less attractive women were put to work making tortillas for the commissary, while ranch people of the surrounding country staggered in on foot, driven by their merciless captors across the scorching plains, for trial and further chastisement.   It was a sanguinary, a memorable punitive expedition.   The Texans acquired one of their most bitter experiences of oppressors from across the Rio Grande and Lieutenant Antonio Lopez de Santa Anna served an unforgettable apprenticeship.

CHAPTER I

AGUSTÍN I

SINCE my earliest years I found myself inclined to the glorious career of arms, feeling a true vocation for it." So runs one of the most authentic sentences in Santa Anna's picturesquely unreliable memoirs. He was born in Jalapa, the capital of the province of Vera Cruz on February 21, 1794, of bourgeois creole parents. His father had a mortgage broker's business in the port of Vera Cruz and Antonio's family wished him to become a business man, but he apparently surmounted their objections and went from a primary school education in Jalapa to a military academy in Vera Cruz from which he was graduated as a promising, if somewhat unruly cadet in the local regiment.

Biographers have dealt so zealously with his early career that only a blurred and most contradictory figure emerges. Shall we believe his advocates who tell us that he consecrated all his days and nights to the study of Cæsar's Commentaries and the contemplation of the magnificence of his future military doings? Or those acrimonious pamphleteers who allege that the San Antonio peculation was but one of many which stained his youth; that on another occasion he was sentenced to have his hand cut off for a heinous larceny; that his military career was one escape from court-martial to another?

Rape, seduction, treason, robbery are charges which clash oddly with stories of impeccable recommendations for promotion, studious habits and noble courage. But so far as the official records go, Santa Anna seems to have passed the hum-drum life of a young officer in a Mexican provincial town, and ascended the ladder of rank in the most conventional manner. It was only when cosmic influences came into play, when the province of New Spain became conscious of itself as a nation that the Vera Cruzan subaltern began to display the traits which made him at once the best hated and most lauded actor in the Mexican drama.

It was not a little fitting that this young fellow who was later to style himself "Napoleon of the West" should be affected by the almost seismic disturbances which the great Captain himself caused. For Napoleon in his promiscuous destruction of European monarchies visited Spain, and finding King Ferdinand VII displeasing and not sufficiently accommodating, abruptly replaced him with another member of his own large family, Joseph Bonaparte. Immediately all Spaniards including the Spanish-Americans discovered an overpowering attachment for Ferdinand, a mediocre and hitherto hardly popular little man.

Ferdinand's viceroy in Mexico City, finding himself without a royal superior, began to assume all the prerogatives of a crowned head himself and became most unpopular with his Mexican subjects. As a result, Mexico enjoyed the rare distinction of revolting for the first time — but in behalf of the legally constituted authority of Ferdinand and against the tyranny of Viceroy Iturrigaray. The viceroy was unseated and a more pliable substitute was found. However, the appetite of Mexicans for rebellion had been greatly stimulated by this *coup,* and two years later in 1810 there was a more profound upheaval.

Hidalgo, a priest in the town of Dolores in the north central part of Mexico, and another cleric, Morelos, in what is now the western province of Michoacan, were the spearheads of a much more serious revolution. For centuries the native-born Mexicans whether of pure Spanish descent or of mixed Indian and Spanish blood had lived in unwilling subjection to the privileged émigrés from the Mother country whom they derisively called *gachupines* — "those who wear spurs." Not only in the professions of the law, church and army but also in commerce the Creoles were hamstrung by laws passed in favor of business enterprises in old Spain.

Hidalgo, by starting a silk industry in his parish and by perusing the works of Voltaire and Rousseau incurred the disapproval of the government. Accordingly, he felt a pardonably Mexican but rather unchristian hatred for the privileged Spaniards and after some preliminary plotting he led a revolt on September 16, 1810, with his *grito* — "cry of freedom" as the Mexicans call it — epitomized by the slogan "Death to the *gachupines!*" He headed a great mob of disaffected of all classes, and the banner which he unfurled bore the figure of the Virgin of Guadalupe — a peculiarly Mexican virgin who had miraculously appeared before a humble Indian three centuries before. Hidalgo's revolution, whatever its defects, was a most indigenously Mexican affair. The Tories who called on the Spanish legions to subdue the revolt took as the divine sponsor of their counter-attack the Virgin of the Remedies which thereafter became known as the *gachupin* Virgin.

The War of the Virgins ! Two dissimilar, antagonistic elements rallying around two different images of the Mother of Peace ! In the little town of Guadalupe, where the cobble-stones were worn by the bare feet of generations of devout Indians, stood the shrine, and within it the simple tapestry bearing the image of the Virgin of Guadalupe. Quite different was the Virgin of the Remedies—a doll-like statue without a nose and tended by a priest without a nose—loaded with literally hundreds of thousands of dollars' worth of jewels, gold, silver, pearls, rubies, emeralds and diamonds—the ornate symbol of the gold-hunting *gachupines*.

Alas, like so many conflicts waged under religious auspices, it turned out to be a most cruel and sorry struggle. The militant curate Hidalgo had no plan save revolt, no charter or any definite constitutional program to substitute for the existing government. He led his rag-tag army— more a horde than an army—into battle with the inevitable anarchy, butchery of innocent Tories and other disgraceful proceedings. The Tories did their best to surpass the excesses of the revolutionaries, and bearing the standard of the Virgin of the Remedies forward with the disciplined aid of the Peninsular legions, they defeated the rebels and captured their leader. Father Hidalgo and his lieutenants met their end before a firing squad.

All Mexico rose under these standards. From the wilderness of Yucatan where thick jungles concealed ancient Mayan temples, to the arid, mesquite-dotted deserts of Chihuahua and from tropical Vera Cruz to the rocky silver-veined mountains of Zacatecas—the country was aflame. Metropolitan Mexico City with its *churiguer-resque* churches and baroque palaces was on the side of the *gachupin* Virgin ; but out in little villages in the mountains of the north and in the fertile, agricultural west, armies of poor folk and bourgeoisie rallied to the image of Guadalupe. Humble curates in bare adobe chapels sympathized, but their superiors in luxurious *obispados* launched denunciations of Hidalgo and his followers.

A greater man than Hidalgo, José Morelos, caught the torch but he, too, met martyrdom at the hands of the Spanish. His followers possessed neither his strength nor his capacities. At the head of little bands they barely existed save as practice targets for the royal battalions. Guerrero in the fastnesses of the southwest, and Felix Fernandez—who had assumed the highly patriotic name of Guadalupe Victoria—in the forests of Vera Cruz kept burning, however faintly, the light of Mexican independence.

Many years later a column rose in Mexico which bore not the names of Guerrero or Victoria but that of Antonio Lopez de Santa Anna and it described him as the *Libertador de la Patria*. The exploits by which he somewhat dubiously earned this appellation will be told in the course of this biography, but at present we must trace the progress of this potential liberator. The train of events which Napoleon started in Spain did swerve Santa Anna's career, but not in the direction of revolution. He became one of the most loyal of the King's janissaries in Mexico. Long since returned from the Arredondo expedition and made a captain for some signal captures and butcheries of rebels in 1817, he enthusiastically pursued the unfortunate Guada-

lupe Victoria and colleagues in the territory around Vera
Cruz.

With such success that in the following year most of the
revolutionary bands had been broken up and Victoria was
living in solitary concealment in swamps and forests, an
almost mythical figure.   Military operations were dull now
and at the orders of the Governor of Vera Cruz, Captain
Santa Anna went to work directing reconstruction in the
wake of the revolutionary disturbances.   Establishment of
the homeless on farms, rebuilding of devastated villages and
farm-houses and stimulation of trade between the peasants
and merchants in the port of Vera Cruz were his tasks.
In one place he built a church and reported to the Governor
that the parishioners were so grateful that they wished to
change the name of the hamlet from San Diego to San
Antonio in his honor, a request which the Governor declined to grant.

But Santa Anna was not destined to go on turning royalist swords into plowshares for peons, because Mexico was
soon to venture independence again, and this time by a
most bizarre and circuitous route.   Just as under Viceroy
Iturrigaray, Mexican Tories overnight found that they
were revolutionists and conservatives and executed the most
nimble about-face, as a result of strange happenings in distant Madrid.   Ferdinand was in trouble again.   Returned
to the throne after the downfall of Napoleon he was forced
by a revolt of radicals to restore the liberal constitution —
a document which made shivers run down the spines of
conservatives and churchmen of the Peninsula.

But if there were fear and trembling in the castles and
sacristies of Castile there was just as much disturbance in

the shadow of Popocatepetl. What a scurrying between chapter-house and Palace, between the Cathedral and counting-houses and what apprehensive conferences among groups of Tories who saw the old menace of Hidalgo and Morelos now appearing from this unexpected quarter. They were unable to influence the Viceroy who wanted only to preserve his office and cared little about the liberal constitution or its consequences. So they turned to the idea of independence,—a new, less radical sort of revolution— separation from Spain but preservation of the old order in religion and privilege. All they needed was a leader and they had no difficulty in finding an accommodating man.

He was General Agustín de Iturbide, a creole, but of impeccable Tory record. He had surpassed most of the other executioners of the followers of Morelos and Hidalgo in cruelty, and his reports to the vice-regal government had been filled with commendable figures of republican captives put to the sword in defense of King and Christianity. One read, "I have signalized with abundant blood, Good Friday, 1813, in the history of this place (Salvatierra)." But he had been just as zealous in peculation and because of a scandal had been forced to resign his command. His sword was now at the service of the plotting Tories and they managed to get him reinstated in the army and sent to a garrison in the south.

A most strategic place. While the old unconquered revolutionary Guerrero sniffed suspiciously at the turn in Tory sentiment, Iturbide performed the congenial task of seizing a large caravan of money which had to go through his district on the way to the sea. Next, he gained an ally in Guerrero by convincing him that he was sincerely for paration from Spain. The old republican overlooked Iturbide's insistence on a constitutional "monarchy" so long he stipulated that all creoles were to share equally with the *gachupines* in honors and privileges. And as a devout Catholic he saw nothing wrong with the promises to preserve the status of the Church. Of such a nature was the Plan of Iguala, which Iturbide published in a little town of that name and to which he won many converts.

The Two Virgins reconciled! It looked that way; it looked like a veritable love feast. All manner of half-hearted republican and temporizing conservatives came out for this Plan and old *guerilleros* discovered that they were comrades of their late persecutors. They thought that Mexico was united at last for independence. It was, and when they perceived the success of their dreams, they were intoxicated. They jumped to the conclusion that they themselves—a heterogeneous crowd of priests, revolutionary patriots, silver-tongued orators, idealistic writers—were the sovereign power of Mexico. They were wrong. Another power, sinister, bloody, selfish, was back of them—a power without which their two Divine sponsors separate or united, were of little help. The sword was more potent than the Virgin's tiara and only because the military elements were hungry for loot, promotions and a re-shuffle for their own fortunes was the independence movement thrust forward. The various generals saw in Iturbide one of their own stamp and they announced their support of the Plan. The vice-regal throne was toppling.

Meanwhile Governor Davila in Vera Cruz remained loyal to the Crown and sent his accomplished rebel-disperser, Santa Anna, to suppress the pronouncers for

Iturbide in the vicinity of Cordoba, a town far up in the mountains near Jalapa. A welcome relief for the bellicose captain. For what after all had the rehabilitation of agrarian settlements to do with a man who felt a true vocation for "the glorious career of arms"? Besides another matter was bothering him. The old affair of the forged cheque in San Antonio had bobbed up again. Santa Anna had neglected to pay the obliging doctor who had made good the 300 pesos and the latter was demanding his money. Whether through stubbornness or lack of funds, Santa Anna had continued to evade payment and the doctor appealed to the highest military authorities. It was the kind of affair to obliterate which, a young soldier would happily rush into battle or revolution.

Action and adventure — and perhaps fear of retribution were the springs which propelled him into his amazing conduct on March 23, 1821. He met a small body of revolutionaries in the early morning of that day, routed some of them and captured the rest, for which feat he was made lieutenant-colonel. But that very afternoon at two o'clock, he himself went over to the pronouncers and was made a full colonel in the forces of Iturbide. A victory over rebels, a pronouncement in favor of them and two promotions from opposing forces, all in one day! It was evident that Santa Anna was destined to be an outstanding figure in the mêlée of revolutionary activity.

An incident that followed this extraordinary *volte-face* showed that he was smart enough to temper his ambition with graceful diplomacy. The good news of Mexico's new struggle for independence took weeks to get to Guadalupe Victoria, and his followers had literally to ferret him out of the protecting swamps. The famous patriot finally presented himself somewhat myopically to his late pursuer Santa Anna and humbly offered to serve against Iturbide in any rank. Santa Anna grandiloquently declined to allow Victoria to be a mere subordinate and saluted him as the commander of the revolting forces. This was very gracious but it did not deceive Victoria. After looking over the personnel and perceiving the real sentiments of the Iturbidists, the old chieftain decided that he would wait for true republicanism and retired again into his sylvan haunts.

The mixed nature of the current political ferment naturally would have disturbed a doctrinaire old radical like Victoria. Creoles of all classes united in a burst of enthusiasm for Mexico's liberation from *gachupin* dominance, but their emotions rallied to different points of the document of Iguala. Clericals dwelt with satisfaction on the promises to preserve the status of the Church ; conservatives liked the monarchical tendencies and favored the concentration of power in Iturbide's hands, while liberals found great comfort in the calling of an elected congress. But the class which had really accomplished the great change, the military, were engrossed in less constitutional preoccupations. They were fumbling, each leader in his own little sphere, for power, for promotions, for money and supplies.

Santa Anna, after the fall of the viceroy was no different, so it seems, than the other members of his caste. As the royal power faded in one of the last battles at Cordoba, he elected to remain cautiously aloof on a hillside at a safe distance from the firing and intervened only at a critical point when he gave the bugler the order to blow the *deguello*—or "no quarter"—a motif that might properly

Idealized portrait of Santa Anna in full regalia

Photograph of Santa Anna
Probably circa 1860

be called the theme-song of his life. After the royalists were routed at this point, he took his troops to his old home-town of Jalapa and established himself as the local *jefe* or chief. The inhabitants cheered him at first but their enthusiasm diminished considerably after he had collected with unusual energy a forced "loan" of 9000 pesos, the customary method which war lords used to fill their purses.

At this stage in his career he was a rude, unlettered soldier, his schooling having stopped at the most elementary stage — and indeed it got little further during the rest of his days. But at Jalapa he became friendly with Carlos Maria Bustamente, a well-educated young man whose historical readings had given him a romantic idea of the destiny of the Mexicans as a people and whose style had that effusive classicism which was the product of an excess dose of both Plutarch and Rousseau. He was an ardent republican and became the Boswell of the revolution. He gave Santa Anna his first lessons in the use of a bombastic and high-flown style for the adornment of proclamations and manifestoes, one of the important items in the equipment of the early nineteenth century militarists.

"Soldiers, come on, change the face of two worlds and recover the famous renown of which we have been despoiled for three centuries. Struggle with a handful of miserable opponents who arrogantly oppose your progress. Stupid creatures! They will soon weep for their temerity. . ." This was the sort of thing Santa Anna put his name to and this particular proclamation heralded a new and audacious adventure. The viceroy had abdicated, and after Iturbide had occupied Mexico City there was only one important center of Spanish resistance holding out—

Vera Cruz. The most important port in the country with a wealthy merchant population and a very lucrative custom house—it was the inevitable goal of a rising young *jefe* like Santa Anna. Without orders from Iturbide, acting absolutely on his own initiative, this twenty-seven year old chieftain set out to capture the queen city of the Gulf of Mexico.

He had chosen a most propitious moment. The garrison was weak and demoralized. Spanish veterans, they had easily succumbed to the annual attack of the dread yellow fever which the natives descriptively called the "vomito"; and further reinforcements from Spain to fill their thinning ranks were long overdue. Davila had pressed into service sailors from the vessels in the harbor and raw town youths who had aroused the town to an uproar by firing on some peaceful farmers coming to market.

Santa Anna, however, was now well supplied with ammunition and artillery, and his men were superb for the time and place. They were called *jarachos,* these rough-riding fighters of the lowlands; impervious to any noxious insect bite, healthy during the most severe epidemics and accustomed to the changes of the cruel climate, they would march for days through swamps and forests content with what rations they picked off the trees and bushes. A motley army whose picturesque variety of costume contrasted with the resplendent uniform of their leader.

They paused long enough at a little port not far from Vera Cruz to foil one of Davila's schemes to seize the *jaracho* Napoleon. A vessel of suspiciously Spanish appearance flying the American flag was in the harbor and its commander asked that Santa Anna come aboard for a conference. But Santa Anna perceiving the ruse, declined and set to work on a little guile of his own. He seduced an obliging Vera Cruzan to open one of the city's gates on the day of his first big attack and by this method led his army into Vera Cruz. Sweeping over the breastworks in the exterior section they gained the Market Place and were commencing to attack the Plaza when a tropical rain-storm interrupted operations. It lasted from eight in the morning until four in the afternoon, and meanwhile the invading troops caroused so intensively in the wine-shops that they were good for little when Santa Anna tried to defend his gains against a brave counter-attack from the garrison. The drunken troops fled ignominiously, abandoning four cannon and getting out of the city as best they could.

Santa Anna had suffered a severe defeat but his dispatches to Iturbide certainly did not disclose the fact — filled as they were with hollow assertions of victory — and only when he rallied his disorderly forces far inland did he betray his true feelings. Bustamente may have polished the periods of his proclamation, but youthful chagrin undoubtedly dictated its sentiments.

"Vera Cruz! The cry for your extermination will be from today on the slogan of our warriors on entering battle; in all juntas and senates the vote for thy ruin will add itself to all deliberations. Carthage's grandeur and fall should place fear in your memory. Mexicans! Carthage did not offend Rome as Vera Cruz has Mexico. Be Roman, for you have your Scipios."

Iturbide who had composed many prevaricating dispatches himself to superiors, doubtless saw through the official reports from the Vera Cruz army and he received with great cordiality the mortified young Scipio when he visited the revolutionary headquarters in Puebla shortly after this repulse. He gave him reinforcements and sent him back to the lowlands again. Vera Cruz was now subjected to a more circumspect attack and trade between the port and interior was so effectively cut off, that by October 1821, the merchants prevailed on Davila to compromise by retiring to San Juan Ulloa, the island fortress in the harbor, and to surrender the city to the revolutionary forces. Davila retired to his maritime stronghold with all his troops and about $90,000 of the town funds while Santa Anna cantered in with his followers and placed the revolutionary banners on the rampart which had so recently defied him.

The Viceroyalty is dead, long live Iturbide ! Although the government of the country was vested in a Regency, composed of several notable men, Iturbide was its dominating figure. As if Mexico had not been able to erase from its imagination the majestic figure of the viceroy, the authorities decreed that Iturbide should be addressed by the title "His Serene Highness" and that he should be generalissimo of the army at the considerable salary of $125,000 a year. Nor did they stop at this ; they gave him the sum of one million dollars and a tract of land in Texas twenty leagues square for his services as a liberator.

No wonder that these honors went to his head, hitherto so cool and shrewd. Perhaps he reasoned that what the Mexican people wanted was not popular government but a gaudy show. It was not long before he took steps to give them just that. He instituted a vast movement of promotions in the army, an advantageous step in a quarter which was of the utmost importance. He got the clericals and conservatives enthusiastically behind him, and he secured the support of a considerable minority in Congress. When the liberal majority in that body became hostile to him he carried off a successful *coup d'état* with grenadiers putting legislators in their place and hirelings crying "Viva Agustín I." So a rump legislature elected Iturbide Emperor and a sumptuous playing at royalty followed. The title was made hereditary and Iturbide's offspring became princes and princesses of the blood ; his father and sister were accorded royal honors too. His bust was stamped on national coinage, and the 19th of May, the date of his *coup d'état,* was declared a national holiday. Even in his household there was a hierarchy with an almoner, master of horse, gentlemen of the bed-chamber and pages.

Iturbide had satisfied the adherents of the bejewelled Virgin with his conservative, semi-monarchical measures and court. So to win the worshippers of our Lady of Guadalupe, he instituted an Order of Guadalupe with castes, ranks, Grand Crosses, knights, etc. More promotions, more uniforms and ceremony. It was a flimsy alliance of the Two Virgins — a tinsel spectacle and, unless the sword was firmly held in reserve, of equally tinsel stability.

The shrewd and observing Yankee, Joel Poinsett, who became our first Minister to Mexico and after whom is named the beautiful Mexican plant, the *poinsettia,* met, or rather had a royal audience with Iturbide in November 1822. He writes about it thus, "I was presented to His Majesty this morning. On alighting at the gate of the palace which is an extensve and handsome building, we were received by a numerous guard, and then made our

way up a large stone staircase, lined with sentinels, to a
spacious apartment where we found a brigadier general
stationed to usher us into the presence.

✕   "The Emperor was in his cabinet and received us with
great politeness. Two of his favorites were with him. We
were all seated and he conversed with us in an easy un-
embarrassed manner, taking occasion to compliment the
United States and our institutions and to lament that they
were not suited to the circumstances of his country. He
modestly insinuated that he had yielded very reluctantly
to the wishes of the people, but had been compelled to
suffer them to place the crown upon his head to prevent
misrule and anarchy.

"In the interval between the defeat of the patriotic cause
and the last revolution he resided in the capital, and in a
society not remarkable for strict morals, he was distinguished for his immorality. . . With a pleasing address
and prepossessing exterior and by lavish profusion, he has
attached the officers and soldiers to his person, and so long
as he possesses the means of paying and rewarding them,
so long he will maintain himself on the throne ; when these
fail he will be precipitated from it. . . Aware of the state
of his funds, and of the probable consequences to himself
of their failure, he is making great exertions to negotiate
loans in England ; and such is the infatuation of the monied
men in that country that it is possible he may effect his
object. . . The professors of botany and mineralogy told
me with great dismay yesterday that they had received
orders from His Majesty to prepare collections to be sent to
England."

Iturbide thought that he had forged an iron chain of

military preferment with his lavish favors, but there was one link that he had neglected—a small, but, he had omitted to note, a most vital link. In the distribution of promotions and emoluments in the army, Santa Anna felt that he had been slighted. Just before Iturbide's apotheosis on May 19th, he had been raised from colonel to brigadier, a grade less than general, a promotion doubtless designed to hold him in line during a crucial time. But others had skipped several grades in their rise to heavier gold braid, and he was still a brigadier while old companions in revolution, or to put it more accurately, pronouncing, such as Herrera and Echavarrí, were full generals. While he cooled his heels, he turned to flattery—to rhetorical libations quite evidently unrevised by the lettered Bustamente.

"Hail to Your Majesty for our glory, and let this expression be so gratifying that the sweet name of Agustín I will be transmitted to our descendants, giving them an idea of the memorable actions of our worthy Liberator. They will immortalize for history how just you are, and I together with my regiment, No. 8, was ready to give such a most worthy and glorious exaltation political support; we feel that we have not merely been the motivators of such a step but the first in this province who offered tribute to Your Majesty; yes, the first who offered our lives and persons to conserve the respectable existence of Your Majesty and the crown which you so worthily obtained, remaining as we are constant subordinates who will shed our blood for the most worthy Emperor."

However he contemplated more than just sycophant adulation to advance himself. He had been named Governor of the Port of Vera Cruz, but was still subordinate to Echavarrí who was captain-general of the province.   In the harbor, lifting its bastioned gloom like a menace to his little fief, stood San Juan Ulloa.   Its Spanish Governor took a large part of the customs duties, considerable sums of money which the Imperial government and Santa Anna should have received.   This Gibraltar was considered to be impregnable to attack but a trick might betray it.   One trick, then perhaps another, and our hero would be undisputed lord of the rich province.

It was an astounding scheme which stamped him as a formidable actor in the Mexican melodrama.   He tried to bribe the Spanish commander to capitulate — so the story runs — and when he failed in this effort he was inspired to a genial stratagem.   He planned to invite the *gachupines* to enter the city, pretending to betray it to them ; but on their entrance he would double-cross them, killing or capturing as many as he could.   Then dressing a body of his own soldiers in Spanish uniforms he would send them back to the castle where they would overpower the commandant and the remaining forces.

Whether legend or history, the Spaniards did essay a sortie on the night of October 25th, 1822, and Santa Anna manifestly did have previous knowledge of it, for General Echavarrí arriving just the day before was asked by his subordinate to station himself with his staff at the Concepcion redoubt where he could command a large force of Mexicans in defense of the Concepcion gate nearby.

But the Captain-General was destined to receive an uncomfortable surprise.   Arriving at the redoubt he found not a strong force of soldiers but a mere handful of regulars. It was the hour of the attack and the Spaniards were already appearing at the gate in formidable numbers. "Treachery" cried Echavarrí as he saw the Spaniards closing in on him. Fortunately he had time enough to get word to a squadron of cavalry nearby which galloped up and rescued him.

Meanwhile at other gates Santa Anna had met the Spaniards, given them a severe drubbing and captured some three hundred prisoners. The remainder of the landing party took to their boats and brought the bad news back to the Castle. So far as it is known, there was no attempt to send the contemplated Wooden Horse into the Spanish stronghold. Santa Anna appeared jubilant at the successful defense of the city, but Echavarrí entertained different feelings. In his report to the Emperor he intimated that his narrow escape at the Concepcion redoubt was a treacherous attempt on Santa Anna's part to dispose of him so that he might succeed to the captain-generalcy himself. Had the young schemer over-reached himself and defeated his chances?

A somewhat ominous answer to these questions was provided by the Emperor's congratulations on hearing of the engagement. Echavarrí was made a marshal while Santa Anna was merely offered warm felicitations. His Serene Highness apparently deemed the young officer's exertions as largely cerebral and of dubious loyalty. Ominous also was the Emperor's visit to Jalapa, as if to inspect a troublesome dependency and still more was his summons to Santa Anna to appear before him there.

It was an historic meeting, a scene of masterly dissembling. The Emperor greeted him with apparent cordiality and offered Santa Anna a post in the capital, saying: "I await you in Mexico, Santa Anna, to make your fortune for you,"

which was a softened manner of announcing that he had
been relieved of his post at Vera Cruz.   Santa Anna later
asserted that he had been warned of his removal and that
he feigned gratitude, asking only that he be given time
to set his affairs in order.   While he was seated at a table
with the Emperor exchanging subtle prevarications, an
aide-de-camp entered and sternly reminded Santa Anna
that he was infringing one of the most sacred rules of the
new Imperial code : "In the Emperor's presence one should
stand at attention."

With this humiliating rebuke in his ears, with the certi-
tude that his military career, perhaps his life, was in danger,
Santa Anna jumped on his horse and galloped night and
day until he reached Vera Cruz.   Fortunately he arrived
in advance of the order for his removal.   But he did not
dawdle.   Part of the garrison was out of the city, but he
assembled the remainder, a slovenly lot of half-clad peons,
in the main Plaza, and brandishing his sword to point his
words, he pronounced for a Mexican republic.

Afterwards speaking of this famous day, he confided to
Riva Palacio that when he shouted for a republic he had not
the slightest idea of what a republic was.   Carlos Maria
Bustamente who was in Vera Cruz at the time, corroborates
this and it seems likely that the idealistic little scholar took
advantage of his friend's uncomfortable military situation
to suggest the new and euphonious slogan "Viva la Re-
publica !"   Indeed Santa Anna was no lone Baptist in an
imperial wilderness.   The minister from the new Colombian Republic was in the port to give him sympathy and
recognition and Guadalupe Victoria appeared like a watch-
dog at the cry for a republic.   Governor Davila in San Juan

Ulloa, desirous of embarrassing Iturbide, offered assistance, and Santa Anna emboldened by aid and encouragement, advanced into the interior to spread the evangel.

But here a check—an anti-climax! He got no further than Jalapa. There Echavarrí, who knew no more about republics than Santa Anna, but who did know his Santa Anna, put up such a sharp resistance that the new *Libertador* was crushingly defeated. Part of his troops went over en masse to the imperial forces and he himself narrowly missed capture, galloping off with an escort of only six dragoons. Meeting Guadalupe Victoria en route he opened his heart, so easily downcast by any rebuff. This plan for a republic was hopelessly lost, he asserted; the best policy for all now was to flee and save their skins; as for himself he was leaving for the United States on an American vessel in the harbor. But Victoria brushed aside these panicky sentiments with inspiriting words, "Go and get Vera Cruz in a state of defense; you can set sail when they show you my head." Rebounding from his despondency at this exhortation, Santa Anna proceeded to Vera Cruz and threw himself into the task which he could do so well, fortifying a city and organizing a force of men.

He was unaware that his *grito* in the Plaza had immense reverberations. He did not know that in the past few months Iturbide's pork barrel for war-lords had been getting low and that the true support of all these tawdry Imperial trappings was shaky. Guerrero had unsheathed his revolutionary blade again and other generals were stirring uneasily in their headquarters. What Poinsett had predicted was taking place; Iturbide had failed to satisfy the avarice of the military and they were turning against him. Iturbide now recognizing the situation, nervously decided to play one militarist against another and sent the vengeful Echavarrí to chastise Santa Anna.

It was this move that resulted in one of the most extraordinary, the most critical and revealing episodes of this conflict. Numerically it seemed an easy thing for Echavarrí to crush his rival for he had 3000 men to Santa Anna's 400. But the latter had effectively strengthened the fortifications of Vera Cruz and Echavarri's forces consisted only of light artillery and cavalry which were useless under these circumstances. It looked like a case of a long siege and Echavarrí began to take thought. He had no love for Iturbide and felt no desire to risk his skin assaulting Vera Cruz. Yet, to march away would be to render satisfaction to the hated Santa Anna. What should he do?

It was typical of the topsy-turvy military standards of those days in Mexico that Echavarrí should find that lifting this impossible siege would "compromise his military honor" and that to avoid "staining" his reputation, he should decide to pronounce against his commanding officer, the Emperor ! He and some other imperial generals added to the mounting list of revolts and "plans" against Iturbide by proclaiming the Plan of Casa Mata, which while disclaiming any enmity for Iturbide and omitting to mention the word "republic," insisted that the sovereignty should rest in an elected assembly.

With this curious dénouement Iturbide's drama commenced to draw to a close. Other generals hitherto loyal saw the shift of sentiment among their own kind and joined the Plan of Casa Mata. No more than the rest did lusty young Santa Anna understand what a republic was, nor, for that matter, care. But he did comprehend this sort of shady dealing ; he did perceive the drift in affairs and he too joined the popular Plan.

So he sat in barrack-room conferences and watched the power of Agustín I crumble, saw the artful prestidigitator of generals and soldiers suffer from his own weapons. He saw the whole army, the whole country flock to the new Plan and he watched Iturbide resign his gaudy crown, his trinkets of royalty and set sail for exile. The idealistic young republicans acclaimed in all this the triumph of the will of the people. The generals with a greater grasp of reality hailed it as a victory of militarism. But Santa Anna rejoiced in the knowledge that it was his own desperate audacity that had tipped over the throne of Mexico's first Emperor.

CHAPTER II

PRONUNCIAMIENTO

UNDER these singular auspices the first Mexican Republic came into being. Of course its formal opening was preceded by a provisional government, a triumvirate *ad interim,* a constituent assembly and the other paraphernalia with which newly-born democratic governments of recent birth the world over seek to put their affairs in order *in perpetuum.* And wonder of wonders these bodies accomplished their work while their provisional leaders squelched the more unruly of their own members who desired to upset matters.

Naturally a flag was designed as well as a national coat of arms. The former was substantially as we know it now, a tricolor of white, green and red in vertical strips; white denoting the purity of the Catholic religion, green for independence and red for the union of the Spanish element with the Mexican. The coat of arms revealed an eagle perched on a cactus and holding in his beak a snake — the famous Eagle and Serpent of Aztec mythology. Some enterprising scholar had exhumed the old Indian tradition that the Aztecs had settled near the present site of Mexico City when they came upon an eagle thus rending a serpent.

All the trimmings had this babe republic and if it boasted

no grave of an Unknown Patriot for the inspiration of florid oratory, it supplied an excellent substitute by digging up the bones of many who died in behalf of independence and placing them in an ornamental urn. What a solemn and incongruous ceremony they held when the keys to this urn were officially turned over to the members of Congress and the executive, when the President proclaimed these heroes "Benemeritos de la Patria" and when the assembled notables and generals, many of them *ci-devant* royalists and themselves the butchers of the patriots, offered wild applause.

Like the many squalling little states which Bolivar had liberated on the southern continent, they chose the Constitution of the United States as their model, interpolating such clauses as seemed proper to fit local conditions. Thus while most of the documents read like the famous compromise of 1787, here and there were scattered provisions — such as the one giving the President the right to assume dictatorial powers from Congress in emergencies — which stemmed from quite a different tradition. Could the Mexicans after so many centuries of despotic rule learn the art of legislative wrangling and tranquilizing compromises, and would the shades of those autocratic viceroys ever entirely desert them ?

Fortunately they elected Guadalupe Victoria as first President of the Republic. In the midst of the numerous scamps, adventurers and opportunists who crowded the public stage in the Mexico of that day, he stands out as a truly noble figure. Absolutely honest, he never profited financially from his office ; scrupulous, he adhered loyally to the Constitution he had sworn to protect ; and he sought to govern with justice leavened by mercy—a rare trait in the fierce struggles of that time.

Unhappily with him was elected as Vice-President his opponent for the Presidency, a practice which led to disastrous results in later years and which almost upset his own reign. His electoral spouse Nicolas Bravo was an old patriot too and almost as popular as Victoria, but he believed in a centralized government with the states under the thumb of Mexico City while Victoria believed in a loose Federal system. Bravo was supported by the conservatives, clericals and Spaniards and opposed Victoria's adherents who were mainly democrats, radicals and critics of the Church. Perhaps the President's was an unwise program in view of Mexico's political inexperience, but it was undoubtedly the popular choice not only of the mass of the people—that is those who could understand what it was all about—but especially of the rabid Jacobins, the anti-Spanish fanatics and of the little provincial *jefes* who wanted to keep their power. Such was the division of forces, and the various adventurers chose the side which they thought would win and interposed their demoralizing uprisings on one side or the other.

One of these fire-brands whom the new Government had to watch carefully was Santa Anna, who now proudly carried the rank of General. He was well known now as the David who had dared to defy the late Goliath, Iturbide, and the pomp and ceremony with which he carried on his role in the lowlands could not help but attract the nervous attention of the new Government in Mexico City. Uneasily then did they watch him career off, independently without their orders, to the North on the pretext that some

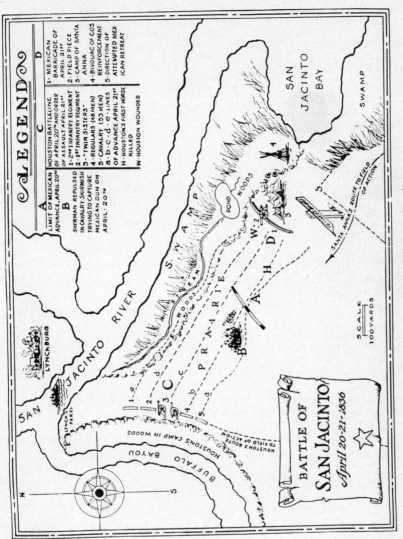

Map of battlefield of San Jacinto

The following text appears within the map illustration:

LEGEND

A
LIMIT OF MEXICAN
ADVANCE, APRIL 20ᵀᴴ

B
SHERMAN REPULSED
IN CAVALRY SKIRMISH
TRYING TO CAPTURE
MEXICAN GUN ON
APRIL · 20ᵀᴴ

C
HOUSTON BATTLELINE
OF APRIL 20ᵀᴴ AND ORDER
OF ASSAULT APRIL 21ˢᵀ
1 - 2ᴺᴰ INFANTRY REGIMENT
2 - 1ˢᵀ INFANTRY REGIMENT
3 - "TWIN SISTERS"
4 - REGULARS (48 MEN)
5 - CAVALRY (53 MEN)
a · b · c · d · e · LINES
OF ADVANCE APRIL 21ˢᵀ
H - HOUSTON'S FIRST HORSE
KILLED
W - HOUSTON WOUNDED

D
1 - MEXICAN
BARRICADE OF
APRIL 21ˢᵀ
2 - FIELD PIECE
3 - CAMP OF SANTA
ANNA
4 - BIVOUAC OF COS
REINFORCEMENT
5 - DIRECTION OF
ATTEMPTED MEX-
ICAN RETREAT

SAN JACINTO RIVER

LYNCHBURG

SAN JACINTO

BUFFALO BAYOU

LYNCH'S FERRY

HOUSTONS CAMP IN WOODS

HOUSTON'S ROUTE
TO FIELD OF ACTION

BATTLE OF
SAN JACINTO
April 20-21-1836

SCALE
100 YARDS

SANTA ANNA'S ROUTE TO FIELD
OF ACTION

SAN JACINTO BAY

SWAMP

SWAMP

WOODS

POND

PRAIRIE

WOODS

N
S

Captive Santa Anna before Sam Houston on battlefield of San Jacinto

(See page 115)

of the elements loyal to Iturbide were active in that direction. San Luis Potosí was some 500 miles away from his base in Vera Cruz, but Santa Anna went equipped with so many provisions and letters of credit that it seems evident that he was determined on a grand campaign which might not keep within mere provincial limits.

But just as in many other enterprises which he started, he commenced in the role of Napoleon and ended up as ignominiously as the White Knight. The Potosians hated his *jaracho* dialect, his lowland love of splendor, his seraglios and courtiers, and in spite of his attempt to set up a rural kingdom by force of arms, rebelled with some success. Finally to attract the aid of the government he proclaimed for Federalism without knowing himself, as he afterwards admitted, what Federalism meant. The local warriors just as ignorant of the new shibboleths as himself, discovered that they were strong Centralists. It was in the midst of this Gilbertian row that the Government forces intervened and rescued — took into custody rather — the disturbing leader from Vera Cruz.

Somewhat sobered now he gave heed to the moral of a popular verse of the day :

> *Here lies a General*
> *Who said one morn,*
> *"Either Cæsar or nothing"*
> *And came out with nothing.*

For he approached the capital in a humbler mood, a spirit more attuned to suing for pardon. Not that Mexico City did not provide fertile ground for one with Cæsarian ambitions. In addition to the conflict of the two main parties, rival Masonic lodges were intriguing, the military were restive and finally the most popular of rabble tocsins, "Down with the Spaniard" was causing trouble. Agitators had tried to form a mob—unsuccessfully, however—to desecrate the bones of the first *gachupin* of Mexico—Hernando Cortez.

While our hero waited in the capital for the Government investigation of his own escapade, he watched the writhings of Victoria amidst this milling throng. But the President had one quality which enabled him to handle his people—courage. When a strutting militarist, General Lobato, headed a revolutionary movement and won over most of the garrison, he absolutely refused to treat with the rebels and organized what few loyal soldiers he could find. And when Santa Anna, seeking to ingratiate himself with the Government, offered to mediate, Victoria blankly refused. This uncompromising attitude together with the as yet undimmed prestige of his office frightened the revolters into submission.

But Santa Anna's move in this matter inspired respect if not gratitude, and the Government, sorely perplexed as to how to dispose of this dangerous young man, decided to appoint him Governor-General of Yucatan, a place sufficiently remote to keep him out of the already too troublous terrain of central Mexico.

A peninsular Eden this state of Yucatan, replete with all the more bountiful flora of Nature, and covering in the midst of the jungle the vestiges of a glorious old civilization. But the descendants of the industrious and peaceful Mayas seemed to have eaten of the fruit of the Eagle and Serpent. For when the new Governor-General took up his post he found the country teeming with the same sort of trivial feuds as in the rest of Mexico. Merida, the inland capital and center of the agricultural interests, was bitterly at odds with the sleepy old banana port of Campeche.

Santa Anna found that he faced a somewhat different situation from the one that overthrew him in San Luis Potosi. He was a stranger here too, yes, but he now held the reins of power in the midst of two factions and they had to come to him for aid. He now learned the first precept of all pro-consuls — *Divide and Rule*. He might have succeeded in ruling this troublous State if the Government had not persisted in treating it as part of the republic, insisting on the collection of Federal taxes and the enforcement of the laws of the land. The history of Santa Anna's term as Governor of Yucatan is one long list of disputes with the Federal Government, of defiance of its authority and refusal even to publish its decrees.

At one time, thwarted by the central government in his internal policies, our hero conceived the reckless plan of conquering Cuba and adding it to the Mexican republic. The Federal Government looked at the project with quizzical but neutral amusement, the foreign minister Gomez Pedraza remarking "If it succeeds it ought to be a great honor to Mexico ; if it fails at least it will rid us of Santa Anna." But Santa Anna, undaunted by cynical observations, proceeded to gather ships, assemble men and even construct the ladders with which he proposed to scale the walls of Morro Castle. Only the news that Havana had been heavily reinforced with soldiers and a fleet moved him to forego this quixotic project.

But meanwhile his *dossier* in the archives at Mexico had

been swelling with complaints and hostile charges, for
many dissatisfied Yucatecans had sent in petitions against
him, nor had various military who envied him his position
remained silent. The Government drew up a formal
accusation against him, accusing him of delaying in an
arbitrary manner the Government's declarations, of having
malfeased funds sent to recruit sailors in Campeche, of
keeping under arms more forces than were necessary.
There was even talk of sending an expedition to Yucatan
to make the independent Governor-General behave.

As he put it, "The hot climate of Yucatan was noxious
for me and I asked to be relieved, which was granted." It
was indeed noxious for him, but not only in a corporal way.
For his term in Yucatan illustrates most strikingly his defects and qualities. Intriguing with two opposing parties
who besought his alliance was indeed his *forte* and he
throve on such a situation. But checked in his rise to
power by a superior force like the Federal Government, he
relapsed into unhappy submission without any plan or system of ideas which he thought worth fighting for. Yet
let him be struck by some dream of conquest, some hare-
brained expedition like the Havana project and he immediately revived.

"Returning to the province of Vera Cruz I was able to
dedicate myself to the progress of my hacienda of Manga
de Clavo." A householder now, a Cincinnatus returned
to the plow but on a farm less distant from the center of
affairs than vaporous and remote Yucatan, better situated
for an ambitious general-politician. For the hacienda was
located part way between the two important cities of Vera
Cruz and Jalapa.

Vera Cruz was then the largest port in the Republic and almost every traveller bound for the halls of the Montezumas had to pass through it.   If he approached it between the months of May and November, he would see the peak of Orizaba thrusting its 17,000 feet up into a cloudy welkin, one of a string of mountains which girdled the safe, healthy plateau region of the capital, a sweet goal for the anxious foreigner.   For the city, low lying on sand dunes and marshes was a plague spot during the hot season and the wayfarer from temperate climes got directly off his boat onto a horse-drawn litter and was hastily conveyed up the foothills to a higher and healthier zone.   The mortality among strangers in Vera Cruz during the yellow fever season was prodigious and only a half-century later was it rendered livable by Porfirio Diaz' renovating measures ; and not until almost a century later did American marines vanquish the malarial mosquitoes.

But despite its noxious insects and sultry vapors, Vera Cruz was a bustling little commercial center.   Its streets were clean — kept so rather nauseatingly by great flocks of vultures or *zopilotes* which perched meditatively on the tops of the churches.   The façades of the churches themselves had a sort of baroque grandeur, and the statuary of the interiors, a succession of horrible bleeding Christs and dolorous *pietas* met the most exacting standards of the sanguinary school of Spanish sculpture.   Curates with their long robes and shovel hats elbowed their way among the marts with English brokers, French dry goods merchants and lean Yankees who at that time dominated the diligence and litter service to the interior.

Out in the harbor lay San Juan Ulloa, the fortress which

Santa Anna had craftily coveted—now no longer a menace, for in 1825 General Barragán with the collaboration of that almost mythical institution, the Mexican navy, had forced its surrender. No longer did it collect a part of the customs receipts, for these rich revenues went to the Mexican government, or perhaps more accurately to the government and to the *zopilotes* in gold braid who happened at the time to be in command of the port.

As for Jalapa, it was an Eden hung high—about five thousand feet—above the hygienic and climatic inferno of Vera Cruz; set in a perfect garden country, convolvulus everywhere, acacia trees, roses in negligent profusion, *palma Christi,* ferns, mango trees, banana plants with their green semaphores, and fruits falling like manna from every branch. There the peons gathered the jalap plant—from which the town is named, and which, as a French traveller put it, is a most "energetic purgative." Do not American babies cry for it in the guise of Castoria?

But Jalapa was also the capital of the State of Vera Cruz where the legislature, that body so troublesome to military opportunists, convened. So it was within convenient distance of these two important points that Santa Anna had his hacienda, Manga de Clavo, whose name translated means Clove-Spike, an aromatic designation well suited to the place, for it was situated far below Jalapa in the *tierra caliente* where the natural beauties and fruits were even more abundant.

He had purchased it for 25,000 pesos, he later said, —it paid to be a General in those days—and there he lived with his wife and family. He had been married in 1824 to Inez Garcia, daughter of a well-off Spanish bourgeois of Vera Cruz. A tall thin woman without any great beauty but doubtless worth more because of her great moral qualities than the 8,000 pesos which she brought him as dowry. Legend has it that he desired her pretty sister, but that he made his proposal to the parents so clumsily that they understood him to mean Señorita Inez, and only when he approached the altar did he note the mistake, accepting it with the remark, "It's all the same to me."

He owned only twelve square leagues of land at this time —but it grew with the years. As he was wont to remark to visitors, he had no garden for the whole country was a garden. There his numerous herds of cattle and sheep roamed. There he kept his prize game-cocks, for cock-fighting was his favorite sport; and in his slight, pretty little house he served sumptuous meals, with innumerable dishes and sweetmeats, wines, liqueurs, on service of fine French porcelain. His splendid litter was there and his carriages, to make those raids on the political scene afterward so famous. And several aides-de-camp and officers were at hand to show visitors in. For past his hacienda ascended many people of importance and visitors from across the sea. There passed Anglo-Saxon bond-salesmen then as in the recent past avid to underwrite rickety republics for huge commissions, Frenchmen who sought to corner the dry goods marts in the capital, Scotch engineers who were on the look out for mining concessions, prelates on their way to their sees and Yankees who sought all manner of enterprise. And many called on this already renowned leader and accepted his liberal hospitality.

J. R. Poinsett, who in 1825 became the first American

minister to the Republic, described him : "Santa Anna is a
man of about thirty years of age, of middle stature, slightly
yet well made and possessing a very intelligent and expressive countenance but evidently suffering from fatigue or the
effects of the bad climate. Our reception was polite and
cordial and when we rose to go he insisted upon our staying
to dinner with him."

Many others had studied that expressive countenance and
had also noted his fine dark eyes, his rampant pompadour,
his thick almost negroid lips, his sallow pallor, his melancholy air, "placid sadness," one called it, and the appearance of unhealthy fatigue. A *tortoro triste*—a sad bull ?
For at rest he did seem sad and thwarted, almost sickly,
and surely dejected. Only in *amor*—and he deceived
Doña Inez frequently—or in action did he thrive.

But action was a different matter. Reverses such as those
in Yucatan frustrated him temporarily and even when fortune favored him he did not always have the opportunity
to mount his charger and lead his *jarachos* to battle. Unless he ignited in one of these bursts of pure action, he
seemed a sick man, the tremendous vital force thwarted,
shut in, secreting bile. He was always pleading sickness,
and while his complexion and the rather insalubrious site
of Manga de Clavo suggested a constitutional disease, his
oldest friend Gimenez avers that he enjoyed perfect health.
Besides he died at an advanced age. There seems to have
been much of the hypochondriac in him, whining over his
imagined ills, and taking drugs until his motor force found
an outlet. Zavala, one of his colleagues, spoke of "a prin-
ciple of action forever impelling him forward."

But it was difficult to go full speed forward in the almost

impenetrable maze of Mexican politics of the latter part of
Victoria's term. Indeed it seemed as if it were Mexico's
destiny to provide the most fantastic political picture of
modern time. The followers of the Two Virgins were
again at loggerheads, but this time under the most extraordinary banners. The country was split into the two factions of the York Masons, called the *Yorkinos,* and the
Scotch rite Masons called the *Escoseses.* But the old
divisions, the old parties were apparent under these new
titles ; the creoles, the anti-Spanish fanatics, the radicals, the
Federalists, were mostly *Yorkinos;* and the former *gachupines,* the clericals, and those who hoped for a despotism
through Centralism were largely *Escoseses.*

One odd aspect of the struggle was that clericals including priests were members of the *Escoseses*—and even
the *Yorkinos* were started by a curate, Padré Arénas. The
explanation of this is that up to 1825—when the Pope
issued his anti-Masonic and secret society encyclical, papal
edicts were not spread throughout the body of the Church
in Mexico. The hierarchy—largely Spanish and myopic
traditionalists had become frightened by the severance of
Mexico from the King of Spain, head of the Mexican
church, and had fled abroad, to New Orleans, to Cuba and
to Europe. The Vatican itself was not of one mind as to
how to deal with the situation, and while the priests and
nuns carried on in Mexico, they had no bishops to direct
them. Seminarians to be ordained had to go to New
Orleans to find a bishop. It was complete disorganization.

So the encyclical did not reach them and we have the
strange spectacle of priests becoming members of lodges and
nuns knitting caps and aprons for the "brothers" who were

devout Catholics.   It was not until the beginning of the
next decade that the bishops returned and brought their
flocks up to date with papal decrees.

Moreover it was the American minister Poinsett—he of
the floral name—who technically started the York lodges
in Mexico.   This extraordinary man, who has been erro-
neously accused of introducing Masonry into Mexico, saw
that the lodges which were breaking away from the Scotch
rite had no direct charter and he sent to New York and
got permission from the Grand Master there to start the
York rite in Mexico.

Far from being personal meddling as it has been charged
against this diplomat, it was to further the interests of his
government.   For the long duel between Great Britain
and America for spheres of influence in the New World
was still going on, and Ward, the British minister in Mexico
City, had strongly fortified himself in the conservative and
Escoseses groups.   In order to advance the interests of the
United States, Poinsett had to deal with the conservatives'
opponents, the Federalists.   Besides he felt that evangelical
itch to uplift foreigners which Americans too often experience ; in this case the elevating of the Mexican despotic
dictatorial government to the blessings of popular and states'
rights government.

But the Mexicans saw in this concern for their civic welfare nothing but a smoke-screen, ill concealing a much more
realistic policy than universal democracy.   On the plains
of Texas a far more dangerous invasion than the roving
bands of Neutral Ground ruffians was taking place.
American colonists in formidable numbers were crossing
the Red River and digging in, establishing their sod houses

and planting their crops. Wise heads in Mexico perceived this with apprehension ; Alamán the bespectacled historian-statesman feared its results and passionate Santa Anna threatened to return to finish the job which he had started on the Medina River in 1813. But for the moment these politicians let loose their anger on Poinsett, blaming him for all the ills of the country, on the basis that "blame the foreigner" was a profitable policy.

It was into this mêlée that Santa Anna gingerly advanced a claw. He had somewhat reinstated himself and had intrigued his way into the position of Vice-Governor of the State of Vera Cruz. He mouthed the proper Federalists' doctrines, although he refrained from joining any lodges, alleging that he was opposed to them — not an entirely original attitude, for many thought that they were indeed a plague and ought to be abolished. He, however, coquetted with the *Escoseses* and watched his chance to jump on the heavier balance of the scales.

The Tulancingo affair gave an interesting glimpse of his seething ambition and crafty talents. On December 30th sympathizers with the *Escoseses* announced a plan demanding the suppression of secret societies, the dismissal of Poinsett and the resignation of the President's entire cabinet. The backer of this movement was none other than the Vice-President Nicolas Bravo whose political fortunes were on the wane. In the following days he and his associates pronounced at Tulancingo, a little town not far from the capital.

Professing the same convictions as this group, one may surmise that when the shouts of revolt went up, Santa Anna was not far away. True enough, he appeared at

Huamantla not far from Tulancingo, but he got no further. For Guerrero, the President's minister of war, exhibited unusual energy, gathered large bodies of troops and advanced on the revolters. When it was apparent that the Government had superior forces, Santa Anna appeared and offered his services. Guerrero looked askance at his being at this spot so remote from his district and without leave, but he made the excuse that he was attending a cock-fight at Huamantla. It was manifest that he was actually on the point of joining his co-mates under the rebellious Bravo, and he received a well-merited rebuke. Bravo's forces surrendered after a short skirmish and the leaders were exiled.

Pronunciamiento ! A vocable that however common it was then getting to be, held yet considerable excitement. Bravo's abortive pronouncement was in the grand manner, with large forces concentrating around that most important of places, the capital. It was almost a "palace" revolution, the most daring of all the genus, such was its proximity, and Santa Anna whose nature was well adapted to this form of action could well study what became his *metier*. Clandestine relations with other war lords, control of the rank and file, financial support, a convenient shibboleth — and then *l'audace, toujours l'audace*.

All over the country *jefes* were practising it. European travellers made notes of the phenomenon and the inevitable German scholar came along and wrote down a study of a *pronunciamiento* which he had witnessed on the Pacific coast. But it remained not for a German but for a French *dozent* named Bazancourt to outline with real Teutonic thoroughness the *genus Mexicanus*. According to M.

Bazancourt, first a general or colonel issues a simple pronouncement. He assembles a company, or perhaps a battalion to hear his *grito* of freedom and liberty. The second
stage consists of the drawing up of the *Plan,* the itemization
of protests and demands for constitutional changes and the
definition of the aims of the movement. In the third stage
the insurgent and government forces face each other.
Under exceptional conditions, there is something that might
possibly be termed a battle. But as a rule, the two forces
feint, feel each other out, exchange emissaries ; if the government forces remain loyal, the chief insurgent de-
pronounces ; if the regulars go over to their opponents,
there is a grand march into the capital. The Presidential
incumbent meanwhile has galloped off to Vera Cruz and
an English packet.

Thus the classic form of the *pronunciamiento.* It had
its variations of course, from the spontaneous uprisings in
the capital, where the city mobs often gave the first impetus
down to mere garrison mutinies in obscure provincial towns
where little generals were upset by their ambitious colonels,
who wielded the cries of *Centralism* or *Federalism* to seize
loot and epaulets. Naturally this form of uprising had its
particular appeal to Santa Anna with his combined love for
impetuous action and florid proclamations. It was an outlet, a means of release for the tremendous force within him
which had almost erupted at Huamantla and which on the
second election of a Mexican president welled up again.

After the downfall of Bravo, Guadalupe Victoria was
enabled to obliterate the *Escoseses* as a political force and
the remainder of his term was marked by factional disputes
between the *Yorkinos.* However, Victoria was successful

in sitting on the lid until his four years came to an end and he retired legally and peacefully from the office of President—a phenomenon not to be witnessed again in Mexico for many a year to come.

Creole versus *gachupin*—that old fight was now shifted to an even more deep-seated racial clash in the second presidential campaign. General Guerrero, the staunch old patriot of the southland, had all the qualifications for the Presidency—patriotic service, fidelity to Federalism and the York Rite, a military career—save one—his blood. He was a mestizo and the Indian blood which ran in his veins made him anathema to most of the creoles together with the now leaderless Spanish element. But his opponent Gomez Pedraza had all Guerrero's recommendations plus a creole pedigree which was traceable back to the most unblemished Castilian antecedents. He won the support of both radicals and conservatives and carried off the election. The defeated candidate sullenly acquiesced but naturally, after the bitterness of a racial campaign, his partisans were ready to revolt. They raised no standards or *gritos,* but their rebellious spirit seemed to need but an audacious leader to pronounce in the name of the chagrined Guerrero.

The instrument was ready at hand and was none other than Santa Anna. That remark of the caustic Pedraza about his projected Havana expedition had come to his ears and had long rankled. Even more so was Pedraza's failure to accord him special ceremonial honors when they met a few years before in Jalapa—a matter which had offended the late Governor of Yucatan's enormous vanity. During the Presidential campaign he discovered a warm affection

for Guerrero whom he had formerly opposed and he elec-
tioneered for him in Vera Cruz, but so ineffectively that
the state went overwhelmingly for Pedraza.

Santa Anna had played his cards and lost; lost not only
for Guerrero but for himself since the legislature removed
him from the position of vice-governor. There were only
two courses to pursue; to "pronounce" or to sink back into
Manga de Clavo in apathy and defeat. But the "spirit of
action" was too strong and, gathering about him some of
his cronies in the army at Jalapa, he collected a battalion
and made for the fortress of Perote, good shelter for a tiny
force, protection until other *pronunciamientos* followed.

It was September and just eighteen years before in a little
village in the north Father Hidalgo had been the first to
declare Mexican Independence. But only Santa Anna
with his sharp sense of the dramatic would have thought
of delaying his rising a few days so that he might shout his
own *grito* on the sixteenth of September — that day on
which all Mexicans commemorated Hidalgo's famous declaration. The fortress of Perote rang with the eloquence of
his *pronunciamiento* and the shouts of the ragged soldiery
who responded to his ready syllables. After the din was
over, the new Libertador settled down to wait for favorable
echoes.

But his call to arms had no answer. Guerrero and his
followers found the uprising premature and bided their
time for a better occasion. The government declared
Santa Anna an outlaw and sent two of its chief generals,
Rincón and Calderón, to subdue him. As they closed in on
Perote, the arch-rebel left the fortress, eluded them and led
his little army toward the south, toward Oaxaca and the

fastnesses where Guerrero years before had been successful in defying the Spanish.

Napoleon crossed the Alps with hundreds of broken caisson wheels and exhausted pack-horses in his wake. His Mexican counterpart left a trail of absurdly long proclamations over the rocky sierras of south central Mexico. When his vanguard encountered a force of the enemy, he would retire to the shade of a tree or a peasant's brushwood hut where in his gorgeously brocaded uniform he would pace up and down as he dictated manifestoes of no less than 10,000 words each; at times calling imperiously on his new adversaries to surrender; at other times, especially when the hostile force was superior, attempting to draw them into prolonged negotiations so that he could find time to escape. Finally, he reached the ancient city of Oaxaca, devoutly packed to its walls with convents, monasteries and churches.

There in the convent of Santo Domingo he fortified himself. The city's churches and religious buildings had been built centuries before to withstand the earthquakes which afflicted it so frequently and their walls were as thick as bastions. With his genius for sortie and quick raids, Santa Anna had the best prospects for holding out against Rincón who finally came up and settled himself leisurely in the Bishop's palace. It was an ecclesiastical duel — episcopal walls replying with shot and shell to nunnery roofs.

Rincón's men were now heavily reinforced by General Calderón and his division, and it was apparent that Santa Anna badly needed assistance. His greatest resource, guile, did not fail him and he sent a band of his followers dressed as monks into the half-deserted convent of San Francisco which was located near the enemy's headquarters. The soldiers well filled their new rôles, tolled the bells for mass, assumed sacerdotal attitudes and, perhaps easiest task of all, sought out the collection boxes.   General Calderón and his staff frequently attended mass in the chapel of this convent but by some chance on this particular day chose another temple for their devotions.   However, foiled in the principal objective of the scheme, the soldiers of Santa Anna took up the collection and made off with not only that money but some more in the strong box of the institution.

As the regulars redoubled the vigor of their assaults, our hero in a last effort to avoid the doom which now seemed inevitable, tried to draw Calderón into an armistice.   After Calderón had firmly rejected his overtures, he was preparing literally to die in the last cloister arch when he was dumbfounded to observe his formidable besiegers marching away.   For in far-off Mexico, the sluggish half-breed Guerrero had finally acted, listened to "the call of his people" and with the aid of an audacious revolutionary named Zavala, chased his enemy—the aristocratic Pedraza—from the Palace after a ferocious little uprising in which soldiers and mobs thoroughly pillaged the capital.

So the second President of Mexico, forced out of his legitimate office by a revolution, went into exile and his rival mounted the throne with all the pomp and military circumstance that now became the inevitable accompaniment of a change of executive.   Officers who had taken the chance of espousing his cause jumped three and sometimes four grades in rank in proportion to the number of ragged privates they brought over to the revolters ; lieutenants and captains became generals over night ; generals who had "turned" at the eleventh hour or recognized the *fait accompli* became ministers if they were powerful enough, or if not sufficiently influential struggled to retain their posts ; the *jefes* who remained loyal had to cool their heels in New Orleans or Havana cafés until the next revolution ; treachery was at a premium from now on in Mexico and elective popular government perished.

The stage, the *decor* was set—was indeed largely the creation of General Antonio Lopez de Santa Anna. He had learned well the technique of pronouncing, the swagger of military bluffing which passed as war in Mexico, the proper mouthing of shibboleths, and best of all his name now, after the downfall of those who opposed him, Iturbide and Pedraza, was a potent and sinister one among the reigning war lords of Mexico. He was only 35 years old and was again installed as the Governor, the Dictator of the State of Vera Cruz. Might not there be a more precious guerdon for his ambitions ?

CHAPTER III

CAUDILLO

AFTER his miraculous escape from Oaxaca, Santa Anna received as his share of the new government favors the Governorship of Vera Cruz and settled down to tasks of a provincial *jefe* (chief). But most restlessly. He might harangue the palm-tree legislators of that tropical State, he might intrigue in the squabbling factions of the assembly which met in the tiny hall of that verdurous capital, Jalapa—but in reality he found administrative matters most uninteresting. The spoils of the new government were too recently divided for important cabals to form in opposition. What was he to do with this indomitable force within him? Enemies? At home— would they ever be wholly downed?—the at present humbled conservatives; abroad—it was obvious—Spain!

He leaped from his state of inactivity with the ever popular cry "Death to the *gachupin!*" Other Mexican opportunists in power were not slow to appropriate this new movement; it was much easier than trying to solve the knotty problems of finance and economy. For Mexico was in a most chaotic condition after this first successful overthrow of the constitutional power. It was less a state than a collection of loosely connected fiefs, suffering under their exacting overlords the Generals. Congress was mainly a mouthpiece for a sonorous flow of Latin oratory — magical to inspire to valor but also to spread confusion and panic.

In Spain meanwhile Ferdinand and his council, little superior in discernment to the Mexicans, thought that the erring daughter after the past years of desperate illness from the grave maladies of democracy would happily return to the benefits of the old Empire. They gave willing ear to the exhortations of the Tories, to exiled priests and various folk who had been driven out by the Republicans — often men who had not been back in Mexico for years. In the spring of 1829 they fitted out an expedition under General Barradas, a force of about three thousand men, soldiers used to salubrious airs of the Peninsula, and with the same sapience which characterized their diplomacy saw fit to dispatch these unfortunate warriors to the pernicious swamps of the Mexican coast in the midst of the yellow fever season. Thus began the war of 1829 between the mother country and the young republic — the counterpart of the War of 1812 between the United States and England.

All through the preceding year there had been rumors of such an invasion, but the Government merely employed them as ammunition against the Tory-minded opposition. The army was not increased nor was equipment put in order. In June a French frigate brought the news that the armada was approaching Mexico, but the Government was still cool to the problem of national defense. When word finally came that the Spanish had landed, the President moved to call an extra session of Congress. Even that feeble measure was attacked by politicians and the Spanish had been on Mexican soil ten days before Congress actually met; and not until the end of August did they give the executive extraordinary powers for the defense of the nation. But there was one public figure who was alert to the danger.

Santa Anna had done much more than utter his harsh *jaracho* war-cry against the *gachupin*. Whether from authentic advices across the water or from his own seventh martial sense, he sniffed the coming invasion. As early as June he had vainly tried to get the Government to appropriate more forces to meet a possible landing party—naturally in the State of Vera Cruz. But when the news burst he dashed from his hacienda to the port of Vera Cruz and plunged into a fever of military organization—a matter which he understood thoroughly. He levied a forced loan of $20,000 on the merchants of the place who, now really apprehensive, bestirred themselves and handed it over within three days.

He gathered about two thousand men and when the word came that the Spaniards had landed on the coast near Tampico, he loaded his infantry in a small improvised fleet, dispatched his cavalry to the north by land and sailed off for Tampico. On embarking an old French veteran of the Napoleonic wars had said to him, "This expedition may prove for you what Napoleon's Egyptian campaign did for him." Whatever its import, a seductive comparison for the man who afterwards announced that he was "The Napoleon of the West."

Yet the Corsican would hardly have set out with an ill-armed and badly disciplined force of two thousand to oppose a seasoned army of four thousand regulars—for such was the number reported in Mexico. Also, in accordance with all the canons of military discipline, Santa Anna should have waited for orders from his superiors in the capital. Furthermore, the Spanish admiral had been given orders—the obvious, the predictable thing to do under these circumstances—after leaving the land forces to patrol the coasts in search of any Mexican reinforcements which might venture by sea. It was a case where courage—or was it crass personal ambition?—was equivalent to foolhardiness.

Nevertheless he launched this audacious, this foolhardy —from a military standpoint—expedition. For other considerations weighed importantly with him. Might not the military log-rollers in the capital anticipate his move and send some other war lord to command the army—some rival who would thus have an excellent chance to seize laurels, power, perhaps even the succession to the Presidency? As for engaging with a superior force, had he not plunged headlong into *pronunciamientos* and emerged the victor? Santa Anna's motto was to act first; if things went badly, he could always negotiate later and extricate himself from difficulties.

When he arrived near Tampico he found an interesting situation. Barradas had taken possession of the town of Tampico without any trouble. The Mexican General Mier y Teran, a most able militarist, had checked his move to emerge from the end of the rocky peninsula on which the city was built. So the Spanish general had resigned himself to issuing proclamations calling on the stubborn Mexicans to yield to the banner of the King and to examining his none too favorable surroundings. Tampico was separated from the mainland by the slimy Panuco River and several miasmic lagoons on the shores of which palmettos and banyans clustered. In the background above the lagoons, and the parrot-infested forests of the mainland loomed the jagged peak of Bernal some sixty leagues distant—beacon light of the road he must pass to the highlands and the capital if he was to conquer.

The salubrious highlands must have seemed a veritable Canaan for the unfortunate Spaniards, for they had encountered a more formidable enemy than the forces of Mier y Teran. The deadly mosquitoes had been at work and the hospital was overflowing with *vomito* victims. The morale of the invaders was badly impaired and Barradas thought that a sortie against Mier who was entrenched at the other end of the peninsula might restore their courage and force a decisive victory. He left a garrison which was largely composed of invalids and went forth.

At this moment Santa Anna slyly introduced himself into the fray. He had landed safely thanks to the Spanish admiral, who had ignored Barradas' orders to patrol the coast, and had taken up his station at Tuxpam across the bay from Tampico. There he put in order his faithful *jarachos* who, bright and healthy, throve on the fever-laden airs. He had received word from the Government that he had been named commander-in-chief of the Tampico forces as a reward for his readiness in starting from Vera Cruz, but he chose to let Mier take the brunt of the open fighting.

For Mier such prosaic combats, but for himself, the arch-dissembler, there was a more spectacular rôle, a quick *coup* which might bring victory to the Mexicans. He sent word to Mier to keep Barradas occupied and then he prepared to cross the river stealthily by night and to surprise the small and genuinely feeble garrison in the town of Tampico. It was a scheme fraught with hazards, for he cut off chances of retreat by crossing the river, and even if he carried Tampico he would have to face the forces of Barradas who would run to the rescue of their base. But tactics mattered little to the impetuous "pronouncer" whose guerrilla training had taught him the efficacy of the rapid, tricky thrust.

With the tireless activity which characterized him he assembled a large number of launches, row-boats and canoes and embarked in them with about six hundred of the best men. It was a dark night, about ten o'clock on August 20th when he set his fleet in motion on the river Panuco. The crossing was effected successfully as well as the disembarkation, which was made on the side of the city least fortified and most vulnerable. He arranged his forces in three groups and was about to advance softly on his prey, when one of the men accidentally fired his gun.

It was enough to arouse the garrison under Colonel Salamon who immediately mustered his troops and disposed them at the most strategic points. He even dragged the sick from their beds, put guns in their hands and bade them fire from the windows and roof-tops. When Santa Anna came up he was met by the resistance of this desperate corps which fought him for every yard of ground. From house to house and from walls and doors the battle went on and the losses were considerable on both sides. Even Santa Anna had his blouse pierced by three balls, but unscathed still cheered his troops on.

But by two in the afternoon his banner flew from only a few of the houses and he foresaw a long struggle before he could conquer. Besides he feared that ere he did,

Barradas would come up and he would be ill able to receive him. He sent a flag of truce and requested a conference.

Colonel Salamon, nothing loath to gain time, accepted for he had sent a messenger to Barradas and was confident of early relief. In the conference room Santa Anna was at his best and he was soon astonishing and intimidating Salamon, a credulous old man, with his tales about twenty thousand men on the mainland, ready to supplement his forces. Meanwhile a messenger sent by Barradas announcing his approach was captured by Castrillón, Santa Anna's adjutant and so could not bring the news to Salamon. Castrillón rushed to the conference room to bring the news to his chief.

When he entered, however, he announced in a loud voice, "Gentlemen, two thousand more men have just arrived." The Spaniards who had been listening to Santa Anna's impressive figures thought that the aide meant that some reinforcements had arrived for the besiegers. But Castrillón made a sign to Santa Anna who understood and gave orders to get his troops ready to embark. Just then Barradas arrived and the situation looked most uncomfortable for the Mexicans. What a folly Santa Anna's expedition seemed now! Caught with water behind him and only six hundred men while his adversaries looming to the number of two thousand needed only to attack to destroy him! It looked now as if he was a failure not only in tactics but also in his own out-and-dash *metier*. What a commander!

And what a warrior Barradas was! More diplomat than warrior, for instead of profiting by the enemy's sorry position he declared that although Salamon had started the parley without his permission he would respect it and simply requested that the discussion should proceed. In the conference room now Barradas glibly poured forth his often repeated Spanish propaganda ; saying that he had been sent not to harm the Mexican people but simply to bring them back to Spain ; and finally that General Santa Anna could depart freely for his base headquarters from which he could carry on further discussions which would prevent the shedding of blood.

Santa Anna subtly answered that he too abhorred the sad scenes of a combat and left the conference room, embarked his troops and took them back across the river, where he prepared not for further parleys but for more persistent attacks on Tampico. Artillery was brought up—and new points of vantage were established to harry the Spaniards. And to spur on his efforts the Government sent him news that it had raised him to the rank of General of Division.

Commenting on this escape and subsequent developments in his Memoirs, he wrote, "Well has it been said, that when fortune gives, it gives with full hands."

Barradas pursued further his conciliatory policy by sending Santa Anna a note recognizing the Mexicans' right to self-government, offering to prevail on the Governor of Cuba to stop sending more expeditions to Mexico and asking an interview on the basis of this proposal. Santa Anna replied with a curt note of refusal and a bombardment. After about a week of this shelling, feeling doubtless that Barradas should be in a humbler mood, Santa Anna sent him another note, more arrogant and menacing. He referred to Barradas' forces as a "handful of adventurers" and threatened that he would "rush upon his (Barradas') garrison with quarter for none" if there were not an unconditional surrender.

The Spanish commander was in a dangerous situation. He had not been able to find a single ship to send off and seek the return of his fleet. His main outpost, the fort at the bar, was imperiled by Mier. Worse than his military state, however, was the *vomito* situation. No less than nine hundred of his men were ill, not to mention the wounded. Tampico was one large hospital. The proud force which landed 2600 strong was now reduced to about 1200 through casualties and illness.

Moved by this predicament, he had sent off a letter which crossed Santa Anna's epistolary defiance and deprived the latter of the satisfaction of receiving an humble reply from the *gachupin*. A confusing exchange of notes followed, one from Barradas in reply to Santa Anna's insulting letter, saying that he did not offer to evacuate through impotence but to avoid shedding blood, while the Mexican wrote that without having received specific orders from the Government to the contrary, he could not vary his proposal of unconditional surrender. Feeling that victory was within his grasp he wished to exploit it to the full with the glory of a haughty triumph. The Spaniard refused to entertain any such terms and parleys broke off.

Pursuing his ambition to force the Spanish to their knees, Santa Anna projected a night attack on the fort at the bar. The wise Mier strongly advised against this, urging a long bombardment and a well-prepared assault, but he could not prevail over Santa Anna's impetuous spirit. Troops were brought up from the mainland and under cover of darkness were hurled against the little redoubt. But the Mexicans had not counted on Spanish valor and after several hours of bloody conflict, the attacking forces had to retire leaving the field littered with dead and wounded.

General Mier now had his own way and made preparations for a sustained cannonading of the Spanish outpost, which had suffered heavily too. Barradas, seeing the fort doomed and deeming that the Mexican loss was so great that their commander might take a different view from his "unconditional surrender," sent another emissary asking for liberal terms of surrender. He stipulated that the Spanish army could march out with drums beating and turn over its guns to the Mexicans, the officers however to retain their swords. The whole army was to be transported back to Havana at Spanish expense, "the lives, honor and property of the Spanish to be scrupulously respected."

By this time Santa Anna, much chastened by his defeat the night before, agreed to the terms. To his honor they were respected and the Spanish army sometime later embarked for Spain. But Santa Anna's recession from his stand of unconditional surrender did not dim his triumph. Coldly considered it was hardly a striking victory. The fatal tentacles of the mosquitoes had worked more havoc than bullets and the impractical policies of Barradas had contributed largely to the Spanish surrender. Besides a veil was best drawn over Santa Anna's two coups and the only generalship on the Mexican side was that of Mier y Teran. But the latter did not write the triumphant dispatches, and the Mexican nation was not in a mood to scrutinize too coolly and closely this decisive repulse of the *gachupines'* invasion.

They lauded to the skies their new national idol and thus

Santa Anna became known as the "Hero of Tampico." State legislatures vied with one another in naming him "Benemerito," conferring on him citizenship and striking off medals in his honor. Others voted him bejewelled swords, and the whole *populus mexicanus* which had never seen their republican standards in conflict with a foreign army rushed to applaud this consul and his triumph. A few weeks later when he landed at Vera Cruz, he was borne on the shoulders of his admirers to the Governor's palace. Te Deums, balls and banquets celebrated the homecoming of Santa Anna.

But the Hero of Tampico was not destined to relax long in the balmy airs of Manga de Clavo, graciously acknowledging the medals, odes, swords and oratory which poured in upon him. A storm was gathering which was much more menacing to Guerrero and his Government than any *gachupin* invasion. Just as he and his partisans invoked the national hatred of the Spanish, so the pure creole class were coalescing to attack the President in whom they saw the symbol of the *mestizo* and Indian. (It was even rumored that Guerrero had negro blood in his veins.)

As was typical of the disordered politics of the time, the Vice-President was the focal point of this opposition. Anastasio Bustamente was one of the most distinguished chameleons of Mexican politics of those days. He had been successively a royalist, an Iturbidist, a republican, a Centralist and a Federalist. He had the most magnificent propensity for building up flimsy governments, constructing impossible cabinets and then imperturbably watching his rivals bring the house of cards down on his head. But these checks never daunted him. After refreshing himself with some tamales, his favorite dish, he would optimistically start to erect new structures. He was cast by Fate to be Santa Anna's foil. Santa Anna hated him with the venom of a temperamental man who is infuriated by a stolid, undiscouraged adversary ; he learned to love him in a peculiar way, as a hero loves the villain who supplies him with a dramatic victory.

At this time Bustamente was a Federalist with Centralist leanings, of the opposite party to Guerrero, but thrown into the executive bed with his rival according to the absurd custom of the time. Naturally his relations with the President were far from conjugal and he began to conspire to overthrow the Government. After playing up to the spirit of race antagonism which the creoles felt for the half-caste Guerrero, he proclaimed revolution against the President in the city of Jalapa, at Santa Anna's very door. He tendered the olive branch to the "boss" of Vera Cruz, urged him to join the rebels. It was a chance for the great opportunist to join what was rapidly assuming the magnitude of a landslide against the President.

But Santa Anna failed to estimate correctly the respective forces of the two combatants and still paying lip service to Federalism he elected to stand by his chief, Guerrero. He issued a long proclamation which reviewed his own glorious career in all its phases, bestowed a few conventional compliments on the President and reached its gaudy peroration with the promise that Bustamente would only conquer over his "dead body." Gathering several hundred men about him, he doughtily advanced to meet the rebel forces. But Bustamente for once surpassed him in machinations and bribery. The soldiers began to grow cold to the ardor of their leader as they neared Jalapa, desertions thinned the ranks and ere very long Santa Anna was in the position of a commander without a force. Disconsolately, he turned his horse about and cantered back to his hacienda. There he issued a lame manifesto recognizing Bustamente's new Government as the rulers of the nation.

Low tide for Santa Anna ! To swallow his boast of the "dead body" was easy enough, but to retire to private life and watch the triumph of the phlegmatic Bustamente, so obviously lacking in his own flamboyant qualities, was difficult. However, he consoled himself with a new hacienda, "Encero." Besides, Bustamente's pitiful struggles with a new cabinet afforded him a compensating spectacle and he learned what he was to have good knowledge of later on — that an occasional retirement, a short interregnum only consolidated the forces of his own popularity.

Indeed the Hero of Tampico still had much prestige. Bustamente after routing, capturing and executing Guerrero, sought to enlist Santa Anna's aid by offering him a post in his Ministry. But Santa Anna resisted his overtures. He either intended to play his rôle as a consistent Federalist or he saw that the Government was not strong enough to last long. Indeed, Bustamente had not the power to keep the army in line, failing to distribute promotions properly and making some unpopular military regulations, notably the suppression of the *soldaderas,* the common-law female companions who marched with the soldiers to battle, cooked their food and even foraged for them, thus serving as a sort of commissary.

While our hero had affected complete absorption in the labors of agriculture, he actually had been watching the situation closely and his ambition to become President in the next election grew with time. He did not formally throw his hat in the ring, but he covertly advanced his candidacy. Thus we find him writing to a Mexican politician, Santangelo, who was then in New York. ". . . the next election of President and Vice-President, if by that time I should deserve a majority of votes, I will be quick to accept the honor and to sacrifice as a gift to the nation my repose and whatever else in the nature of a private gentleman can make me creditable. It is my fixed intention to be called, comparing myself in this respect to a modest maiden who prefers to be longed for rather than to show her longing." He continues coquetting with Santangelo who is also a journalist, subtly suggesting that he spread propaganda in the United States for his election.

Two years of retirement had made Santa Anna careful and cautious, unwilling impetuously to utter a *grito* or empty a barracks on the least provocation. When popular hatred had gradually accumulated against Bustamente and the inevitable military cabals began to form, he adopted a coy and disinterested attitude. A Colonel Landero in Vera Cruz for a long time tried to win him to an uprising, but he resisted his solicitations for some time. Finally he grudgingly accepted, but said he would reserve his own freedom of action in the matter. What he meant by this was speedily discovered after Landero's pronouncement in January 1832, when he wrote to the President referring to the rising and offering his services as a "mediator."

It was a clever trap and the clumsy Bustamente fell into it. Little did he know that Santa Anna was simply trying to ascertain if the Government had any backbone, and by this time nervous about his security, he assented to the parley. In reply Santa Anna backed up Landero and pronounced against the Government. With his customary sense of financial realities he seized in Vera Cruz the funds which the Government had sent that far in payment of the external debt and he dispatched a heavy mail to potential pronouncers in other parts of the country. Viva Santa Anna ! — cried the Vera Cruzan rabble. He was off on adventure again.

He did venture forth and offer battle at Tolome, not far from the port, but his old rival the loyal General Calderón decisively defeated him and sent him fleeing back to Vera Cruz. Behind the walls of the great maritime city, however, he found the best outlet for his talents. He mounted no less than 120 pieces of artillery, mended the fortifications and organized a little fleet. The situation somewhat resembled his previous encounter with Calderón in Oaxaca, for Santa Anna harassed his opponent with volatile and effective forays.

Apprised through spies that Calderón was expecting a train of provisions, he sallied forth, captured not only the supplies but also a chest containing some 30,000 pesos. An English traveller arriving in Vera Cruz at this moment to find to his dismay "a state of alarm and military movement," wrote down his astonished observations on the appearance of Santa Anna's *pronunciados* as they came back to Vera Cruz amid pomp and circumstance after their successful raid.

"Heroes exhibiting so unmilitary and extraordinary an appearance, I never witnessed before. They were attired in shreds and patches formed of every color in the rainbow.

Some had no uniform at all, and many of them, leaving out of consideration altogether this warlike distinction, seemed pretty nearly divested of all clothing whatever. The cavalry, so to call them, were a complete mob of half-starved peasantry; numbers of them were without either stockings or shoes; others were deprived of both coats and jackets, and their nether garments torn in rags and tatters, seemed ready to be carried away with the first good breeze that might blow. Their accoutrements corresponded in fanciful variety with the rest of their motley attire; and rusty swords, broken pikes, and worn-out firelocks, apparently kept for show rather than use, constituted the mortal weapons of this ragged cavalcade. It reminded me of Falstaff's ragamuffins with whom he refused to march through Coventry and who [were] charged with less reason than would have been Santa Anna in the present instance with having unloaded the gibbets on his line of march in order to press men into his service."

About all the investing forces could do was to cut all communications of the city with the interior and exchange shells with the besieged. They had to divide their men around the city in such fashion that their own communications were none too good and they suffered much from the deadly sallies which Santa Anna knew so well how to make. After several weeks all they had accomplished was to stave in the top of a church and to capture one of the ships. Meanwhile the yellow fever season had come on and many cases of sickness arose.

Well might Santa Anna be defiant, for unlike the last fight with Calderón he now had a strong ally on his side. The Government troops gathered from the *tierra fria,* the high and salubrious plateau region, fell by the hundreds under the attack of *vomito* and it was not long before about one thousand had perished not to mention those who dragged themselves in various stages of sickness ; whereas Santa Anna and his *jarachos* were as healthy as ever.

Finally after a covering attack on May 11th, the Calderón forces retired to the highlands around Jalapa, leaving Santa Anna not only with the honors of the field but with $400,000 taken from the customs charges. These he employed to spread the revolution, and with such good effect, that by Autumn it was in full swing.

For a while it looked as if this amorphous wave of feeling against Bustamente might be crystallized into some orderly reform movement with General Mier y Teran, the real hero of Tampico at its head. He was a true leader of men, strong of will, wise of purpose and free from venality or personal ambition. But his tragic end just at this particular moment symbolized in a sense the plight of Mexico. Brooding over the deplorable state of the country and perceiving in this new outbreak naught but another cynical revolution, he committed suicide.

Another personality loomed through the smoke of revolution. In the north a scholarly lawyer, Gomez Farias, filled with shame at Mexico's chaos, and painfully aware of the military abuses which caused it, had led the anti-Bustamente revolt in Zacatecas. He, like Mier y Teran, was pure of heart and purpose, but he was filled with hope of reform and thought he saw in Santa Anna the proper instrument to forge a new system of affairs.

Meanwhile the latter had been winning a few skirmishes and a great many allies among his own tribe, the military.

Generals all over the country dissatisfied with Bustamente went over to the revolution and by November the *jaracho* Napoleon was in the highlands, threatening the capital. Bustamente saw it was all over and abdicated. Triumph again for the famous throne-wrecker! —but a qualified triumph. For the lawyer from Zacatecas, stickling for constitutional procedure insisted on fair play in the new régime. He made Santa Anna consent to Gomez Pedraza's return to the Presidency.

But his triumphal entry into Mexico City on the 3rd of January removed the wry taste of associating with his hated rival, for his cortège resembled that of a victorious Roman consul. He was met at the gates of the city by four carriages in the first of which was an attractive young girl beautifully arrayed and carrying a shield which was adorned with a portrait of the Hero of Tampico; with her were various other girls bearing symbolic burdens and one of them carried a picture representing the battle of Tampico. Others followed emblematic of the Nation, the constitution, etc., but his honors came first.

High tide for Santa Anna! He knew that the menace of Pedraza would not last long, for in accordance with the rather picturesque effort to make the Government legal, his rival was to serve out the remainder of the term for which he had been elected four years before, and which was cut short by his exile—and the remainder consisted of only one month. High tide for that dramatic ability which won the impressionable Mexicans! Knowing full well that his partisans would soon elect him President to succeed Pedraza, he threw himself into the attitude of the modest retiring patriot. Turning his horse's head for Manga de

Clavo, he cried with studied humility, "My entire ambition is to exchange the sword for the plow. If any hand again disturbs the public peace, Mexicans, do not forget me; I shall return to your call and we will make the world see that tyrants and oppressors cannot stay in the Mexican Republic."

The call came a few months later when by an election in Congress he was named President with Gomez Farias as Vice-President. But he only partially answered it. It must have required no little strength of will to make the decision he did, for it would have been pleasant to stand on the Palace balcony April 1st and be sworn in as President, with salvos of artillery, and more symbolical maidens to stroke his vanity. But pursuant to a sort of Fabian policy which he was to find most effective, he thought it wiser, while accepting the Presidency, to plead illness and to name Gomez Farias as Acting President until he "recovered." For Pedraza, prompted by Farias, had roused a tempest of passions and dissensions which Santa Anna would rather not attempt to still.

Indeed it was a tempest, for now loomed a fight which was to be carried on for the next thirty years, plunging Mexico in the worst kind of civil war whose implications and problems have not been settled to this day. The Church like a huge leviathan was stirring uneasily, disturbed from its repose by new conditions and a changing environment. Up until the advent of the Republic it had truly lived in the manner of the mediæval Church in Europe, the dominant power in national life with the State as its inferior, and virtually the agent of police power.

It had reached its height of spirituality and usefulness

in the seventeenth century, humanizing the colonization of the Spanish conquerors, a protector of the people from occasional rigorous and grasping viceroys, and at times acting as the civil power itself through the Archbishop who often became viceroy for short terms. But whether as primate or viceroy, the head of the Mexican Church was appointed by the King of Spain—a centuries' old arrangement between the Pope and the Spanish Crown—a link not easily broken by the independence movement.

But its very efflorescence in Mexico with innumerable orders and societies of priests had its seeds of decadence. For the secular clergy, Benedictines, Dominicans, Jesuits, Bethlemites and numerous other orders could not live in harmony and by the eighteenth century reform measures had been taken which definitely sapped the vitality of the great body. The most useful of all, the Jesuits, the best of the teaching and missionary orders, was suppressed by the Spanish Crown, with the consent of the Pope, and the best rejuvenating blood of the Church was lost. Then followed the independence movement which broke the link between Spain and its colony and upset those immovable traditionalists, the Church hierarchy. Frightened from their mediæval sacristies by this new era, they fled precipitately from Mexico. So the disorganization of the Church reached its height and was not helped by a dilatory Pope who took no measures to put order in its chaos.

Now returned to their *Obispados* and altars, the clergymen looked apprehensively at the civil chaos. The adventurers and opportunists who went in and out of power had not only upset the administrative order but had wrecked the finances of the State. London was reluctant to underwrite their revolutions and there were so many drafts on the ordinary revenues that they had to look about for another place to dip their greedy hands. The Church had enormous properties, a truly prodigious wealth, and this mass of money potential and real was naturally the best pie for the militarist-statesmen to cut.

Gomez Farias was to be the agent for this raid. He was well aware that the military had to be curbed before domestic peace was to come, but thought that he might with their aid begin reform with the Church which undoubtedly did need renovation. This Jacobin leader was no Marat or Danton, but a strictly confessional Catholic. Scrupulously honest in his personal affairs and a sincere and unswerving constitutionalist, he sought to curb the wild militarists. He put his programs and plans ahead of his own personal advancement and aggrandizement and thus shone as an exceptional man among the other time-servers and pushers who swarmed in Mexico.

However, reputed to be a mountain of learning and erudition, he was in reality only moderately well educated; and as a thinker, obviously half-baked. He probably best represents the confused and unfortunate character of Mexican liberalism of that time. He was a student of the United States government and policies but he seems to have learned little — particularly from our happy tradition of religious tolerance and separation of Church and State. Living long in this country he never seems to have understood our institutions or dominant trends of popular policy — witness his die-hard attitude on the Texas question and the Mexican-United States War — an attitude worthy of the most purblind Mexican conservative.

This imperfect student of American affairs and professed admirer of our institutions, capped his new program of reform of the Church with placing the *patronato,* the appointive power of bishops and priests in the hands of the State, a throw-back to the old Spanish system under which the King had the power to appoint the hierarchy. The bishops myopically peering from their bookish and eighteenth century retreats at this menacing state with its greedy generals and venal politicians naturally took fright and opposed many measures which they might better have compromised with, such as toleration of other sects, abolition of the collection of Church revenues by the Government, etc.

While Farias was acting as if it were 1933 and the clergy as if it were 1517, our hero reposed in Manga de Clavo, watching with interest the struggles of his Vice-President. He kept in constant communication with Farias, assuring him that he was well able to deal with the situation and asserting that the principles of Federalism — did he ever exactly understand what these meant? — would prevail. But more than the Federalists and Farias had his ear, for the clergy so recently vilifying the rebel of Tolome now approached him and tried to reach an understanding. Revolts now arose in the more devout sections of the country and not a few talked of Santa Anna the dictator. Intoxicating talk for such an inflammable egotist. For Jean Garat, the old veteran of Bonaparte's campaign was one of his intimates and full of yarns and anecdotes about the great Emperor of the French. It was at this time that he commenced his collection of Napoleonana, pictures of the great man, statues (representing him in the famous pensive attitude, hand in his bosom), and books about his regal glory. They filled his haciendas and they filled his all too impressionable mind.

So we may picture him returning to the capital alert for some new way to deal with the troublesome Farias and his visionary measures. He arrived none too soon, for a week later, on May 26th, a serious revolt broke out in the western states, its leaders assailing the anti-clerical measures and calling on Santa Anna to be the protector of the Church. Within a few days other risings occurred nearer the capital in the State of Mexico and Santa Anna turned over the Presidency to Farias, assumed control of a small army and went forth to quell the revolts.

To quell them? He was now indeed in a confusing predicament, advancing on those who proclaimed him as dictator, who flattered his ambition for power—and how he longed for just that—and yet bound by his oath and previous policies to support the Government. He seemed to yield at first to duty. He hesitated, attempted to compromise and to smooth the troubled waters.

On June 3rd from Tlalpam where he had gone with his troops he wrote to Farias begging him to influence the Senators and Deputies to mitigate the drastic anti-clerical program, to postpone the dreaded exercise of the *Patronato* until "better circumstances prevail." Also he urged Farias to stop the editor of the *Demócrata,* a radical paper, from discussing ecclesiastical questions until a more convenient time. He was apparently endeavoring to act the moderating executive and to stick to constitutional procedure. At the same time vaulting ambitions were troubling him. But the dilemma was soon to be resolved.

It was on June 6th that this agile prestidigitator waved his wand in one of his most surprising tricks — one of those mysterious affairs on which there is no documentary evidence but whose suspicious nature points to Santa Anna's duplicity. A curious piece of adventure — for Santa Anna was apparently taken captive by his own troops at Zuchi. His extraordinary captors immediately proclaimed their imprisoned charge dictator of Mexico. It looked like a scheme for upsetting Farias by Santa Anna himself, for the former had been deserted by many of his supporters in Mexico and seemed unarmed and helpless. Moreover, much evidence seems to strengthen this conclusion, for Arista, our hero's alleged jailer, later declared that Santa Anna was not held in durance vile, but allowed to go or come as he pleased.

But Farias was not without energy or resolution ; within a few days he had organized a strong force and resuscitated the power of his Government. He put down with great severity the *pronunciamiento* in the capital, imprisoned the leaders, restored order and raised an impressive force of about 6,000 civic guards. Martial law was declared and the capital put in a strong state of defense.

The game, in the expressive language of melodrama, was up, and a few days later Santa Anna "escaped" from his appreciative guards and was next seen attending mass in Puebla in preparation for prosecuting war against the Church and its military partisans. For the game was really up ; he had no other course, now that the surprisingly determined meddler Farias had shown fight and strength, than to prosecute the campaign against his erstwhile captors. No longer vacillating he jumped into the fray. The leaders of the rebels, among them General Arista, were finally captured after a prolonged summer and fall campaign and sent into exile. The coup had failed.

It was no time to intrigue for another, so our hero again adopted the policy—which became famous—of retiring to his hacienda until affairs changed. It was these periodical retreats which inspired Guillermo Prieto, the illustrious poet, to write in his memoirs, "The names of Santa Anna and Gomez Farias who alternately occupied the power appeared now like those of two impresarios of theatrical companies, one with his committee of soldiers, ignorant gamblers and profiteers, a disorderly group; the other with eminent liberals, with freemasons, anarchic patriots, and men of action, each with his Virgin of Guadalupe and his plan of regeneration between his coat and his skin."

The following table illustrates this curious policy—a policy due partly to a latent cowardice of his nature—a fear of facing big issues and critical events:

May 16, 1833 to June 3, 1833—Santa Anna, President.

June 3, 1833 to June 18, 1833—Gomez Farias, Acting President.

June 18, 1833 to July 5, 1833—Santa Anna, President.

July 5, 1833 to October 27, 1833—Gomez Farias, Acting President.

October 27, 1833 to December 15, 1833—Santa Anna, President.

December 16, 1833 to April 24, 1834—Gomez Farias, Acting President.

April 24, 1834 to January 28, 1835—Santa Anna, President.

He was now the unofficial leader of the clericals although he still professed adherence to the Government. He was acclaimed as their champion by the Government enemies in spite of his action in putting down the rebellion, and this popular view of the situation created an irritability between him and Farias—who was now dubbed "Furias" (Furies) by the opposition.

"What will the public think of the discord between the President and Vice-President?" he asked in a rather querulous note to Farias in March 1834. "You think that there is someone who is irritating my sensibilities and you err because no one attempts that nor am I a child who allows himself to be surprised." He seems more concerned about military and patronage matters than the great issues of the day. He complains because the Government forces have not entirely quelled the revolters and complains rather surprisingly that the large number of promotions had upset military organization. He defends the collector of the port of Vera Cruz—that fat position of graft—against Farias' charges of dishonesty and he assails the Vice-President's recent harsh treatment of the late Iturbide's family. All was not well in the official family.

Finally in April 1834 he resolved the situation. He had lined up behind him all the impressive wealth and spiritual prestige of the Church. The wealthy conservatives, alienated by the Farias taxes, were also by his side. By the methods which he knew so well, he reached this general and influenced that ; the military were secured. The mass of the people were restive now and saw in the idealistic Farias only a troublesome dreamer. Moreover, to the north the United States was looming as a more formidable danger. What better stroke than to seize the power and defy the Anglo-Saxons? Returning to the capital, he assumed the Presidency and treated Farias, Zavala and the other anti-clericals as supernumeraries.

After some preliminaries, he came out frankly for a conservative program. He denounced the religious reform measures as impious and demoralizing. With an imperious gesture, reminiscent of his Corsican model, he dissolved the national Congress which had not shown itself subservient to his wishes and with true theatricality marched up to the doors of the legislative halls, locked them and put the keys in his pocket.

Master in his own house ! The protean President in one of his rapid convolutions had changed from anti-clericalism to clericalism, from Federalism to Centralism, and most of all from a democratic republican to the exponent of despotism—a true Dictator at last.

The "reluctant maiden," less modest now, appropriated every distinction which his new situation afforded. He had himself named "Benemerito of the Nation" for this title had previously been given to him only by certain states ; and the Battle of Tampico was honored by a special decree authorizing the erection of a memorial shaft on the shores of the Panuco. The town of Tampico itself was renamed in his honor "Santa Anna de las Tamaulipas," a cumbrous name that time and local custom erased from usage.

He ousted Farias from the Vice-Presidency, sent him into exile and replaced him with General Barragán, a pliable tool. He had now brought under his will the entire Republic with the exception of the State of Zacatecas where Farias' partisans stubbornly held out for Federalism. Leaving the capital the *Benemerito* advanced against his late allies whom he now termed "miserable rebels" and on the 11th day of May joined battle.   The regional patriots, unfortunately for the cause, were led by General Andrade, a typical member of the military log-rolling clique and they little suspected that Santa Anna had a secret understanding with their commander.   Accordingly, they obediently bivouacked at his orders in a most untenable position near the city on the night of May 10th and then went off to sleep while Andrade went about dismissing sentinels and putting the horses to graze at an inconvenient distance.

However, one officer was more vigilant, a German soldier of fortune named Harcourdt who commanded the artillery. He noticed the stealthy approach of the Government forces, gave the alarm, and poured a murderous fire on the attackers with his field pieces.   But his resistance was not enough, for the Zacatecan infantry, taken by surprise, were wholly disorganized and when their opponents were found to have cut off their retreat, surrendered.   Santa Anna, furious that his surprise had not been complete and learning the cause, gave orders that all foreigners were to be executed, an evidence not only of his mounting xenophobia but also of his impatience — now grown to a bloodthirsty degree — with all opposition to his will.

After sacking the town thoroughly and confiscating vast quantities of its chief product silver, the President tarried only long enough to hear mass ere returning to Mexico City.   There he was received by the conservatives exultant that the last vestige of Federalism had been stamped out. But their joy was premature.

CHAPTER IV

THE VILLAIN OF THE ALAMO

AMONG the many acts which attended Santa Anna's grand march to tyranny and Centralism was his dissolution of the Coahuila legislature. The State of Coahuila was a wild and uncultivated district in the north and the President possibly did not notice,—if he ever knew, which is unlikely—that he was also disfranchising the entire area of Texas which was combined with Coahuila. Since his youthful campaign with Arredondo Santa Anna had had no reason to notice that region where disciplined Spanish troops had upset a ragged horde of American border ruffians in 1813—a mere outpost of the Mexican empire.

The Texans would not be thus ignored. They had changed radically since the days when rascals from the Neutral Ground roved the *llanos,* and had come to form a respectable and fairly homogeneous settlement. The great migration had begun in the early 'twenties when the Mexican Government encouraged colonies of Americans under the leadership of Moses and Stephen Austin to settle in what is now southern Texas. Serious tillers of the soil and honest husbandmen these and for many years they were loyal and quiet citizens of the Mexican republic.

But the capital of Coahuila was distant weeks of weary

leagues and the business of governing the new settlements was sadly hampered by this arrangement. The officials in Mexico City gave them little attention and when they did, their acts were so ill-advised and so quickly impaired by other measures that Texan dissatisfaction became acute. When Santa Anna swept into discard the Constitution of 1824, which however imperfectly, gave the Texans some rights, Stephen Austin went to Mexico to negotiate for a new arrangement of Texan affairs, for which insolence he was summarily clapped in jail.

There appeared in the province of Texas about this time a fascinating and important personage. Speaking English fluently and for that matter French and German almost as well as his native Spanish, with his cultured address and plausible eloquence he made a great impression on the simple ranchmen who were perplexing themselves with the question of whether or not to revolt against these intolerable conditions. Lorenzo de Zavala, the hero of the famous Acordada revolution which saved Santa Anna's hide when he was invested in Oaxaca in 1829, had more than eloquence to ignite the Texans' potential rebellion. He was a firm and sincere believer in Federalist principles, a crony of the exiled Farias and a bitter enemy of Santa Anna.

When Austin returned after three months in jail, convinced that there was no means other than force of obtaining justice for Texas from the Mexican Government, he founded the Republic of Texas. Zavala was named Vice-President under Burnet, the new President, and although he lost his position some time later when hatred of all Mexicans was highest among the Lone-Star citizens, he had served his purpose in exciting them to revolt. This participation of one of Mexico's leading Federalists in the Texan revolution emphasized its nature as an internal affair within the Mexican republic. Instead of the Texan revolt being merely a rebellion subsidized and supported by United States citizens who desired the annexation of Texas, it was to a large extent a revolt of Mexican citizens of Anglo-Saxon descent who were enabled to succeed where Zacatecas and other Federalist states of the Mexican republic failed.

But all through the fall of 1835 the more intrepid spirits had been attacking Mexican garrisons and the mutineers had been joined by many volunteers from the States. Perhaps it was this that inspired an outburst from Santa Anna when the French Minister mentioned the Texas situation to him. "If the Americans do not beware, I shall march through their own country and plant the Mexican flag in Washington." By October he could not ignore the matter any longer and he left Mango de Clavo for the capital. November found him in San Luis Potosi attempting to form a punitive expedition to put down these presumptuous Texans who wished for rights which Mexicans had so recently lost.

There he showed such zeal in gathering troops and outfitting them — no small job at that time, for the treasury was virtually empty — that the Government authorized him to float a loan to cover the costs of the expedition. This he did with his usual fine disregard of governmental economy and alert consideration for his own pecuniary betterment.

Thrusting aside the house of Esnaurrisar which had floated other government issues and which offered more advantageous terms, he made arrangements with a grasping firm of *agiotistas* — as the Mexicans called profiteers —

Rubio and Erraz, to underwrite the expedition. $400,000 was the principal and it bore the humane rate of 4 per cent — that is 4 per cent monthly. A year later we find some of these bonds unaccountably in Santa Anna's own trunk.

Furthermore he gave the House of Rubio and Erraz permission to pay customs duties at Matamoros with other worthless bonds which they held and turned over to these rascals the concession to supply the army rations. They did this so efficiently that even in the earlier part of the campaign the soldiers had to exist on half-rations. As a matter of fact, they introduced through the customs house of Matamoros — which being on the Rio Grande would be the nearest point to the center of the campaign — various contraband goods instead of food.

Aside from these matters he busied himself with other and for him equally important measures. He had his minister Tornel issue proclamations commencing, "The Mexican government desires vengeance," treating the Texans as "execrable adventurers," and — how much he loved this sort of thing and relied on it to excite the soldiers to valor ! — he created a special "Legion of Honor" for those who were to serve in the Texan campaign. Simple crosses of silver for the ranks and cavalry, gold for the officers — resplendent crosses with five double radiants, national arms on one side and an inscription "Honor, Valor, Country" on the other. A higher grade, The Grand Cross, permitted its wearers to carry double colored bands over each shoulder.

But with all his activity he had not mustered any more than 6,000 when he left San Luis Potosi in December. They went to Saltillo where they stayed several weeks, still girding themselves and gathering further gifts — one of one thousand pesos from the Bishop of Monterrey. Meanwhile came the news that General Cos, the commander of the Mexican forces in Texas, had been humiliatingly defeated by the "execrable adventurers," had been captured and released with the provision that he and his men would not serve against the Texans again. Ominous information which the "benemerito" did not send on to the National Government.

More reviews and speeches and a little nepotism. Santa Anna had appointed his brother-in-law quartermaster general of the expedition and given him ample funds to provide for two months' rations and supplies. Yet even by the time the army set out from Saltillo provisions were running low. Where had they gone? Only the commanders knew this and it was not until early in January when the wretchedly clad men from tropical Mexico were marching through the cold desert between Monterey and the Rio Grande that he reduced the rations to half and announced that the privates were to be paid a *real* a day. As for the officers, they had to provide themselves with supplies out of their own pay without extra allowance.

Famished and chilled by the bitter northers which swept over the barren plain and whistled through the inhospitable chapparal, the men suffered terribly. Every few miles some had to be picked up more dead than alive and placed on the munitions wagons and gun carriages. Many did die and were left on the road while their comrades marched on.

At the Rio Grande they encamped at Laredo and incorporated with themselves a brigade from Zacatecas which had also had difficulty in getting to this point. There they waited for Cos to return with his defeated troops. Further humiliation waited the unfortunate General for Santa Anna was vexed with him for his debacle at San Antonio. He forced Cos, in spite of his protests, to break his word not to fight against the Texans and to turn back.

The combined forces crossed the Rio Grande and marched on San Antonio across the semi-desert of southern Texas—the same country through which Santa Anna had marched under Arredondo twenty-two years before. But this time the invading forces did not proceed with the serenity or confidence of the Spanish army. Blazing hot days alternated with spells of winter weather when the cold, wet northers swept across the barren ground chilling the soldiers to the bone, and sometimes immersing them in blinding snowstorms. Colonel Andrade's cavalry lost their way in one of these and struggled for hours in a mesquite thicket.

But our hero pressed them on with imperious disregard of advice or mercy. One of the principal Generals urged him not to take this road but to proceed down the Rio Grande to the coast, a far better route, but he swept these suggestions aside. He fell into a towering rage when he discovered his advance guard under Colonel Mora walking their horses and packing saddles ; and he ordered Mora to be court-martialed forthwith. Only after it was pointed out to him that the Texans had burnt all the grass in this country, thus depriving the mounts of fodder and reducing them to exhaustion, did he yield and rescind his order.

The march went on. Fifty oxen perished from the icy blasts and snow. The *soldaderas* who accompanied their ill-clad paramours on this expedition were unable to forage for their mates in this barren land and suffered pitiably. But the ruthless commander pressed them on. Perhaps he was charging himself with the righteous resolution to duplicate the victory at which he had assisted two decades before, to punish severely, nay to exterminate these troublesome North-Americans, to surpass the cruel vengeance of Arredondo.

As if to give point to these reflections, on February 20th he reached the Medina River, scene of the horrible butcheries of Arredondo's soldiers. A priest and a Mexican met him there and informed him that 250 Americans held the Alamo at San Antonio but that they were diverting themselves at a fandango that night and could be easily surprised. An excellent chance for a forced march and a sudden victory !

But the ammunition train had been left on the other bank and as the troops were making ready to leave, the Medina River suddenly rose as the result of a wet norther which had blown over the country on that day. The swollen river was dangerous and it was impossible to make a crossing to get the ammunition, so the enterprise had to be abandoned. His Excellency was enraged again when he saw his trick spoiled, but there was no other course but to wait. Finally on the following evening, the river had subsided sufficiently to bring up the ammunition and cross.

On February 26th Santa Anna entered San Antonio de Bejar and found but few people in the town, most of the inhabitants having fled at the approach of the Mexicans. Those remaining informed the General that 156 Americans had fortified themselves in the Alamo. The Mexicans proceeded to invest it but so deliberately that 32 more

Texans who had come up from Gonzales not far away were able to pass easily through the besiegers and join their comrades in the fort.

A bristling and most military stronghold the Alamo must have seemed to those in San Antonio de Bejar who could remember when it had been the peaceful mission of San Antonio de Valero, nicknamed the Alamo for the cotton-woods (*alamos*) which grew near by. But the friars had left it years before and it became a fortress. The walls were castellated and the outer appearance of its thick masonry belied the lines of the contemplative cloisters which still survived within. Most military, and defiant too, it must have appeared to the Mexicans on that February day, for like a stern reproachful reminder there floated above its walls the Mexican flag with the date "1824," representing the liberal constitution of that year, which Santa Anna had just destroyed.

Santa Anna, seeing the commanding position of the fort, was in no hurry to attack it and waited for General Tolsa to come up with reinforcements. He disposed troops to close the circumference of the siege and encountered no little trouble with the then turbulent San Antonio River which passed through this zone and which had claimed the lives of several of his men who made bold to cross it. To bridge this stream he gave orders to dismantle for timbers several houses which stood below the Alamo. It was while inspecting these buildings that he is said to have found other reasons to postpone the attack.

There is a story told by one Juan Becerra, a sergeant in the Mexican forces, which has come down with the force of a rather vivid legend. To a critical eye it seems at first likely to be simply the expression of Texan rancor, for Becerra afterwards became a citizen of Texas, yet the account is surprisingly repeated in a biography of Santa Anna printed ten years later in Mexico City. It is therefore permissible to relate the matter here not as authenticated history but as a quite possible episode in the life of this man who at times seemed bent on emulating the rascalities of those heroes of Spanish picaresque novels, of Gil Blas and his companions.

The story goes that General Castrillón entering one of these houses met the occupants, a middle-aged lady and her daughter, the latter strikingly pretty. They seemed panic-stricken at the imminent destruction of their dwelling and all the more helpless in that they appeared to be well-bred and intelligent. And the girl was very pretty. Castrillón bore the news to Santa Anna whose curiosity and amorousness were inflamed. He begged Castrillón to get the girl for him, but the officer with honorable stubbornness refused to be his procurer, saying that he obeyed only strictly military orders.

But our hero got a more accommodating officer, Col. Miñon, to make his lecherous proposition to the lady. The mother replied hotly that she was respectable, etc., furthermore that her deceased husband had been an officer in the Mexican army ; and finally to put the discussion on a somewhat more moral basis stated that Santa Anna could have her daughter only by marriage. On that she was inflexible. Miñon, a sly rascal as well as a zealous sycophant of his commander, told him the disappointing result but suggested a stratagem.

He said he had a man in his company, a great scalawag

but well educated and versatile, furthermore not unwilling or unable to execute a good impersonation. The man was sent for and replied that he would do anything to oblige His Excellency. Going to a priest and brandishing the name and prestige of Santa Anna he obtained the necessary vestments and missal according to the prescribed rites of the Roman Catholic religion, in order to impersonate a priest and celebrate a bogus wedding.

In Santa Anna's own headquarters the fake marriage took place and the honeymoon lasted as long as Santa Anna stayed in San Antonio. When he left he sent the deceived girl to San Luis Potosi where she presented His Excellency with still another of the many by-blows which littered his amorous career. The story has been corroborated several times and seems to have some basis. Whether history or legend, the sequel runs that years later the sinful impersonator of the priest was hounded and hissed in the streets and public places of Mexico.

The diary of Col. Almonte gives an excellent picture of Santa Anna's less private activities after he settled down to the siege.

"February 27th. It was determined to cut off the water from the enemy on the side next to the old mill. There was little firing from either side during the day. The enemy worked hard all day to repair some entrenchments. In the afternoon the President was observed by the enemy and fired at. In the night a courier was dispatched to Mexico informing the Governor of the taking of Bexar.

"March 1st. At 12 o'clock the President went out to reconnoitre the mill site to the northwest of the Alamo. Col. Ampudia was commissioned to construct more trenches. In the afternoon the enemy fired two twelve-pound shots at the house of the President, one of which struck the house.

"March 3rd. The enemy fired a few cannon and musket shots at the city. I wrote to Mexico directing that my letters be sent to Bexar — that before three months the campaign would be ended."

A good transcript of the life of the Mexican army, but volumes could be written portraying the anxious days and hours of the besieged garrison ; the messengers they had dispatched to Houston, to Fannin at Goliad, to other Texan bands summoning aid ; the heroic letters that Commander Travis wrote proclaiming his intention to die rather than surrender and to inflict mortal losses on the enemy, in case they assaulted the Alamo. "I am still here in fine spirits. With one hundred and forty men I have held this place against a force variously estimated at from fifteen hundred to six thousand ; and I shall continue to hold it till I get relief from my countrymen, or I will perish in its defense." And again, "I feel confident that the determined valor and desperate courage heretofore evinced by my men will not fail them in the last struggle ; and although they may be sacrificed to the vengeance of a Gothic enemy, the victory will cost so dear, that it will be worse for him than a defeat. God and Texas ! Victory or death !"

But whether the novel sort of honeymoon palled or whether he felt his honor stained by so much preparation before the "execrable adventurers," Santa Anna voted down a proposal to wait for more artillery. Generals Cos and Castrillón, the former having had experience with Texan marksmanship and the latter a clever officer, wanted to wait until two twelve-pounders came on the 7th. But the rest-less bridegroom, supported by the impetuous Almonte, over-ruled them and the attack was planned. Desultory skirmishing and cannonading had gone on long enough for His Excellency, impatient and angry too, for the impudent Americans had fired rather closely to his person several times and had made one or two impudent sallies.

Preparations were made, scaling ladders were con-structed, ammunition was got ready and by the 5th all matters were arranged for the conflict. The Matamoros battalion was marched to a point near the river and above the Alamo, supported by about 2,000 men under Gen-erals Cos and Castrillón, while General Tolza stationed himself at the head of an equally strong force below the Alamo, with His Excellency overseeing this portion of the work. The troops were to march forward at the bugle sound in silence and without firing a shot until the enemy lines had been reached.

The night of the 5th Santa Anna kept a long and anxious vigil. With Almonte for company and the negro servant to serve black coffee, he was enabled to stay awake all night. About midnight, the two men left their quarters to oversee the preparations. They returned at two o'clock and Santa Anna betrayed much agitation especially when Almonte re-marked, "It will cost much." To which Santa Anna re-plied, "It is of no importance what the cost may be, it must be done."

On the morning of March 6th, at five o'clock the bugle sounded the advance — the advance, yes, but it also trilled out clearly the terrible strains of the *deguello,* for Santa Anna was determined to exterminate this force, to make an example of them and to frighten the colonists into submission. Those wild, not unpleasant notes for centuries had been associated with "no quarter." Spain had used the call in her long wars with the Moors and it meant wanton destruction of not only lives but property so that it also earned the sobriquet of the "fire and death call." The very derivation signified "beheading" or "throat-cutting."

But whether the defenders understood the significance of this ominous music or not, they were ready to face the worst. The word "gallant" seems to have been especially invented for the description of Travis, the red-haired, quick-tempered young man of twenty-seven, desperate, careless of his life, driven perhaps by the thought of his wife from whom he had been estranged. He had, from the first, refused any suggestions of treating with the enemy, resolved to hold out until the end. With him were Bowie, whose name itself was a menace — the true frontiersman, fierce in the use of his famous knife in hand-to-hand combat; and valiant Davy Crockett with coonskin cap and buckskin trousers. As for the rank and file, they were just as determined as their chiefs.

When the Mexicans planted their scaling ladders and started to climb, these courageous men fought them back so fiercely that the attack was a failure and the enemy had to retreat. "It seemed that every cannon-ball or pistol shot of the enemy embedded itself in the breasts of our men" wrote a Mexican soldier after the battle. A second charge and more slaughter was necessary before a column under General Castrillón gained a position in a sort of courtyard of the Old Mission. But the seeming advantage was but a mere prelude to greater attacks and more abundant carnage.

The besieged had prepared sandbag barricades in every part of the building, on roofs and in courtyards and doorways. The Mexicans now returned to the assault with added energy. One of them said, "The Texans fought like devils ! It was a short range conflict—muzzle to muzzle —hand to hand, musket to rifle—bayonet and Bowie knife :—all were mingled in confusion." Here a charging squad of Mexicans, there a kneeling, aiming Texan. The crash of firearms, the shouts of defiance, the cries of the dying and the wounded made a din almost infernal. The Texans defended desperately every inch of the fort; overpowered by numbers they were forced to abandon one room ; they rallied in the next and defended it until further resistance became impossible.

Eleven Texans manned an improvised turret on a roof top. From behind uneven rows of sandbags they poured a deadly fire on the besiegers. Well did a Mexican soldier say after the battle, "When a Texan's rifle was levelled at a Mexican, he was considered as good as dead." This little group on the roof had a few small calibre cannon and their fire on the attackers, particularly the cavalry, was lethal. When the cannon balls were exhausted they rammed pieces of scrap iron and nails down the muzzles to send them ricochetting among the Mexicans. At last the Mexicans brought their cannon to bear and the little redoubt was finally silenced too.

The Church building followed this same sickening process. There a hospital had been improvised and the defenders, some too mortally hurt to move, fired from the floor until their pieces were exhausted and they could reach for no more ammunition. A small artillery piece was placed near the door of the hospital by the Mexicans, loaded with grape and cannister and discharged. It obliterated all opposition and the attackers rushed in to find the corpses of fifteen Texans. They had left forty-two of their own men on the ground outside, so they gave little quarter to the feeble few who tried to fire from a sitting or lying position.

The bugler entered another room of the hospital and raised his gun to kill a man sitting on the floor among the feathers of a demolished bed, but the man screamed in Spanish, "Don't kill me, I have plenty of money." He pulled out from a pocketbook a large roll of bank bills which he gave to the greedy soldier. The latter was about to leave when the wounded officer addressed another soldier who had just come in asking him to find General Cos. At this juncture General Amador came in and asked why this man had not been killed in obedience to the orders of the President. He wrenched the bills from the soldier's hand and was about to dispatch the American when General Cos, followed by Almonte and Tolza, entered.

As soon as Cos saw the wounded man he rushed to him and embraced him. Turning to his brother officers he informed them that this man was Travis and that another man lying beside him was Crockett. He explained his affectionate demonstration toward Travis by relating how well the latter had treated him when he himself had been captured recently, how Travis had looked after his comfort and loaned him money. He asked his colleagues to join him in securing the lives of not only the big-hearted Travis but Crockett as well.

As the group left the room they encountered the Presi-

dent and Castrillón. General Cos besought the President
to spare the lives of the two men, saying "Mr. President,
you have here two prisoners. In the name of the Republic
of Mexico, I supplicate you to guarantee the lives of both."
The only answer was a burst of rage from the insensate
conqueror, "Generals, my order was to kill every man in
the Alamo," and turning to some privates near by said,
"Soldiers, kill them."

But Travis was not through yet, for when the soldier
pointed his gun, he seized the bayonet and bent it down
out of harm's reach near the floor. But other soldiers
opened fire and Travis was struck in the back. Standing
erect, he folded his arms and looked without flinching at
his executioners. Crockett joined him in this position and
they both fell, heroic to the last.

Thus runs the version of Juan Becerra. Travis' negro
servant, however, maintained that his master, seeing himself surrounded and in danger of capture, committed suicide by shooting himself through the head.

Just then a burst of shots in the courtyard scattered the
group of officers, Santa Anna running away and Castrillón
squatting down to avoid the singing balls. Eight more
Mexican soldiers fell before this last spurt of resistance was
quelled. The hunt for fugitives had now begun and five
Americans were found concealed under some straw stacks.
Castrillón, who had discovered them, asked for their pardon
from Santa Anna. But the latter only reprimanded his
subordinate for such a request and turned his back while
the soldiers finished off these last surviving wretches.

The sun was high now ; it was nine o'clock and the five-
hour struggle was over. The bodies of 183 Texans—it

was not difficult to count them — were scattered in bizarre and horrible postures in the midst of a much larger number of Mexican slain.   Examination of their wounds revealed the nature of their death combat.   Many knife scars, gashes and bayonet holes, for the most part in the head or neck, were evidences of the fierce hand-to-hand character of the battle.

But the terrible vengeance of Santa Anna did not stop. Viewing the horrible panorama — Almonte possibly uttered his thoughts, "Another such victory will ruin us" — he ordered wood to be brought.   The cavalry went out to cut timber and even the non-combatant inhabitants of San Antonio were pressed into service to gather logs, branches, anything inflammable.   A large pile was then erected and the bodies of the Texan dead were placed between upper and lower layers of wood.   It was the summit of Santa Anna's bloodthirsty rage against the Americans — perhaps against the stubbornness of Barradas, against *pronuncia-miento* rivals, against the obdurate inhabitants of Vera Cruz, against all who did not accede to his will.

But in the midst of this horrendous operation, His Ex-cellency stopped before a mass of flesh and bones.   It was the mutilated body of Bowie, for his corpse as well as those of Crockett and Travis had been tossed from bayonet to bayonet like a pile of hay by the savage soldiery.   One last fiber of mercy, one last compunction of military gallantry, responded to this horrible object.   He hesitated, saying "He was much too brave a man to be treated like a dog." But the mood passed and he gave the order to place the body with the rest; "Pues no es cosa, escase !" — "Well it is of little consequence."

So the pyre burned all day and it was sunset before the mass was reduced to ashes. Today the cremation of dead bodies would not evoke any indignation ; indeed it would be commendable from the standpoint of sanitation. But in those times it was the worst indignity that could be heaped on a fallen foe and it was so intended. It was significant that the Mexicans dug graves and buried their dead.

And they were many. Estimates differ widely, from three hundred dead and wounded up to two thousand. It is likely that Santa Anna suffered the loss of about five hundred in dead and wounded, which was a serious reduction of his forces. Thus the strategic contribution of the Alamo defenders to the Texan cause rested in these figures and in the two weeks during which they prolonged the defense. Like the forts at Liége in 1914 they stopped the invasion, delayed the enemy and inflicted heavy losses on him, thus permitting the troops in the country behind them to assemble and organize. Their heroism is of course immeasurable and perhaps the more lasting gift. "Thermopylæ had its lone messenger of defeat. The Alamo had none." Thus runs the most succinct and eloquent epitaph inspired by this heroic stand.

Not a white male of the Alamo garrison survived. Many tales have come down to us of one or two men who escaped, but the truth is that only a few negro slaves and women and children were spared. Among the latter were Mrs. Dickinson, wife of Lieutenant Dickinson, who fell in the defense, and her little daughter.

She and her daughter were brought before Santa Anna in the home of Musquiz, the political *jefe* of the Mexican town where His Excellency was holding a sort of court, hearing the stories of the survivors. To each of the Mexican women and slaves, he gave a blanket and two silver dollars. When Mrs. Dickinson and her child were brought up, Santa Anna reassured them of their safety. He took a keen and affectionate interest in the little girl, putting questions to her, asking her if she had been afraid, etc.

He proposed to the grief-stricken wife and mother that she allow him to adopt her daughter, explaining that since she was a widow, the little girl needed a protector, that he could bring her up in his own family, educate her and provide well for her future. To this delicate proposal the widow of his victim replied with as much restraint as she could muster in refusal. With many expressions of courtesy, Santa Anna sent mother and daughter off to Gonzales, where many Texan rebels and fugitives were congregated, after asking them to present his compliments to General Houston and to tell him that the treatment of the Alamo would be the treatment which the rest of the country might expect.

But the maniacal fury of Santa Anna had not abated and he sat grimly in his headquarters during the following weeks and answered notes from General Urrea who was active farther south near the coast chasing the small detachments of rebels who were operating in that territory. Urrea announced that he had defeated the rebels near San Patricio and had taken several prisoners. Instead of congratulations on his victory he received a severe scolding because he had not immediately executed the captives.

Then His Excellency learned that Urrea was closing with Colonel Fannin near Goliad and a bit later came word from Urrea that Fannin after some parleying had surrendered unconditionally. And would His Excellency please grant clemency to this brave officer and his four hundred men? Again the merciful subordinate was reprimanded for his magnanimity and the vindictive Santa Anna not only expressly ordered Urrea to execute the unfortunate Americans but, to make sure of their death, sent a duplicate order to the commandant at Bahia where Urrea had left the captives while he proceeded with his campaigning. The Bahia officer having received these irrevocable orders had to carry them out and the prisoners were taken outside of the town and shot, but so carelessly that about fifteen escaped.

Nor was that all. This executioner later reported that he had taken eighty-three prisoners in Copano harbor. A few days previously he had captured five men who were making their way to Goliad to join Fannin, ignorant of that officer's fate. On learning of events, they were persuaded to return to their main force which was domiciled in a vessel in Copano harbor with an offer from the Mexicans to accord these Americans "all consideration" if they surrendered. The whole eighty-three accepted the terms and gave themselves up.

Santa Anna was about to send the usual reprimand and reiteration of the execution orders, when the bearer of the message pleaded for clemency toward the captives. He received a bitter reproof, but he had the satisfaction of knowing he had checked Santa Anna's vengeance. His Excellency compromised and ordered a court of investigation to look into the case. Subsequently the captives were permitted to live.

Lest this story of Santa Anna's conduct seem too much

like the rôle of a Jack Dalton villain, it should be said that
he deemed his adversaries genuine "adventurers," and inasmuch as the old colonists among the rebel forces were in
the minority and the leaders were more or less recent ar-
rivals from the United States, there was some foundation
for his conception.   It is impossible not to view Santa Anna
in these frantic days as a man possessed with the memory
of the events that took place in this territory in 1813, with
vivid pictures of the rapscallion filibusters of the Neutral
Ground whom he had assisted in defeating and mercilessly
executing.   Early impressions and the sanguinary example
of Arredondo bore fruit in the Alamo and Goliad victims
and Santa Anna's failure to discriminate between the heroic
men of Fannin and Travis and the border ruffians of
Captain Perry, while no excuse, gives in a measure an explanation of his conduct.

CHAPTER V

SAN JACINTO

AFTER the fall of the Alamo, the Mexican armies spread out like a line of hunters, beating up the Texan plains in a fan-like movement reaching from the bayous and strands of the Gulf of Mexico to what was then the northern-most settlements of the province ; Urrea in the south along the coast, Filisola in the center and Cos scouring the northern area where the most important quarry was considered to be lurking. For there the old fox, Sam Houston, was leading the Grand Army of the Texan Republic in full flight and in his wake came crowds of refugees, their stock and household goods piled on carts and pack-horses, terror-stricken by the horrible news from San Antonio.

It was to join this northern army that Santa Anna left the scene of his victories in war and light-love. Apparently he anticipated an easy campaign, for with colossal self-confidence he had given the order for the Mexican man-o-war *El Bravo* to wait for him in Copano port on the Gulf. Clearly he envisioned himself sweeping through the guerrilla-infested country, scaring Houston into flight, reaching the Sabine River where his presence would impress the mean-spirited Americans in Louisiana, and finally the coast and Copano. From there his triumphal procession would start—Vera Cruz, Jalapa, Mexico City with bands, cheering crowds, more medals, larger statuary—another exploit added to that of Tampico.

He departed from San Antonio on horseback, leaving behind his magnificent coach. That started out the next day with "some passengers" for San Luis Potosi. "Decency and public morals," writes the President's secretary "do not permit further mention of the matter."

He overtook his northern army at San Felipe on the 6th of April. There he should have felt great satisfaction with his situation. Under him was the stolid General Cos with about thirteen hundred veterans. To the south the alert Italian, Filisola, and Urrea with their respective armies were converging on a point in the network of bayous and rivers that reach up to the present site of the city of Houston, a good place to trap the fugitive General Sam.

His Excellency's staff rubbed their hands smugly, and the rank and file, up till now shaken by the heavy losses at the Alamo, found new enthusiasm at the prospect of military operations so manifestly easy. All they had to do was to strike directly forward, chase the panicky Texans toward the Gulf where the southern armies would bottle the remnants up and put an end to the rebellion.

Strike directly forward! In front of them was the Brazos River and on the other side, a little band of rebels under Colonel Baker, easy prey for the Victor of Tampico. The Texans were deadly sharp-shooters, true enough, and here was no chance to wade across and join them in straight battle. But two large barges would be sufficient to get the men across the Brazos and some American carpenters were found and pressed into service to build them. Assisted by Mexican helpers these mechanics worked so rapidly that after a day and a half they finished one of the units. Another two days and everything would be ready for the assault.

But stay! His Excellency countermanded the order for the second barge, saying that it would take too long. His officers were disappointed but looked for the wily strategist of Tampico to take another step, the obvious if less valorous move. He could send a force up the river, let it cross at a shallow spot and fall on the rear of Colonel Baker's band. It was a simple maneuver and the officers were already mentally on the march. But again their commander lifted his arm in negation. No, that would not do!

Astonished and puzzled, the army waited. The Texans opposite sniped monotonously, the Brazos rushed tantalizingly by, but within the marquee of their commander, there was silence. What was the matter with His Excellency? Was it a spirit of obtuse stubbornness which moved him to these inexplicable refusals? He had quarreled with his staff, it was true, especially with Castrillón, and the latter had left His Excellency's mess taking the cook with him, so that Santa Anna had to put up with another and less able chef. A general, too, marches on his stomach. Was it dyspepsia? Or the lethal marksmanship of the Texans?

Whatever his motives he would not attack Colonel Baker's force. Assembling the cream of his army and leaving Cos with about six hundred men to exchange pot-shot with the Texans, he marched southward along the banks of that exasperating Brazos which at some places described serpentine curves, at others fantastic hair-pin turns, its reddish sinister waters eating treacherously into steep clay banks. Skirting the thickets which bordered the stream they sighted a small group of horsemen who galloped off and disappeared. The enemy? A negro living with his wife in a little house not far away gave them a hint. He said that the fleeing riders were doubtless part of a small force of Texans that held the east bank at Thompson's Crossing.

Desirous of surprising this guard and fearful that they had been warned of his approach, Santa Anna offered the negro one hundred pesos if he would go to the Texan camp and tell the enemy that the Mexican force had turned away from the Crossing for another route. The negro accepted the offer and accomplished his mission. Returning, he reported his success and joined the Mexicans as a guide. Legend has it that Santa Anna refused to give him the one hundred pesos. Hardly likely. Santa Anna always found it paid well to reward treachery.

The Thompson's Crossing force was easily routed as the Mexicans forded the river. They were a small fragment of Houston's army which, rebelling together with Baker's men against Houston's tactics, left the main body. For Sam Houston had been having his troubles too. Only lately installed as Commander he had so far resolutely avoided battle, which did not inspire confidence in his zealous men. It was rumored that he intended to lead the army back to the Sabine River which meant virtual abandonment of Texas. Thus hot-headed Mosely Baker and his followers, Captain Wily Martin and his detachment — about four hundred men in all — deserted him with no little bitterness, but promised to hold the Crossings if they could. The rumors which caused this defection were unfounded. The Raven did not intend to leave Texas; he meant to join battle with Santa Anna, but only when he was good and ready. Under his leadership the Texan army, too, wound south with Harrisburg as an objective.

Santa Anna had been up till now an enigma to his officers. He had thrown himself with but seven hundred men and one cannon in a territory of confusing bayous, swamps and woods. Houston? He was pursuing him, he asserted. As a matter of fact, with both forces heading southward, the opposite was true and Santa Anna was actually in the position of the proverbial Ghost followed by the Fleeing Darky. But through these unheroic ma- neuvers, his real plan began to appear, to the relief of his entourage. Fight these annoying Texans? No! They were unworthy of notice. But, to march through Texas, to frighten the rebellious settlers, to make a demonstration of his military force along the international border for the Americans' benefit, to reach the coast finally where a ship would transport him to Mexico and glory — that was a plan in the grand manner.

However, a chance encounter modified this course. As the army proceeded through the barren plains, they came upon a little ranch whose proprietor, an aged Texan, was in the act of packing his belongings preparatory to leaving the country. He insisted that he was too old to be involved in such war-like movements as were disturbing Texas and that he only wanted to leave. Santa Anna reassured him of his safety and questioned him about the movements of the Texans. The old man told him that he had just re cently seen a newspaper which stated that Burnet, President of the Lone-Star Republic, together with his entire government was in the town of Harrisburg.

Santa Anna was now only sixteen leagues from this town and he felt that his opportunity for a decisive stroke was too good to be missed. He would swoop down on the town, capture the ramshackle Government and best of all get his hands on the hated Federalist and renegade, Zavala, now Vice-President of the Texan Republic. Thus the rebellion would collapse and his triumph would be assured. He did not stop to consider that Houston would still be in the field with the reputed force of eight hundred which would have to be defeated ere the revolutionary movement was suppressed.

But he was in good humor now as he contemplated the capture of the upstart Government of the so-called Texas Republic. At Oyster Creek as they raced on for Harrisburg, the infantry crossed successfully on a log but the cavalry, the cannon and the supply wagons, experienced great difficulty. Officers and men struggled in great confusion, some fell in the water and two mules were drowned. All of which appealed to Santa Anna's sense of humor and sent him into fits of hearty laughter. His considerable wagon train has given rise to the legend that he carried with him a vast treasure of gold captured in the Alamo and which he buried somewhere along his route. There is no evidence that he brought with him on this campaign any large amount of money and so this story must join the mass of lore which has drawn the gullible "Coronado's children." On the 15th he burned a farmhouse and a cotton gin and pressed on, for by this time he was near his goal.

Leaving his army and accompanied by sixteen dragoons he dashed at eleven o'clock that night into Harrisburg and found — nothing but a deserted town, empty save for three printers, a Frenchman and two Americans who were setting type for the *Texas Register and Telegraph* in a small building. They informed him that President Burnet and his colleagues had taken a steamboat for Galveston and that Houston was at Groce's Crossing with eight hundred men and two pieces of artillery.

That night the disappointed General and his dragoons slept in Harrisburg while their main force did not arrive until the next day. As his troops straggled in dejectedly on the morning after, their low spirits were reflected, it seems, in their Commander's mind. As was so frequently the case with Santa Anna, a check threw him into black pessimism. He seemed to vacillate between different plans and emotions. News that Houston was not far away did not stimulate him to a confident spirit of combat; on the contrary he timorously dispatched orders to General Cos to join him. Harrisburg, a collection of little shanties, was certainly no magnificent prize. Yet only a few miles away a bayou lapped the woody shores with partly briny water and there was a salt freshness in the breeze from the south. The sea! His Excellency awoke to action again.

He sent Colonel Almonte with fifty horse to the town of New Washington with orders to head off any member of the Texan Government, in case they had not yet embarked for Galveston. There in the little hamlet situate on a woody bluff overlooking the pea-green waters of Galveston Bay, Almonte discovered no Texans but did find warehouse filled with military stores. The message he ser back about this capture was just enough for Santa Anna. At the head of his army he marched to New Washington — to protect the stores, he said.

But when he got there, he seemed little concerned about the booty. Other matters appeared to be revolving beneath his handsome brow. He scoured the shores of the bay, looked at ships and made inquiries about sailing. A German, owner of a little schooner anchored in the bay, came in and parleyed with him. After some discussion, His Excellency struck a bargain with the German for the purchase of the schooner. His motives seem clear now.

He would avoid any precarious encounter with the troublesome Houston and, sailing off with the German for Mexico, he would leave the responsibility of his little army in the hands of his subordinates — Castrillón, Cos and Filisola. Why risk his fortunes on this uncertain terrain? His most important battleground, he well knew, was in the scheming, treacherous field of Mexico City politics and a return with the trophies of the Alamo and Goliad would ensure his Dictator's berth. This seems the most likely interpretation of his strange actions. If this was so, his plan was not exactly courageous but it was crafty.

Crafty, almost diabolically so, seemed the act by which the Texans blocked this plan, as if they had knowledge of it and were intent on drawing him back to his fate. The Texan navy, paltry group of tiny sloops, sailed up the bay and proceeded to burn the German vessel before the eyes of the helpless President of Mexico. As the cloud of smoke curled lazily to the sky, he desperately turned to his former scheme and sent an aide, Captain Barragán, north to Lynchburg Crossing, not many miles away, to arrange for barges.

He would foil them yet—he would get across San Jacinto River and follow out his former plan : the demonstration along the Sabine, the march to the coast and, at last, relief and safety on a Mexican vessel bound for Vera Cruz.

Houston meanwhile had been headed south from Groce's Crossing in the direction of Santa Anna and on the 18th reached a point on the Buffalo bayou where he rested after his forced march—a distance of fifty-five miles in two and one-half days. Deaf Smith, the ferocious scout who believed in no quarter for Mexicans, reluctantly brought in two prisoners, one of whom was a courier. His leather bag bore the name of Colonel Travis—a grim souvenir of the Alamo. The contents gave Houston the information that Santa Anna had failed to capture Burnet and that he was in the vicinity of Harrisburg.

The pouch contained a letter from the Secretary of State of the Mexican Republic congratulating Santa Anna on his triumph at the Alamo. "Providence is propitious to us and has destined your Excellency to be the savior and preserver of the Republic. Glorious with these titles and ever patriotic your Excellency has garnished your temples with laurels of everlasting fame." With this reminder of the fate of the Alamo in his hands, Houston was emboldened to press on in pursuit of Santa Anna and on the 19th as he came upon the cold ashes of the Mexican camp-fires he wrote to a friend, "This morning we are in preparation to meet Santa Anna. It is the only chance to save Texas."

The next day, Santa Anna was standing among his staff in the long, narrow lane, Main Street of New Washington, which was filled with soldiers, pack-animals and camp impedimenta. He eagerly watched Captain Barragán gallop up. The aide delivered the first part of his news: Some Texan Tories at Lynchburg were ready to ferry the Mexicans across—so far so good. But the second announcement had a sinister ring: Houston was advancing on the Crossing and had that very day captured and dispatched some Mexican stragglers.

Santa Anna horrified his staff by losing complete control of himself. Mounting his horse, he galloped up the narrow lane knocking down and riding over anyone who came in his way, throwing the soldiers and pack-animals into great confusion as he shouted at the top of his voice, "The enemy's coming! The enemy's coming!" Was it just temperament? Or a fear of retribution?

Under such a panicky leader the Mexican forces were slow to assemble in proper order, officers shouted contradictory commands and His Excellency contributed to the pandemonium by ordering the soldiers to drop their knapsacks on the road and leave them there. Groping their way through the woods and swamps that line the San Jacinto River, they reached, about two o'clock in the afternoon, some gently sloping savannahs covered with long grass. As the Mexican pickets emerged from the underbrush they sighted Houston's men on the edge of a wood on the other side of the prairie. On the right of Houston was the crossing to Lynchburg and Santa Anna had to traverse this peaceful stretch of open ground to reach the river. Mexican bugles sounded and the fidgety Mexican general formed his skirmish lines.

A bit intimidated by the appearance of the enemy, Santa Anna advanced his lone field-piece between the skirmishers.

It was none too soon for the Texan four-pounders, the "Twin Sisters," had already fired their first shot.   A second crash came before the Mexican gun got in position and barked back in reply.   It was an unequal artillery duel for Santa Anna's lone piece was badly impeded by its defective carriage.   However, it inflicted some damage and would have continued if the Texan rifle fire had not made the Mexican front lines waver.

Santa Anna decided not to start a general engagement ; it was getting on towards five in the afternoon and he sent a detachment of cavalry to bring back his cannon.   The Texans sallied forth with a raiding party themselves to dispute for the field-piece but were severely punished and retreated.   As a finale to this day so unsatisfactory to both sides, Santa Anna retired about one thousand yards to a shady spot where he encamped, the soldiers raising a little barricade of pack-saddles and camp paraphernalia.

It was a very flimsy redoubt in a most precarious position. For over the advice of his staff, Santa Anna had settled down with the enemy in front blocking the way to the Crossing, and the treacherous swamps of the San Jacinto River in his rear.   If Houston chose to cut off the road to Vince's Bayou which ran at right angles to the field, he would be in a *cul-de-sac*.   General Sam himself had the Buffalo bayou at his back and was established on no enviable site, but he was on an eminence with a full view of the country, whereas Santa Anna had retired to a grove five hundred yards back from the crest of his hill so that even the most lynx-eyed picket on the barricade could not descry an advancing Texan until he was virtually on top of him

The following morning, while Houston was vacillating

uncertain whether to attack or not, General Cos with his six hundred men marched boldly and in full sight of the Texans into Santa Anna's camp. They had been up all night and being greatly fatigued they proceeded to go to sleep. Santa Anna now had about thirteen hundred men, and feeling sure of his superiority postponed action until the next morning. It was a hot Texas day and he pitched his tent under some giant oak trees, festooned with drooping trailers of Spanish moss.

But the arrival of this last force roused the Raven to action. He foresaw the fatal results if Filisola himself came up with another thousand. He ordered Deaf Smith and his scouts to destroy Vince's bridge and thus cut off any chance of further reinforcements reaching Santa Anna. As a further admonition, he added, "And come back like eagles or you will be too late for the day."

The Day began at three-thirty in the afternoon, when Houston formed his little army for the attack — eight hundred men against thirteen hundred. But eight hundred men nourished on the slogan "Remember the Alamo" and waving an oriflamme which crudely but appropriately represented the figure of liberty. The General from the saddle of his white horse rode through them cautioning, "Hold your fire, men, hold your fire!" For ten minutes they advanced, down the slope of their own hill, then up the gentle savannah of the enemies', bending down to avoid balls that did not come, alert for "Quien Vivas" never uttered, unheralded, unnoticed.

Under the arras of the Spanish moss, in his sumptuous marquee Santa Anna slumbered, slept the untroubled sleep of the Mexican siesta hour, always sacrosanct in the *pro-*

nunciamiento scraps. Most of his men especially Cos' regiments which had marched all night, did likewise. A few were awake, cooking, performing camp chores, taking the horses unsaddled to water at the river, delightfully and unconcernedly puttering about when a drowsy sentinel at the barricade saw the line of Texans approaching and gave the alarm. The befuddled Mexicans were hardly on their feet when a blast from the "Two Sisters" opened a breach in the breastworks.

The Texans—fury personified—leaped over the barricade scarcely opposed, screamed their battle-cry—"Remember the Alamo" and fell on their enemy—their prey—with fierce gusto. Easy objects for their vengeance were the Mexicans, running aimlessly about shouting "Me no Alamo." For every sign of organization and resistance was promptly crushed. Cavalrymen hoisting their saddles, artillerymen grasping their ramrods, privates reaching for their stacked muskets—all were instantaneously butchered. General Castrillón fell trying to rally his men.

Santa Anna rushed out of his tent and ran up and down wringing his hands. Shouting a few futile orders, he secured a horse and galloped out of the mêlée in the direction of Vince's Bayou. Almonte alone out of the surviving officers acted the man and was able to bring some order out of the panic-stricken mass of Mexicans. He saw it was useless to get them to fight and he herded them together only that they might surrender in a body. He gathered about four hundred whimpering fellows and looked down at the field.

Below the little hill where he was trying to calm his men a horrible sight met their gaze. The bulk of the fugitive:

had reached the bank of a little creek which ran back of the camp and as they crowded at its edge in a vain effort to cross, the brothers of Travis and Fannin descended on them and slaughtered them mercilessly by the hundreds. The stream bed was so filled with bodies that a fortunate few were able to clamber across this human bridge to Almonte's position.

The rank and file of the Texans were vengeance incarnate. It did not occur to them that the poor Mexican privates were innocent of the crimes of Goliad and the Alamo, that they were paying dearly for the insensate orders of their commander. They only saw in every Mexican uniform a bloody reminder of the massacre of their fellows. To their honor some of the Texan officers tried to stop the butchery, but their men ignored their orders. Only when Almonte waved a white flag, was a civilized surrender possible ; and the day of carnage and valor ended.

Less than an hour after the Texans had sneaked up the savannah, Sam Houston, nursing a wounded leg, was able to survey his victory. The statistics were astonishing. The Texans had lost three killed and eighteen wounded, whereas about four hundred Mexicans lay dead on the field, two hundred were wounded and seven hundred thirty were taken prisoners.

As Santa Anna pressed his steed on in terror-stricken flight for Vince's Bayou, one may imagine that an old illusion was rapidly disappearing from his mind — a mental picture of a horde of ragamuffin adventurers fleeing before files of triumphant and well-disciplined Spanish infantry, Anglo-Saxon filibusters bowing to the superiority of Hispanic courage and civilization. Did he realize that his

rudely interrupted siesta had settled the fate of the Southwest, had turned back forever the thin, the thinning skirmish line of Latin-America?

Hardly possible, for our hero was too absorbed in flight
for any other thoughts. Finding Vince's bridge cut off,
he turned back followed by his faithful secretary who had
kept close to him all this time. After awhile he dismissed
the man, got off his horse and plunged into the thickets.
Walking on—where he knew not—he finally came, according to his account, to a deserted farmhouse. There he
took off his uniform and disguised himself in a blue jacket
and white cotton trousers. With the heavy conscience of
the guilty he divined from the cry "Remember the Alamo"
that the Texans were looking especially for him.

The next day a troop of Texans sent out on a scouting
party with orders not to kill any prisoners, noticed a Mexican making his way in the direction of Vince's bridge.
When he saw them he fell down in the long grass and
concealed himself beneath a blanket. Coming up, the
scouts ordered him to get up but he only peeked from
under the blanket. After several more summons he arose
and advanced, offering to shake hands. With a timid
gesture he took the hand of one of the scouts and kissed it.
Emboldened by their peaceful reception, he produced a
valuable watch, some jewelry and a large sum of money
which the men refused.

He then asked where General Houston was. The men
replied that he was in camp and asked him who he was.
A private soldier, he answered, but the discerning Texans
pointed out an expensive stud in his coat whereupon he
burst into tears. Poor, weak, dejected little fellow crying

and complaining of pains in his chest and legs, the Texans
felt pity for him, hoisted him on one of the horses and took
him back to camp.

But as his captors approached the stockade where the
Mexican prisoners were kept, they noticed a commotion
and heard a murmur run through the body of captives, at
the sight of their strange little charge. "El Presidente!
Sant' Anna! Sant' Anna!" they cried, and the rough
frontiersmen, if they did not recognize the Mexican pronunciation — with elision and open vowels — of their hated
enemy's name, knew that they had captured the President
of Mexico. So the Texans came running up yelling in
their own dialect, "Santy Anny." As the President was
borne off to Houston, in his terror he is said to have given
the Masonic sign of distress to some of the Americans.

Then ensued the famous scene depicted by the Meissonier
of Texas, Huddle. It hangs amid official grandeur in the
State Capitol at Austin and hundreds of Texans admire it
daily. On the canvas — completed in 1901, already black-
ening — General Sam is represented lying underneath a
moss-hung oak tree, his bandaged leg stretched out before
him and a surgeon with his kit in the foreground. Deaf
Smith, a rough frontier figure, sits with his hand cupped
to his ear, while in solemn official attitudes all the Texan
leaders, Lamar, Rusk, Wharton, Zavala, et al., are conscien-
tiously grouped behind the recumbent Houston. The
Lone Star flag of the republic — first designed a year later,
floats above Mr. Rusk's forehead, while on the side an angry
man — presumably a relative of one of the Texan martyrs
— is being restrained by one of his comrades from attacking
the central figure of the picture.

Mr. Huddle transcended himself in his portrayal of Santa Anna. The President, in blue jacket and white wrinkled trousers which look very much like under-drawers is standing in a bashful, dejected attitude, appearing more like a truant schoolboy waiting for a reprimand than the proud despot of the Halls of Montezuma. Houston with a benign expression on his face hardly compatible with the pain he was suffering from his leg, is motioning Santa Anna to a seat.

According to some of the more reliable witnesses, Santa Anna ran up and squeezed the hand of the sleeping President, saying rapidly in Spanish, "I am Antonio Lopez de Santa Anna, President of the Mexican Republic and General in Chief of the Army of Operations." Moses Bryan translated for the awakened Houston who was supposed to have replied, "Ah, General, take a seat, take a seat."

Such is the official version. But just as in the case of many other great events there is also an apocryphal version. At Waterloo, Marshal Cambronne is said to have hurled at the English, "The Guard will die rather than surrender"; but every French schoolboy smirks in the knowledge, prompted by folk-lore and Victor Hugo, that he said something disgracefully different. Texan historians are not of the same stuff as the compatriots of Rabelais and they have no author such as Victor Hugo. Fitting therefore to fill the gap, to report that the suffering Houston roused from his relieving slumbers and being told that this disturbing fellow opposite him was Santa Anna is said to have found one of the most ready words in his long vocabulary of profanity, the English equivalent of the French unprintable expletive "merde."

Santa Anna did sit down, however, on the box indicated by Houston. He seemed much agitated, placed his hands to his chest as if in pain and asked for some opium. A considerable quantity of the drug was procured and he promptly swallowed it. Apparently benefited, he now regained his composure. Colonel Almonte was brought up to act as interpreter, and there ensued a discussion which, according to some of those present, took the following form :

Santa Anna opened with some of the glib flattery he was so ready with on all occasions that demanded it. "That man may consider himself born to no common destiny who has conquered the Napoleon of the West ; and it now remains for him to be generous to the vanquished."

Houston : "You should have remembered that at the Alamo."

Santa Anna : "You must be aware that I was justified in my course by the usages of war. I had summoned a surrender, and they had refused. The place was then taken by storm and the usages of war justified the slaughter of the vanquished."

Houston : "That was the case once, but it is now obsolete. Such usages among civilized nations have yielded to the influences of humanity."

Santa Anna : "However this may be, I was acting under the orders of my Government."

Houston : "Why you are the Government of Mexico."

Santa Anna : "I have orders in my possession commanding me so to act."

Houston : "A dictator, sir, has no superior."

Santa Anna : "I have orders, General Houston, from my

Government commanding me to exterminate every man found in arms in the Province of Texas and to treat all such as pirates, for they have no government and are fighting under no recognized flag. This will account for the positive orders of my government."

Houston : "So far as the first point is concerned, the Texans flatter themselves they have a government already, and they will probably be able to make a flag. But if you feel excused for your conduct at the Alamo, you have not the same excuse for the massacre of Colonel Fannin's command. They had capitulated on terms proffered by your General and yet, after the capitulation they were all perfidiously massacred, without the privilege of even dying with arms in their hands."

At this point Houston found it difficult to restrain his indignation. It is said that his eyes flashed "like a wild beast's" and in his immense effort to curb his wrath cold sweat ran off from his brow in streams.

Santa Anna : "I declare to you, General (laying his hand on his heart) that I was not apprised of the fact that they had capitulated. General Urrea informed me that he had conquered them in a battle and under this impression ordered their execution."

Houston : "I know, General, that the men had capitulated."

Santa Anna : "Then I was ignorant of it. And after your asseveration I should not have a shadow of doubt if it were not that General Urrea had no authority whatever to receive their capitulation, and if the day ever comes that can get Urrea into my hands I will execute him for his duplicity in not giving me information of the facts."

General Rusk then interpolated : "Colonel Almonte, you can say to General Santa Anna that if he has no better excuse or apology to make than this, the less he says about the matter the better for him, for we all know that General Santa Anna was Dictator of Mexico and did as he pleased."

Rusk's interruption had expressed the mounting anger of the Texans at Santa Anna. Some of the survivors of the Goliad massacre were present and they cried out for Santa Anna's instant execution. Only the authority of Houston, unquestioned now after his brilliant victory, restrained the Texans from forming a firing squad. Rusk accordingly pressed the captive for severe and humiliating terms. Santa Anna, gathering some of this, was frightened enough to concede a great deal.

In his great fear he offered to stop the war and order Gen. Filisola to retreat out of Texas. To Rusk's taunt that Filisola would not obey his captured superior, he insisted that his soldiers were so attached to him that they would obey any of his orders.

Rusk, pressing his advantage, then wanted Santa Anna to order Filisola to surrender his men as prisoners of war. This was a bit too much for even the trembling President. He replied bluntly that he would do anything that would not be disgraceful to himself or Mexico, that he was but one Mexican and that they could do with him as they pleased. Col. Almonte quickly translated this in a more tactful way, saying to Rusk that Santa Anna was willing to order Filisola to leave Texas but that he could not order him to surrender inasmuch as the Mexican force was superior in numbers to the Texan.

It was late in the afternoon at this juncture and Santa

Anna, offering to send instructions to Filisola, asked for his
writing materials. His secretary who was among the prisoners then was summoned and sent to the battlefield to find
the General's effect. Stumbling amid the corpses he came
upon the marquee of the famous captive, and his elegant
escritoire was brought back to Houston's camp.

There in Houston's presence Santa Anna eagerly went
through the humiliating rôle of commanding the Mexican
troops to retreat from Texas. He dictated these orders to
the secretary Caro, with details as to the disposition of
regimental funds in Matamoros when Filisola should arrive
there. He also gave orders for the release of Texan prisoners at Goliad, and injunctions to the Mexicans to respect
the armistice. And to them all he had placed his inevitable
subscription, "God and Liberty !"

Houston's deportment and treatment of the captured
President was more than humane. He spared him every
humiliation he could ; he prevented the Texans from firing
a salute celebrating the capture, and he saw that most of
his personal effects were respected. His marquee was
brought to camp with all its elegant furnishings ; silver
teapots, cream pitchers, monogrammed china, glass tum-
blers and decanters with gold stoppers, a considerable fortune in itself when it included his diamond studs valued
at $1,700. Last but not least in importance was the Gen-
eral's bed and it came to pass that Santa Anna had a bed
that night when all the Texans, even the sick Houston
slept on the ground.

But Santa Anna did not sleep. The wild yells of Texan
soldiers revelling on the champagne which they appropriated from his baggage disturbed him ; but there were oth-

cares. Guarded in his marquee, he sat up with Almonte, his brother-in-law Nuñez and his secretary Caro all night, discussing in troubled tones the condition of the rest of the army, and especially the possible results that news of this capture would have on political events in Mexico. But he was to have more immediate worries ere very long.

CHAPTER VI

CAPTIVITY

NOW follows one of the most painful—and revelatory—periods in our hero's life. In Mexico, enthroned in splendor as President or galloping about in the revolutions he emerges only as a pamphlet character—a stout hero to his partisans, a virile monster to his enemies. His military position, his quondam political offices, cast about him even in temporary defeat a mantle of grandeur, however tawdry. Balloon-like from the lips of the stiff figure emerge the lush, formal proclamations, the only recorded expressions of his thoughts. But vicissitudes among sharp analytical foreigners bring sketches and side-views—another dimension to make understandable his curious character.

After the battle, the dead for some reason—probably the almost boyish joy of the conquerors who could think of little else save their miraculous victory—were left on the field to decompose. The stench was so offensive and quite evidently so unhygienic that some measure obviously had to be taken. Santa Anna, eager to extenuate his behavior at the Alamo, suggested that the bodies be burned, maintaining that he always employed this method of disposing of the dead. But the Texans avoided the difficulty by moving their camp about nine miles north.

The defeated President had good reason to volunteer excuses for his past policies for he came to realize now the true danger of his position. Relatives and friends of the Alamo and Goliad victims were clamoring for his execution. Of the fifteen men who escaped from the Fannin massacre "each one" as Caro the secretary puts it, "became a tiger in his persecution of us." Efforts were made to induce Caro to relate the true story of Urrea's and Santa Anna's exchange of notes in regard to the executions. If he had not kept loyally silent, his master might have faced a firing squad. Meanwhile Zavala, the Texan Vice-President, appeared and when his distinguished countryman attempted to start a cordial conversation with him, he not only administered a chilling snub but informed him that he might expect the supreme chastisement for his crimes.

However, with the magnanimous Houston covering him with his protection and Rusk, the Minister of War, happy over his success in getting Santa Anna to order Filisola's retreat and eager for more concessions, His Excellency caught at the drifting straw of hope. As he later put it, "In the critical position in which I was placed, this proposition was to me what the rays of lightning would be to a poor traveler, who having lost his way in a dark and stormy night, avails himself of the rapid flashes of light in order to trace an unknown path."

The proposition he referred to came from the zealous Rusk and stipulated that Texan independence should be recognized and the boundaries of the new republic should reach to the Rio Grande. Also, indemnities were to be paid to Texans for lives and properties lost, all prisoners to be exchanged, the Mexicans to leave the country and the

United States to act as intermediary and referee to see that
all these provisions be observed. Santa Anna should be
held as an hostage until these terms should be fulfilled.
Otherwise — execution. Harsh demands, but obviously
open to modification and Santa Anna, scenting a chance to
barter and haggle, brightened up.

The party which had dealt with the retreating Filisola
had come back bringing with them the Mexican General
Woll who pretended that he wished to negotiate further
about matters, but whose real purpose was to spy on the
condition of the Texans. Houston, divining this and in-
tending that the Mexican forces should not know the real
nature and extent of the Texan strength, held him as a
prisoner, just as he was about to return to his army.

But the negotiations went on and there was to follow an
opportunity for Santa Anna to gain time and to give full
scope to his ability at parleys. For on the 5th of May it
was deemed best for the distinguished captive to go on
board the steamship *Yellowstone* together with Houston,
Rusk, Burnet and the whole Texan Government, and travel
to Galveston Island. Finding accommodations bad there
they repaired to Velasco, principal port of the new Re
public, a better stage for the diplomatic drama.

One of the passengers gave a very good picture of him
on this voyage, — a revealing character sketch: "He in
dulged in a singular self-delusion in regard to his own in
fallibility; for when talking of his reverses of fortune, h
attributed all to a blind and wayward destiny, a tyrann
over which human wisdom and human power had no ir
fluence. 'For,' said he, 'the same troops who fled in terrc
and dismay at your first fire, only the day before, the unite

efforts of myself and others could scarcely restrain from attacking you. They were old soldiers, fought bravely with me in Zacatecas, were familiar with and had been fearless of danger in all its shapes. It was destiny.' After the armistice was entered into and he was permitted to hope that his life would be spared, his conversation assumed a tone of gaiety little to be expected in one who had suffered such a sad reverse. . . He displayed great diplomatic skill, firmly (at first) opposing every measure by which Mexico was likely to suffer, and Texas be benefited, declaring that he had no such power, but finally giving a reluctant assent.

"His conversation, afterwards, turned upon matters indifferently, in the discussion of which he displayed a strong and versatile mind, and very general historical and political information. He never spoke of military matters, or the relative merits of his officers, except on one or two occasions, referring very contemptuously to General Cos (Martin, as he called him). He professed a warm admiration of female character, and said 'women were the gravy of society.' In passing down the bayou from San Jacinto to Patrick's he made a great many observations upon the scenery along the river and seemed sensibly alive to the force of natural beauty. It was his invariable custom to send his compliments to General Houston and to inquire into the state of his wound every morning."

Well he might, for it was Houston who stood as a protector between Santa Anna and the bloodthirsty horde yelling for vengeance. His protection of the Mexican president and his support of the treaties which Rusk was drawing up seems to have been an attitude representing a combination of generosity and policy. It is perhaps improbable that he placed much reliance on Santa Anna's promises to recognize Texan independence or his power to enforce such measures if he could do anything about them. More likely is it that the shrewd old Indian fighter deemed it silly to kill this famous man and so to draw down on the young republic European and American censure when there was a bare possibility that some bargain might be made out of the preservation of his life.

Rusk drafted two treaties, one a severe and drastic document for public consumption, the other a secret one which Santa Anna was to sign and stand by. The first required that hostilities should cease, that the Mexicans should retire beyond the Rio Grande, that property taken should be returned (a modification of the indemnity demand which undoubtedly Santa Anna had gained in the parleys). More important in the eyes of the suspicious Texans who would peruse this treaty, Santa Anna should agree not to take up arms against the Texans in the future and should be sent to Vera Cruz "as soon as may be thought proper."

The secret treaty which the illustrious prisoner was to sign made no mention of property but required the Mexicans to retire beyond the Rio Grande. Other provisions reveal how much the sharp Mexican had obtained in concessions from his captors. Instead of recognizing the new Republic, Santa Anna was to "prepare" things in the cabinet at Mexico for the reception of a Texan mission to negotiate a treaty. But most important of all for the impatient captive, "The present return of General Santa Anna to Vera Cruz being indispensable for the purpose of effecting his solemn engagements, the Government of Texas will provide for his *immediate* embarkation for said port."

But at this point our hero overstepped himself.   Having regained some of his old confidence and nourishing this on the fuss which Rusk and other officials were making to get him to sign, he became insolent and balked at placing the signature to the secret treaty, alleging that his word of honor and good faith were sufficient.   This produced an uproar in the Texan cabinet and instead of impressing them as Santa Anna had meant, it made them all very angry at the troublesome captive and strengthened the proponents of execution.   Seeing how matters lay, His Excellency yielded and affixed his florid rubric to the document.   But he had lost the good will of most of his protectors.

Together with Nuñez, Almonte and Caro, he was now lodged not in the state-rooms of the steamboat but in a small room in Velasco with a sentinel outside whose presence suggested, under the circumstances, less detention than protection from mob violence.   For it was only after the utmost difficulty that the moderates prevailed and made arrangements to place him on a ship in the harbor, the *Invincible,* preparatory to sending him to Vera Cruz. But on the morning of June 1st, just as he was to be taken on board, the soldiery rebelled and Rusk had to devote several hours to pacifying them.

In the afternoon a storm came up—ominous threat of what was to follow—and Santa Anna was hurriedly taken on board, aided by Zavala who had by this time begun to have his troubles with the Texans and was then about to be ousted as Vice-President.   Perhaps mindful of this situation he became conciliatory towards his former enemy and aided him in his plans.   On board the *Invincible* our hero, his impressionable soul moved, dictated a premature proclamation to the Texans expressing gratitude : "My Friends : I have been a witness of your courage on the field of battle, and know you to be generous. Rely with confidence on my sincerity and you shall never have cause to regret the kindness shown me. In returning to my native land, I beg you to receive the sincere thanks of your grateful friend. Farewell ! Antonio Lopez de Santa Anna."

Premature gratitude, premature rhetoric ! For when it was known that Santa Anna was on the ship, popular feeling ran high — a Texan high — and a mob gathered. Possibly no small part of this was directed at President Burnet for his release of the captive. But it all came to a climax through an unforeseen event. At this juncture a party of volunteers who had been long overdue from New Orleans came into port two hundred thirty strong in two ships.

Their leader joined with the anti-Santa Anna party and his weight in the balance upset Burnet's plans. This man, Thomas J. Green, promising the President that the captive would come to no harm from the mob, influenced him to send an order to the *Invincible* requesting that Santa Anna should be sent back on shore. Our hero, agitated by the delay in the sailing, was greatly upset by this message and refused to move saying melodramatically that he would never leave the vessel alive.

An almost feminine hysteria seized him now and when Green with some others went on board to get him, they found him lying in bed, crying, "Mercy! Mercy! Oh God! If they wish to kill me let them come and shoot me here. Don't let them take me on shore." An officer on the ship wrote, "Santa Anna is the greatest coward ever produced. He referred constantly to the 'new army

which was going to kill him and said he would commit
suicide."

No amount of explanation could persuade him that he
would be safe ashore. He rushed around and took some
opium — more opium, he said — he had taken so much, he
averred, that he would soon die anyway. Almonte who
stood out in serene and tranquil contrast, was asked to add
his powers of influence to get the raving General to leave
the ship. But Almonte who knew his Santa Anna, replied
that it was impossible to advise him, that he was obsessed
by this idea of execution, and diplomatic as ever in smooth-
ing over his superior's scrapes, suggested that they wait a bit.

But the resolute Green had to be shown. He had a surgeon examine the General's pulse and had the satisfaction
of hearing it pronounced normal. Then he tried his own
remedy. He ordered irons to be brought and when the
formidable chains appeared, his prescription worked. For
the sick man jumped up readily from his bed, adjusted his
collar, put on his hat and announced that he would leave
the ship. Emerging from his cabin, however, he almost
collapsed when he saw the sentinel on deck; he bared his
bosom dramatically and offered to die then and there.
More expostulation, more persuasion until he reluctantly
descended into the gig-boat weeping bitterly. As the ob-
servant naval officer paraphrased,

"His coward lips did from their color fly
And that same eye whose look doth awe all Mexico
Did lose its lustre."

Approaching the shore, his captors had another struggle
with him, when he noticed a crowd gathered at the dock

in Velasco and threatened to drown himself unless the boat landed somewhere else. Green tried to calm him, saying that the crowd was not violent, only curious and, "If Your Excellency still wants to show himself the Napoleon of the West, you should take the Texan flag and wave it at the crowd on shore." Placing the emblem in his quivering hands, and indeed practically moving his arms for him, the crew gave three cheers as he feebly waved the banner.

But Green thought it safer to land his man across the river from Velasco in the small hamlet of Quintana where his fears were allayed and where President Burnet made Green responsible for his safety.   The latter decided to feast his famous prisoner in the only manner the little town could offer.   The erstwhile banqueter in the halls of Montezuma, who customarily dined off monogrammed silver and china sat down with the rude soldier of fortune on a rough pine bench and sopped up some beefsteak and gravy from a tin pan.   The elegant Almonte stood behind his august master and served him coffee in a sooty tin cup.   But Santa Anna, delighted at what he considered his escape from death, sat astraddle the uncomfortable bench as if it were the upholstered throne of Iturbide.   When Green jested that he might take a trip to Mexico and that he expected Santa Anna to serve him with better coffee cups, the President of Mexico laid his hand on his breast and with all the earnestness which he knew so well how to assume, said "Ah yes, my dear General, I do long for this unfortunate war to be over, and then I want to see you in Mexico where I can reciprocate your kindness."

But his terror returned when he was taken across to Velasco on the 7th of June and put under the guard of

Captain Patton who was to be his jailer for some time to come. Someone had told him that there were four desperadoes among Patton's troops who had sworn to kill him. At this news his secretary, even more agitated than his master, collapsed. But Santa Anna recovered his composure sufficiently to write a protest to President Burnet, saying that he was being treated "more like an ordinary criminal than a prisoner of war, the head of a respectable nation." With the scene of his humiliating breakdown and approach to shore in his mind, he protested about the "act of violence" to which he had been exposed and the "abuse" in being forced to go to shore. He also complained about his present lodgings and the "privations" which almost rendered life unsupportable. Burnet replied with dignity and moderation.

But while he was enduring this unpleasant captivity, he made his first effort to escape. A young Spaniard who worked in a saloon in the town came to him and said that as he was going to New Orleans he might be able to arrange for an escape if given the necessary funds. He was given some rather equivocal letters to the Mexican consul there but they contained no direct mention of funds. Evidently Santa Anna did not know how far the Spaniard could be trusted, and he relied on the rumored intention of the Mexican Government to pay huge sums for his rescue to facilitate the plan.

Shortly after Patton removed the President and his suite to a house in the nearby town of Columbia. He seems to have been somewhat careless of the safety of his charges for an incident took place in Columbia which provoked Santa Anna to further alarm and hysteria. A drunken man stag-

gered up to the house and asked for Santa Anna. Obtaining no satisfaction from the sentinel he approached a
window of a room in which Almonte and Nuñez were
sitting — Santa Anna was in a chamber adjoining —
gurgled out his demand again and as the Mexicans either
did not understand or would not answer, whipped out a
revolver and fired into the room. The shot went wild,
hurting neither of the occupants, and the assailant was
arrested. Santa Anna protested bitterly against this attack
and also against the breaking of the treaty he had signed

But his protests meant little to President Burnet who was
overcome with the new problems arising from the situation
He had tried to temporize by making Santa Anna's position
indeterminate until the Constitutional Convention met and
decided his fate. But the die-hards among the army were
at work, insisting that Santa Anna be turned over to them
and finally the San Jacinto veterans who had at first yielded
to Sam Houston's orders to respect Santa Anna's life, now
joined the rest who yelled for his blood. This move was
made by none other than Rusk himself who seems to have
been won over by the execution party and took the form
of an order to Patton to bring Santa Anna to the army
which was at Victoria. This was equivalent to a death
warrant and he was never in greater danger.

But he had powerful protectors. Burnet put up a stiff
fight against his Pretorian guards, and now Stephen Austin
returned flushed with his success in rousing sentiment in
the United States favorable to American recognition of the
new Republic. He displayed a keen interest in Santa
Anna's plight and allayed the popular fury by a new stroke
of policy — the suggestion that Santa Anna write President

Jackson asking him to start mediation between the new Republic and Mexico and to exert his own influence to bring about a settlement. Perhaps Austin himself anticipated little from this but at least it was an excellent measure to gain time. Meanwhile Sam Houston was returning to Texas from New Orleans where he had spent some time treating his injured leg. When he heard of the move to take Santa Anna to the army he correctly interpreted it as an order for his execution and he wrote an energetic protest. It was a noble letter and must have had its effect, for Santa Anna was soon after moved not to the army but to a place called Orozimba, a ranch owned by Dr. Phelps, about twelve miles from Columbia.

There at last the much disturbed lodger found a quiet, happy haven. Dr. Phelps and his family were kindness itself and hospitably did everything to make him comfortable and happy. His spirits revived and he received many visitors with all his pristine affability and capacity to please. Stephen Austin dropped in and he gaily scolded him on his defection from the cause of Mexico. Sam Houston came and the captive fell on his neck, watering the manly shoulders with the tears of gratitude. Grateful, yes, and happy too with a virile defender like old Sam and the prospect of enlisting Andrew Jackson's aid. Another visitor was Colonel Bernard Bee, a wealthy backer of the Texan Republic. He had recently met J. R. Poinsett during a tour of the United States and conveyed a rather reproachful message to Santa Anna from his friend the former Minister to Mexico. Poinsett lamented the fact that Santa Anna had turned against the principles of Federalism and had unkindly remarked that the former President deserved his fate, for he had "turned from liberty to despotism."

In good form now, Santa Anna replied with a rare burst of honesty : "Be kind enough to say to Mr. Poinsett, it is very true that I threw up my cap for liberty, with great ardor and perfect sincerity, but very soon found the utter folly of it. Sir, for a century to come our people will not be fit for liberty ; they do not know what it is. Unenlightened as they are and under the influence of a Catholic clergy a despotism is the proper government ; but there is no reason why it should not be a wise and virtuous one."

Happy days, destined to be rudely broken. For one day the Spaniard who had approached him in Velasco appeared. He told Caro that the plan he had worked out for Santa Anna's escape was impossible now since Orozimba was too far from the coast. Furthermore, he disclosed that the authorities in New Orleans had become suspicious and that he had great difficulty in leaving that port. He offered however to return another day with some supplies and articles for the General's comfort.

But Patton's suspicions were aroused and he had the Spaniard arrested. The local judge freed the man of any complicity, but meanwhile news had reached Texas from New Orleans that a vessel had been sent to rescue Santa Anna, and Minister Rusk ordered both the General and Almonte put in irons. A heavy and most uncomfortable ball and chain was placed on the leg of our hero — on Almonte's too — and it was kept there for "fifty-three days" as he mentions with circumstantial bitterness in his letter.

In this melancholy condition Santa Anna received another blow. Old Hickory in Washington had been advised by the Mexican Minister there that no act of Santa Anna while a prisoner would be held binding in Mexico. Accordingly he wrote an evasive letter saying he would talk to the Mexican Minister privately but that he could do nothing, being on friendly terms with the Mexican Government; furthermore Texas had not yet been recognized by either the United States or Mexico. With some finality he stated that he felt that he could not enter into negotiations as suggested by Santa Anna.

It should have been a rude rebuff, but Santa Anna with his usual elasticity rebounded from it with great art. He pretended that Jackson had not understood him and on this basis began to agitate for his release so that he could journey to Washington and personally carry on negotiations with Jackson himself. This impressed Houston as well as Austin who were both anxious to get Santa Anna away from their vindictive colleagues. By October their moderating influence was such that the President decreed that the ball and chain should be removed. Patton received instructions to treat his prisoner with all manner of indulgence.

"A misdirected magnanimity, that would turn loose upon the world another Ate, hot from hell. Such is the magnanimity now proposed Santa Anna, the slayer of our friends and brethren, the pirate, the robber, the murderer, the all-horrible demon in human shape whose march through the world is to be traced by the BLOODY TRAIL he leaves behind, is to be screened from justice, is to be turned loose again like a hell hound upon his race for the all-glorious purpose of exhibiting his conqueror in the exquisite attitude of a *magnanimous hero*. Spirits of Bowie, Travis and Bonaham, and all ye gallant martyrs of Goliad and Bexar, what think ye of this?"

Apparently others beside Santa Anna possessed the gift of florid oratory.   For a storm was blowing in the Convention at Austin.   The Demosthenes was Senator Everett and he was supporting with all his words and will the party which opposed the release of Santa Anna.   Fortunately for the latter, Burnet, Austin and Houston were working hard not only for his safety but his release.

Meanwhile he experienced concern about the shifting forces in Mexico.   The keen old hunter could hear from afar the notes of the political horns in the valley of the Aztecs.   He was gratified that the government had decreed that the soldiers should wear a band of crepe on their collars during his captivity and that all flags should be half mast.   But it implied that he was politically dead and indeed some newspapers had begun to refer to His Excellency as the "late" President in a satirical vein.

His nature did not appreciate these sallies and he noted that scurrilous pamphlets had begun to appear: "Don Antonio, like Icarus in attempting to soar too high, was precipitated into the abyss below.   We would ask, who is this Protector of Religion?   A man loaded with vice in all its forms.   His aim was always disorder, etc. etc."   There were enemies undoubtedly forming combinations against him and for all the loyal defense of his friends, Tornel and Sierra y Rosso, he was eager to get back and into the game again.

Finally the movement to keep him was quelled in the Convention and Sam Houston, now President, took on himself the responsibility of releasing Santa Anna so that he could visit Jackson in Washington.   On the 25th of November, 1836, he set out escorted by Colonels Bee and

Hockley and Captain Patton, in a stage-coach. As he passed by the field of San Jacinto, he gave a shrug of relief, but he must have heaved a great sigh of satisfaction as he crossed the border into Louisiana where his companions were no longer captors but charming associates on a happy journey.

He created a sensation wherever he stopped, the curious coming down to the landings on the Mississippi to lure him out of his cabin on the river boat which was carrying him to Louisville. He exerted his great talents for courtesy and compliment so that even in Kentucky the home-land of many of the Alamo victims, he received warm attentions. Almonte with his less demonstrative manner, his cool poise and his policy, no less brilliant than his Commander's, was much more popular. Besides our hero was taken with ills, probably real this time, for the country was strange and the weather in the dead of winter was often severe.

Perhaps for this reason he did not appear at his best for the Louisville correspondent of the *New York Express*: "Imagine to yourself a man of full ordinary stature, forty years of age, weighing about one hundred sixty pounds, of graceful form and step, round shouldered, with black glossy hair, tolerable full white face and round forehead, a short, squarish, inferior looking nose and a round dark eye, somewhat sunken. Suppose him dressed in a genteel trail-bodied black coat and blue pantaloons, walking about or sitting cross-legged in a pair of slipshod pumps ; tolerable, pleasant of countenance and speech (which is exclusively Spanish), very polite, and using stately compliments. Such is the appearance of General Santa Anna. He has in my view nothing military in his appearance and nothing indi-

cating great talents.   He would readily, I think, pass for an
active intelligent merchant or man of general business.
He is very reserved, plain, modest in his conversation and
manners as far as I have observed him, I can see nothing
villainous or deceitful in his countenance."

The farther north he got, the more popular he became,
especially after he passed the Mason and Dixon line.   For
the anti-slavery partisans felt that the whole Texas war was
but part of a conspiracy to bring another slave state into the
Union.   Accordingly it was no surprise that the Woon-
socket, R. I. *Patriot* should salute him in the following
terms : "Santa Anna !   How can we style him a tyrant
. . . who opposed the efforts of rebels and used them with
deserved severity . . . fought and bled to contravene the
efforts of those who wished the substantial, the horrible
system of slavery ?"

In Kentucky for the first time he saw the "cars," as they
called the first steam railroads of that day, and he boarded
them at Louisville, going as far as Lexington where a huge
crowd met him at the depot.   Whether he mistook their
curiosity for some other violent feeling, or whether the
"cars" made him dizzy, is not recorded, but Almonte
hustled him to a hotel saying that the General was unwell.
His fastidiousness and ill-health was costing Colonel Be
not a little by this time, for with the Texan treasury empty
their Mæcenas had put up two thousand dollars for the
expenses of the trip out of his own pocket.   Santa Anna
drew a draft on Lizardi of Vera Cruz, saying he knew he
had no money but hoped that Lizardi would honor it.   He
arrived in Washington on January 18th, 1837, and put up
at Mrs. Ulrick's boarding house.

He found Old Hickory in a vigorous mood and especially ready for a Mexican, for he had just scored off the Mexican Minister Gorostiza when the latter had run to the President to protest when he heard that Jackson was going to recognize the Texas Republic. "Sir," said the Minister, "it looks as if you were going to recognize the Texans. Don't you know that there are treaties which prohibit this government from intervening in a dispute of our family?" To which Jackson had retorted: "Sir, it looks as if you were thirsty for American blood. Don't you know that such an appetite occasions indigestion?"

In a private interview the American President lectured Santa Anna severely on his desertion of the Liberal cause, and on his conduct at the Alamo and Goliad. They discussed in detail the future of Texas and a possible treaty for the cession of Texas to the United States. Beyond these facts Old Hickory would not divulge any further details of the conversation.

But Santa Anna discussed with great freedom and candor the situation with Wharton the Texas envoy who was trying to obtain recognition from Jackson. Yes, certainly, he hoped for American recognition of Texas, it would facilitate matters for himself when he returned to his country. And why not a treaty selling Mexican rights to Texas to the United States for a sum — say thirteen million dollars? Then, jocularly, he hoped the Texans would not put anything in the way of his getting a few millions from the Yankee treasury.

In fine fettle now our hero rattled on. Texas could never be conquered by Mexico, he knew now. The rumored invasion which had been agitating the Texans for the past month? Humbug—and if there were anything to it, he would put a stop to it when he returned. Ah, when he returned, he would show the Texans that he was their friend, that he was not the perfidious and ungrateful monster they pictured.

Why wouldn't such an accommodating and gracious fellow become popular in Washington? For had he not asked—rare gesture among Latin-Americans—for a copy of all claims for damages inflicted on United States citizens in Mexico so that he could arrange for payment when he reached his capital? He was eager to return and he even declined a banquet invitation from Jackson himself so that he could take the "cars" to the sea port.

It was none too soon, for a disquieting incident had occurred. The Minister Gorostiza had left and the Mexican *chargé* who was staying in Philadelphia wrote to Santa Anna about the newspaper accounts of his mission to Jackson for Texan recognition and a treaty with Mexico, reprimanding him for his policy and lodging formal protest against his proceeding with the matter. Santa Anna incensed, ordered *his* diplomat to appear before him at once. But the *chargé* refused and immediately sent off a report of the matter to the Mexican Government.

So as Santa Anna approached Vera Cruz he felt no little apprehension. Was the home government, as this incident indicated, unfriendly? His friends themselves were a little uncertain for they provided a vessel at the port for him to go elsewhere if his reception was unfavorable. But temperamental Vera Cruz responded with joy to its former tyrant's return and proclaimed a holiday. Salutes were fired, citizens met him with acclamations of rejoicing and he was borne in triumph to a hotel where a banquet was given in his honor. The crepe had been removed from the soldiers' lapels and the flags hoisted to full mast. Outwardly it seemed that all was well.

But he learned that there had been a strong party in Congress which tried to declare him a traitor and to remove him from the nominal occupancy of the Presidential chair. This measure had been defeated but the suspicious Congress voted that he should send them an accounting of his actions and promises in Texas. He sent a letter reassuring them of his loyalty and promising an early report on the whole affair, and started off for Manga de Clavo escorted by his friends in Vera Cruz.

He had no small task before him now — an explanation of his actions in Texas that would not only clear him of the charge of betrayal but regain some of his lost popularity. No one reading his long "Manifiesto" can say that he did not do his best; dramatic references to his wife and children, to the marks which the chains left on him, his victories in former years, his services to the Republic. His résumé of the fatal campaign was comparatively easy and his authority as commander carried him through numerous prevarications. But in his explanation of the negotiations with the Texans during his captivity, he had to fall back on the distinction between what he promised his captors in his own name as a private individual and what he promised as President of Mexico. He excused even these *personal* concessions on the ground that he was saving the lives of his fellow captives. It was all very ornate and abounded in such periods as this, "Santa Anna, whether conqueror or conquered, whether free or in chains, yea, I swear before the world, did not in Texas debase the Mexican name in which he glories and takes pride."

It was to shrill motifs like this, accompanied by the apologetic diapason of his co-plotters in the capital, that he resigned the Presidency and retired to Manga de Clavo. As the music died down, Anglo-Saxon ears were cocked to hear if there was any coda, in a diplomatic key, from the glib and obliging guest of Houston, Rusk and Jackson, but they heard, what they should long ago have expected, nothing, absolutely nothing.

It is agreed that no man can be a hero to his valet, and poor Martinez Caro, while a secretary, had all the intimacy of a lackey. This in itself should have restrained His Excellency from assailing the humble fellow and what was worse of accusing him of stealing a costly shirt stud. Caro who had hitherto loyally kept the many incriminating secrets about his employer, now flowed over with bitterness and published his own account of the disastrous campaign and its humiliating sequel. In lengthy and circumstantial detail he refuted innumerable statements in Santa Anna's *Defense* and with cool narration of facts gave a terrible picture of the General's conduct. No wonder then that Colonel Almonte and another officer, doubtless at the instance of their chief, seized the indiscreet scribe and threw him in prison. But Caro's pamphlet had started the ball of controversy rolling. Filisola who had published his own *Defense* was assailed in another pamphlet by Urrea and neither could say much in Santa Anna's favor. It was well that the Clove-Spike hacienda was far from the capital and that other clouds on the horizon were rolling up to cloak the too recent and ugly spectacle.

CHAPTER VII

$600,000 WORTH OF PIE

DEAR FRIEND : Half the world seems to be in revolt. In Guadalajara and in Oaxaca and various other points there have been *pronunciamientos ;* although they have been stifled yet always the rebellion stays warm ; in the latter place there have been many troubles and much pillaging, etc. etc." (Then more importantly) "This year looks prosperous. The sowing went off well, and if in the months of August and September there will be no change of the usual weather conditions, the crops will be most successful." In this manner did a Mexican country squire describe the situation in 1838.

Thus Mexico went on for the most part lending only half an ear to the petards of the pronouncements, suffering their aftermaths of commercial stagnation and robbery, but returning joyously to the stability of nature and its fruits. The cornucopia-shaped Republic was still rich in the soil and subsoil products and came to look with a calmer eye on the antics of its sanguinary politico-clowns. But if Mexicans were submissive there were others who were not.

Sometime in the year 1833 as a detachment of Santa Anna's troops was about to leave the capital on a campaign, several of the officers went out to celebrate at Tacubaya, that pleasant suburb replete with gaming houses, restaurants and places of pleasure. In the Restaurant Rémontel they revelled far into the night, until at the height of their orgy they locked the French proprietor in his room and proceeded to pillage the establishment. Seizing almost every object they could get their hands on, money, silver, even the contents of the larder, including of course the pastry, they dashed off to rejoin their corps. A military prank but destined to have serious results, for M. Rémontel had his Minister file a claim for eight hundred pesos damage.

So arose the legend of the Pastry War of 1838 between France and Mexico — the legend that a French pastry cook being robbed of some of his pies filed a claim for 30,000 pesos, which added to other claims formed the total of $600,000 demanded by the French Government. The truth was that M. Rémontel's little bill was but one small item in a long list of claims for loss of life, property, mob violence and especially forced loans which every *jefe* from Santa Anna down was wont to levy on all inhabitants whatever their nationality.

Feeling may have been accentuated because France had never cast a friendly eye on the Mexican Republic and had been one of the last of the great powers to recognize it, or perhaps because King Louis-Philippe was keenly aware of his Orleans blood and his kinship to the Spanish royal family. Whatever their motives the French Government began to press their claims with more energy than other long-suffering nationalities. The various Foreign Ministers who alternated with as much frequency as the transitory Presidents themselves, displayed amiable courtesy to the insistent French envoy but filed away his *dossiers* and promptly forgot all about his guarded threats.

It seemed an unheard of thing to the *politicos* that they should be expected to protect foreigners, much less their own patient subject-victims, and most incredible of all that a war might be started to collect money. Consequently their complacency received a decided shock when a French fleet sailed into Vera Cruz harbor in 1838 and declared a blockade of all Mexican ports. The admiral was not as patient as his nation's diplomat, however, and abruptly issued an ultimatum demanding the $600,000 payment.

The Mexican Ministers' amazement at such a procedure grew to anger as they looked from the amount of the claim to the balance of their own depleted treasury—depleted largely through their own peculations, and their rage was quickly translated to the plebs who were ready for any good opportunity to sack and pillage. French? A name unknown to this mob who were no better versed in geography than in popular government, and they stormed French houses yelling "down with the Jews" and organizing veritable Sicilian Vespers. Many French nationals who were, next to the Spanish, the most numerous of the foreigners, flocked in confusion to the protection of the French guns in Vera Cruz.

England and America looked on with neutral approval for their own people had suffered greatly and their own bills had been met with the same amiable indifference. The Bustamente government found that they were in for trouble. They sought first of all to tie the matter up in a legal wrangle about the validity of treaties. Then they whistled valiantly to their courage by assuring the world that San Juan Ulloa, that Gibraltar of the nation, was impregnable. The rabble meanwhile with just as much misdirected energy, finding that the French were Catholics, joyously yelled "Down with the Saxons," a name which came to comprehend for them all foreigners including Italians and Turks. Riva Palacio, afterwards a statesman of some merit, and who should have known better, made popular the following chestnut: "The French want 9 679 177. They will get" (reversing the paper on which these numerals were printed and discovering that they made out a crude representation of the French word *merde*).

It was rather fun while it lasted until Admiral Baudin, tired of parleying, raised the indemnity to $800,000 and trained his guns on Ulloa with a twenty-four hour ultimatum to put up or fight. Even then the Bustamente government did not come to terms but prepared in their clumsy way to fight, secure in their feeling that the fort at Vera Cruz could withstand any bombardment.

On the afternoon of November 27th the French fleet took their positions with Admiral Baudin in his huge flagship, named somewhat inappropriately the *Nereid,* firing the first gun. The Crown Prince of the French Monarchy, Prince de Joinville, was second in command and followed suit with the rest of the frigates and corvette adding their thunder. But it was much more than noise for the effects on the old fort were devastating. The battlements, never in repair, were even less so now and French marksmanship was surprisingly good.

The ancient limestone which formed the matrix of the

stone defenses was broken into myriad fragments by the
French shells and killed more Mexicans than did the steel.
After an hour's bombardment, from the tremendous smoke
pall which covered the bay and made difficult the aiming
of the cannon, came a tremendous explosion. Crash !
went the powder magazine of the fort and virtually demolished the citadel. The fire from the walls slackened
and after another magazine exploded it dribbled down to
not more than three guns a minute.

At sunset the firing ceased because of darkness and the
French fleet proceeded to make a few paltry repairs, bury
its eight dead and prepare for another bombardment on
the morrow. But the Commander of the Castle, together
with Rincon who commanded Vera Cruz, decided the position was untenable and a very humble deputation waited
on Admiral Baudin for terms. They were permitted to
leave the fort and continue their occupation of the city
with only 1,000 men ; all other forces had to retire to the
back-country ; and hostilities were suspended. The Mexican Gibraltar had fallen !

Commander David Farragut who stood by in an American war-vessel and made notes which were afterwards to
inspire him to the exploits of Mobile Bay during the Civil
War, looked on and marvelled at Baudin's bombardment.
'I visited the Castle to ascertain the cause of its early surrender and a single glance satisfied me that it would have
been impracticable for the Mexicans to stand to their guns.
The very material which formerly insured their safety was
now a means of destruction, for the Castle is built of a sort
of limestone resembling coral . . . a shell . . . would ex-
plode and rend the stone in immense masses, killing and

wounding the men at the guns, in many instances shatter-
ing the walls from summit to foundation. I am perfectly
satisfied that in a few hours more it would have been a
mass of rubbish. Only picture to yourself a shower of two
hundred shell and shot falling into a castle ! Davis told
me a man might stay there and be killed, but it was impossible to do anything, for he was not on his feet five
minutes before he was knocked down again by a fragment
of wood or stone."

But where was the Hero of Tampico ? The situation
was very similar to that during the Spanish invasion, with
Bustamente just as dilatory and inefficient as the lamented
Guerrero was at the outbreak of that war, and the people
disgusted with their leader clamoring for a strong man, a
man of action. But Santa Anna did not dash front and
center as he did in 1829. The ignominy of San Jacinto
hung over him and when the French fleet sailed into the
harbor he doubtless felt that he would be greeted with no
wild applause if he rushed out in the rôle of military tacti-
cian. Indeed, when he humbly offered his services to
Rincón, the latter rebuffed him so churlishly that he retired, mortified, to Manga de Clavo to watch the progress
of events.

His revenge on Rincón for such insolence came when
the bombardment ceased on that sanguinary sunset of the
28th. Gaona, the commander of San Juan Ulloa, insisted
that he must capitulate, that there was no other alternative
to evacuation save death. Rincón saw that as well as any
one, but thought he could escape the full responsibility of
a surrender by having Santa Anna inspect the fort and give
his opinion. It was Santa Anna's golden opportunity

Leaving his hacienda, he swooped down like a *zopilote* on the ruins of Ulloa. The situation was clear to him, too, but from an angle that neither Rincón nor Gaona could appreciate, and when his report appeared the latter had little reason to be grateful. For the wily old soldier-politico wrote a masterpiece of equivocation and rhetoric, which made it appear that he had upheld the retention of the fortress against the combined protests of Rincón and Gaona. He spoke much of how the "entire world has its eyes on Ulloa" and he emphasized how difficult it would be to regain it. Less a report than a proclamation, intended not for the embarrassed commanders but for the seething mob in Mexico.

His calculations were excellent, for Rincon, facing the inevitable, consented to the evacuation and reluctantly reported it to the capital. Immediately, the hysterical Government, instead of recognizing its defeat, declared war on France. The patriotic street crowds hissed Rincón — whom Bustamente perforce relieved of his command — and intoxicated by the syllables from the oracle of Manga de Clavo, clamored for Santa Anna. Bustamente, who seemed to rely entirely on the shouts of the *leperos* for governmental wisdom, supinely acceded to this demand too. The late craven of San Jacinto was to have his chance to redeem himself.

Santa Anna was at his hacienda resting after his arduous labors of inspecting Ulloa and of framing his sly report when "the people" summoned him to their succor. He proceeded to Vera Cruz on the 4th of December, sending his aide Gimenez ahead with orders to close the gates of the city both on the land and water side and to allow no one to leave. As it happened, on the morning of that day the Prince de Joinville with some of his men, taking advantage of the armistice, had promenaded on the quais. The Prince himself had gone back to his ship by the time that Santa Anna approached, but some French officer: tarrying were taken into custody by the obedient Gimenez. The French were enraged for they more or less correctly surmised that the tricky Mexican leader had sought to trap their Prince.

The Prince brought the battleship *Creole* in near the city and aimed its guns on the Plaza, sending word tha he would level the perfidious city if they did not liberat all the French officers. A difficult situation, for Sant Anna had come to talk and not to fight, but he promptl released them.

Indeed a fatiguing and trying day, for he had to ar nounce to the French commander the fact that his Goverr ment had declared war. A fine situation in a defensele: city with less than 1,000 men and a terrible fleet in th harbor training its guns on the land ! All his diplomat skill had to be exerted to avoid some untoward action, an French suspicion had to be allayed. He worked energet cally all day sending ambiguous letters, playing desperate for time. He demanded an armistice until the next mor: ing—what time he was so neglectful as to omit specifyir —and he finally wrung a grudging consent from the su picious and angry Admiral in the harbor.

General Arista with his staff arrived, the vanguard one thousand more troops which were still some leagu away and could not be brought up until the next da The two old pronouncement veterans met after a sepa tion of five years, a separation, it is true, made somewhat unwillingly on Santa Anna's part after that picturesque but abortive attempt to upset Farias' apple-cart in '33. Doubtless they had lots to talk over : Santa Anna's mock "imprisonment" by his own troops on that occasion and the painful necessity he had to undergo of capturing Arista in earnest and of sending him into exile. They talked until three in the morning when Arista, who wanted to gallop back to his troops, was prevailed upon by Santa Anna to stay and catch a nap in His Excellency's quarters.

So Santa Anna slept, succumbed to the perfidious Morpheus who had cruelly tricked him at San Jacinto. A sound sleep too, for he went to bed confident that he could josh the French through another day and come out of it with laurels. But the French with vengeful technicality observed the armistice only until dawn. While Santa Anna slumbered Baudin armed his men, formed a landing party and brought them up to the very gates of the quais.

When five o'clock of December 5th struck, the ghostly visitors crept up through the fog which had protected them from discovery and overpowered the guards of the gates. To the cry of "Vive le Roi !" they ran through the streets shooting the yawning Mexican guards and seeking the quarters of General Santa Anna.

Apparently Baudin desired not only vengeance but perhaps a bit of the policy which the Texan Rusk had used the year before. The famous Santa Anna in their power, what could the Mexican Government do against them? His men dashed down the gray streets bayoneting, firing and seeking. One of these shots awakened Arista who thought it was simply the *reveillé* gun of the French and turned over. But not so Santa Anna who, doubtless pricked by a guilty conscience, sprang from his bed and ran out into the hall.

The French marines were already in the patio below and as he descended precipitately, clad only in his under-clothing, a marine shouted to him, "Where is Santa Anna ?" "Up there," he replied to the Frenchman, pointing to the upper floor. He made his escape to the street, directing his somewhat inadequately covered figure with all swift-ness through the town toward the barracks which were on the outskirts. Arista a few minutes later emerged gaping into the hall and was seized by the delighted Gauls who thought they had taken Santa Anna.

After this capture the sailors and marines combed the little city, patrolling the ramparts for any doughty Mexi-cans who might want to fight. There were few enough of these left save in the great barracks where they had al taken refuge with their chief. The French not having brought any field artillery, saw it was useless to storm thi fortress and retired into the town, waiting about a con siderable time for evidence of the enemy. But Santa Anna did not emerge from his stronghold.

Finally the French embarked and commenced to row back to their ships. Only at this moment, when the dan ger appeared to be over, did our valiant hero make his ap pearance. Now in full blazing uniform on a white charge he rallied his men from the barracks and cautiously ap proached the shore ; a good opportunity to make a brav show of resistance when the hazards were less and to b able to write a glowing report to Mexico on the way h broke up the embarkation.

But the French frigates had now come in to cover the rowboats and when they saw the horde of Mexicans approaching the pier they loaded their guns and took aim. Charging dramatically through the streets that bordered on the shore, Santa Anna undoubtedly presented a heroic spectacle. On went the Mexicans protected by walls and warehouses and finally out into the open of the pier and quai. Just then a French gunner on a ship fired an historic shot,—a most political shell, for it shifted the course of Mexican Caesarism.

Bursting at the head of the comically heroic little column, it killed our hero's white stallion, shattered his own left leg and disabled a soldier beside him. It was no playacting now, for the French fleet poured a murderous fire on the Mexican soldiers. They retreated precipitately, dragging with them their wounded leader.

Suffering, yes, but not too much, however, to delay the proclamation which he had planned for the Government. It was to be written virtually in terms of blood, in terms of his blood which would perhaps inspire the people to fight against the invader and revenge him; and on that precious issue of his veins he would rise again to political fame and power. In this exalted mood he composed his famous "last words" to "his" people. It has been alleged that he had a clever journalist string together its lurid syllables for him, but in appearance and color it is undoubtedly his own.

After a preamble apologizing for the success of the French surprise attack and alleging treachery on the part of Baudin, filled with the usual inaccuracies and prevarications, he plunges into the real stuff: "We have conquered, yes, we have conquered ; the Mexican arms have gained a glorious triumph in the city and the Mexican flag will remain triumphant ; I was wounded in the last effort and it will probably be the last victory which I shall offer to my country. When our vengeance was satisfied and when our flag floated victorious over our ramparts, I believed it necessary to evacuate the place. . . The enemy in their chagrin commenced an extraordinary fire on the abandoned city, the cowards, to cover their ignominy. I do not doubt the sacred fire which animates the defenders of national independence ; I do not doubt that they know how to conserve intact the honor of the nation's arms. . . I die happily because Divine Providence has permitted me to consecrate my blood to my country.

"At this moment of ending my career I should express the happiness which I have felt of having seen the commencement of the reconciliation between Mexicans. I have embraced for the last time General Arista with whom I had had a misunderstanding. And now I salute you Your Excellency, President of the Republic, as a mark o my gratitude for having honored me in the moment o danger ; I conjure my compatriots in the name of th *Patria* to put aside their resentments and to all unite forming an impenetrable wall on which will break the French audacity.

"I also ask that my body be buried in these same Mec anos (parapets) so that my companions at arms may know that here is the line of battle which I have traced for then May all Mexicans forgetting my political errors, deny m not the only title which I wish to leave to my son, that a 'Good Mexican.' God and Liberty, Antonio Lopez de Santa Anna."

The effect of this on the impressionable inhabitants of the capital waiting eagerly for news from the front was prodigious. All the cafés were agog with the name of Santa Anna, anew a hero and this time a martyr. Poets reeled off verses, Congress seethed with resolutions of thanks and his friends were jubilant. The Government, which knew the real facts, simply tried to ride the wave of enthusiasm. They expressed concern about the condition of the hero, and two of the most learned surgeons were dispatched to care for him. Reports of death alternated with those of his miraculous recovery until finally it was ascertained that the surgeons had successfully removed his badly mangled left leg below the knee. As the patient convalesced, the leg was buried in the grounds of the hacienda and pious deputations from the capital deposited wreaths on this grave; but more of that anon. For the moment, Clio smiled and as a climax to the Pastry War, Mexico's Napoleon recaptured popular favor by a successful amputation.

His name now transcended all; — as a newspaper put it "his laurels of former days had obtained new verdure." It grew in importance at the end of the Pastry War. The French, through the intermediation of the English, came down on their terms and Mexico consented to pay the $600,000 in installments through the year. In this wise the Mexicans won a minor diplomatic victory of which the tottering Government tried to take full advantage, while the foreigners, especially the French, felt that a sufficient humiliation had been wrought on the careless Republic so that thereafter they would be more careful of foreign nationals and foreign property. But the greatest result of the war was the projection of the mutilated Santa Anna again into the center of the political ring.

His triumphal entry into the capital was delayed by his recovery and other considerations so that he did not approach the city until February 17th. The American Consul wrote: "Public expectation is on tiptoe waiting the result of the arrival of this near prodigy who it now appears holds in his grasp the destinies of this nation." It was suggested his slow approach with stops at all the principal cities was to ascertain the amount of public sentiment in his favor. But few gave him credit for a great faculty of dramatic suspense.

When he arrived at last great crowds went outside the city to give him welcome and he was escorted by squadrons of cavalry to the music of military bands—playing a new hymn written in his honor—while the bells rang out and the rockets flashed. He took up his quarters in a house in San Cosme offered by Count Haral, where a constant stream of sycophants and military shook his hand and fawned upon him. General Valencia, one of the most daring, spread the cry of Dictator—heady wine for such as Santa Anna.

Indeed he was all but a Dictator, such was the Olympian way with which he dealt with the uneasy Bustamente. The latter had been worried by an especially serious *pronunciamiento* in Tampico, but had hesitated to act wondering whether the danger in that province was any greater than the Napoleonic peril on his doorstep. With compelling abruptness, Santa Anna resolved the President's inde cision by an ultimatum which was, in effect : either *you* go forth to put down the rebellion, or *I* will. Bustamente foreseeing that another affair like that of the 5th of December with Santa Anna in the center of the stage would put him out completely, readily took his army and departed for Tampico. Before he left, however, with a wry grimace he yielded to the clamors of the people and appointed Santa Anna President *ad interim*. Hobbling into the National Palace, our hero crowed exultingly, "Companions at arms, the national will calls me to rule temporarily. The will of my citizens is irresistible and I am duty bound to renounce the honor of conducting you to Tampico."

But the revolt in the provinces took on large proportions and seemed to be too much for the President in the field. Santa Anna pursued one of the *pronunciados,* Colonel Mejia, towards Puebla. Mejia was foolish enough to believe in Valencia when the latter joined him as a rebel. Not far from Puebla this tool of Santa Anna's treacherously turned on his companion and captured him. Facing court-martial, Mejia was told he would be executed in three hours. "If it were Santa Anna I held captive I would shoot him in three minutes," replied the defiant captive. Santa Anna arrived only in time for the firing squad and victory and got all the plaudits in the capital.

He took advantage of his situation to distribute two thousand promotions in the army and to outfit many regiments with bright new uniforms. He well knew where the "supreme power" lay. According to the report of the American Consul, he filched some $100,000 from the treasury during the *ad interim* term and he placed heavy forces in the Vera Cruz district. His creatures were given

Government positions, strategic posts for a serious uprising. And through all these months the trial of Yañez, the dashing young lieutenant who had killed and robbed the Swiss Minister dragged on—a sinister *obligato* and characteristic motif for this ruthless military reign.

But the wizard of Manga de Clavo elected to return to his haunts in the tropics.   He foresaw serious clerical trouble and preferred Bustamente to handle such a hornets' nest.   The latter had returned now and was busy forming and reforming cabinets, but each new one bore disquieting traces of Santa Anna's hand and influence.   Seemingly a net was drawing in on the old Centralist.   Not surprising then that another revolt broke out the following year.

As usual it resulted from his lenient treatment of depronouncers.   One of these, General Urrea, had been given a light sentence and was cooling his heels in prison.   His friends outside managed to aid him in escaping and he straightway proceeded with a force of picked men to the President's Palace, surprised the guard and mounted to the President's door on the top floor.   The noise awakened Bustamente who got out of bed and was reaching for his sword when the rebels entered and covered him.   He surrendered and was placed under arrest.   This exploit was a match to tinder, mobs formed throughout the city and Farias popped up to lend a hand.

Only the lyre of an Offenbach could do justice to the events of this revolt.   The loyal government forces now squeezed out to the suburbs, were led by Valencia and the polished Almonte.   Urrea, the story goes, almost captured Almonte who escaped by a hair's breadth.   The former was returning to the center of the city when he happened to pass Almonte's house where Señora Almonte was sitting in a balcony. Undisturbed and adhering to the canons of Mexican courtesy, he lifted his hat and remarked to the lady, unaware of events, that it was a fine day !

Bustamente's own forces now bombarded the Palace, sending with accuracy unusual among pronouncers, a cannon ball into the main dining-room as the incarcerated President was eating his dinner. Without betraying the least emotion, the old veteran of a dozen revolutions remarked, "I wager our friends do not suppose we are calmly enjoying our meal."

This painful period of revolution is best described by Madame de la Barca, "The cannon directed against the Palace killed people in their beds, in streets entirely out of that direction, while this ball intended for the citadel takes its flight to San Cosme (in the opposite direction) ! Both parties seem to be fighting the *city* instead of each other ; and this manner of firing from behind parapets and from the tops of houses and steeples is decidedly safer for the soldiers than for the inhabitants. One would think that if the guns were brought nearer the Palace the affair would soon be over. This morning all manner of opinions are afloat. Some believe that Santa Anna has started from his retreat at Manga de Clavo, and will arrive today—will himself swallow the disputed oyster (the presidential chair) and give each of the combatants a shell apiece."

In fact amid such wild sparring it was not at all surprising that Santa Anna should announce that he was on the way to "help" the President, an aid that Bustamente feared more than his captors. The bombardment of the city and the genial sport of the *pronunciados* went on.

But a little less confidently now, for Farias and Urrea thought that they could negotiate better with Bustamente if he were released. They found that they were right in their surmise, for after Bustamente was set at liberty he feared the advent of Santa Anna so much that he hastened to come to terms with his opponents, assuring them that no punitive measures would be taken against them if they laid down their arms and promising some of them places in his cabinet. So the curtain was rung down on this bit of *opera bouffe*.

"Soldiers; the star of the 5th of December"—the day he lost his leg—"shines always for you. Patria! Liberty or Death!" Santa Anna was at work again with such flights of oratory and in the capital at night, and secretly, pamphlets floridly worded, demanding Santa Anna as dictator were spread through the city. The harassed president was in for more trouble. Lacking funds he was unable to curry favor with the military—a grave handicap. To overcome this he imposed unpopular taxes and forced loans, which alienated the wealthy. Little *jefes* all over the country were restless, and pronouncements this year reached the honest average of two per month.

But it was not the hero of the 5th of December who was destined to light the fuse of one of the most brilliant pyrotechnic displays of *pronunciamientos* which had thus far been seen. It was Paredes, the commander of Guadalajara who had not been a follower of Santa Anna but was understood to be in constant communication with him, who started the affair by "declaring" in August 1841, alleging inefficiency of the government, tyranny, and especially which affected the western and northern provinces more weakness of Bustamente in dealing with Indian raids. This declaration seemed to point to Santa Anna for it demanded a "citizen worthy of confidence" for the head. It further demanded the revocation of the "Conservative Power," an executive device which Bustamente had set up for the consolidation of Centralism and his own dictatorship, and freedom from legislative interference.

Guanajuato joined Paredes and Querétaro and the garrison of Ulloa. At the start it was only the typical *pronunciados'* revolt which might either roll up a large movement or subside with the rebels retiring, bribed by more powers or money. But as the weeks wore on it showed no signs of subsiding. On the contrary, it gained new adherents.

Valencia declared in the capital ; Valencia who had supported Bustamente during the last revolution, but also the same Valencia who had betrayed Mejia and was known as a friend of Santa Anna. Bustamente measured strength with his late supporter and the street-to-street warfare that marked the fighting a year before was repeated.

A veritable *pronunciamiento* folk-lore sprang up from these struggles. A soldier boy stationed as a sentinel in his native *calle* shot and killed his mother who did not understand his order to stop. Another directed his "Quien Vive" at a daughter of joy who approached him. She replied "The Supreme Government." And as he demanded what regiment, she riposted, "The Prostitutes."

Meanwhile our hero had moved his troops to Perote although the entire coast near Vera Cruz was aflame with revolt. He wrote to the President announcing his advance and offering his services as mediator. Bustamente sent him a sharp reprimand for his unauthorized movement and reminded him that the tropical section of his province required urgent attention.

Injured astonishment ! He had calmed all the revolutionary excitement in his State, he wrote in reply, but he wished to warn Bustamente that he should recognize the widespread movement for reform and that he, Santa Anna, would hold the present ministry responsible for any blood spilled in suppressing popular rights.

The Government took the hint and Santa Anna's old aide Almonte wrote a letter couched in a dignified manner objecting to such imperious language from a subordinate. The Government desired to say that they would give due attention to complaints about executive actions and—accepted General Santa Anna's offer of mediation. Santa Anna simply read the sad plight of the Government in these words, threw aside his mask and openly allied himself with Paredes.

Bustamente now rushed about with eleventh-hour preparations. He tried to call a meeting of Congress to propose a peaceful arrangement of difficulties and to compromise with the sweeping democratic movement. But it was a bit too late for constitutional action ; his move created no popular shift of feeling in his favor. Leaving the irresponsive capital to Canalizo and his loyal troops he roamed about the vicinity seeking more allies. But instead his own troops began to desert him.

Here lies a General
Who said one morn
"Either Cæsar or nothing"
And came out with nothing.

As Santa Anna stumped up and down among his troops, he seemed determined to belie this ditty. After taking Puebla in his by no means one-legged stride, he established himself at Tacubaya, dangerously close to Mexico City and his goal. Madame de la Barca describes his approach :

"We have just returned from an inspection of the *pronunciados*; they are too near Mexico now to call them rebels. The infantry, it must be confessed, were in a very ragged and rather drunken condition ; the cavalry better, having *borrowed* fresh horses as they went along. Though certainly not *point device* in their accoutrements, their good horses, high saddles, bronzed faces and picturesque attire had a fine effect as they passed along under the burning sun. The sick followed on asses and amongst them various masculine looking women (the *soldaderas*) with *sarapes* or *mangas* and large straw hats tied down with colored handkerchiefs, mounted on mules or horses. The sumpter mules followed carrying provisions, camp-beds, etc., and various Indian women trotted on foot in the rear carrying their husbands' boots and clothes. There was certainly no beauty amongst these feminine followers of the camp, especially amongst the mounted Amazons who looked like very ugly men in a semi-female disguise."

But Bustamente still had something up his sleeve. He obtained an armistice from his opponents and while the two armies were resting he conceived the brilliant idea of declaring for Federalism as a way of blocking the conquering march of Santa Anna. What a solemn and comical sight it was on September 30th to see Bustamente and his associate Canalizo, old Centralists and haters of the states-rights heresy, declaring for Federalism in the midst of the Plaza to a vast crowd of people and to the sound of bells and artillery salvos!

Santa Anna, vexed at this move, proceeded to bombard the city from the outside with the aid of Paredes who had now joined him and of Valencia who had gained a foothold on the inside. A little Scotch woman who had learned her chess in the United States, had chosen a husband in Spain and now was following with sharp gray eyes the national sport of Mexico, observed pithily, "Check from two knights and a castle, Santa Anna, Paredes and Valencia." Bustamente quite evidently could not hold the capital much longer. Several of his Ministers had taken French leave believing Santa Anna's power irresistible, and the President, withdrawing to Guadalupe, decided to make a last stand there.

Here occurred an amusing bit of by-play. While Bustamente passed out of his headquarters his sentry respectfully presented arms, saying, "Soldiers of the Guard! The President!" But while the President took a walk in the garden, the report was spread that Bustamente had become reconciled to resigning his office and when he returned he was met with a somewhat less respectful salute and different words, "Soldiers of the Guard! Old Uncle!" But the sentinel was not far wrong, for when Santa Anna and his combined allies drew up before the struggling President, Bustamente surrendered and was allowed peacefully to depart for Europe.

It was now felt that a political incantation called The Organic Bases of Tacubaya—drawn up there a few days before by Paredes and Santa Anna—would dissipate the clouds of revolution and establish once and for all a re public at once democratic and conservative, both pious and anti-clerical, stable and elastic — a convenient piece of mumbo-jumbo to replace the Conservative Power which had drawn such odium during Bustamente's reign.

These Bases provided that Santa Anna should select deputies from each department — a nice gesture for the sake of the Federalists — who would convene and choose a provisional President, none other than Santa Anna himself, for the cards were all stacked, and within eight months this body should mill about and add still another constitution to the many which had passed into the rubbish heap, violated and killed by their own makers. Almost immediately his self-appointed body of electors sat and declared him provisional President.

The usual triumphal entry in a splendid carriage — loaned by a prominent profiteer — and drawn by four white horses, escorted by other splendid equipages and a large detachment of cavalry. The usual bells, salvos and a Te Deum and then the customary fount of oratory. "The *pronunciamiento* of Paredes," announced Santa Anna, "has ushered in a new era of glory and fortune," whose fortune we shall see — "In the annals of the world there has never been mentioned such a revolution" — naturally ! — "What uniformity of ideas ! ! !" "What generosity ! What conduct ! The triumph has hardly cost a drop of blood. Those who were yesterday our enemies in the field, today embrace." And then as a grand finale, "Placed for the third time on this elevated seat, which is also a precipice, I offer myself as a fellow citizen."

CHAPTER VIII

THE APOTHEOSIS OF A LEG

A RATHER indiscriminate admiration for the works of William H. Prescott had led Americans to call Mexico City the "Halls of Montezuma" just as a century later their descendants were to dub it clumsily "The Paris of North America." True, the twin volcanoes named so indigenously, Popocatepetl and Ixtaccihuatl, looked down on the city like old *teocalli;* a line of pre-Cortesian aqueducts reminded the curious of other, older tyrannies and the descendants of Cuatemozin transported the merchandise of the city on their copper-colored backs But otherwise Mexico City was about as Aztec as a stree in Madrid. Let us look at Santa Anna's capital in 1842.

The famous calendar stone is nicknamed "Montezuma' Watch" and with some levity has been cemented into the façade of the great baroque Cathedral, a basilica whose line follow closely similar edifices in Tarragona or Castile. A with the Cathedral so with other buildings. Transoceani influences not only dominate the architecture but also th manners and customs of the Mexicans. Cavaliers on ex travagantly decorated saddlery doff sombreros to señorit —or for that matter someone's else señora—standing o ornamental iron balconies, while within the patio the who intense life of the household goes on. As *caballeros* cant

Return of Doña Tosta de Santa Anna to Mexico in 1846
(From an old print)

Old print of General Zachary Taylor refusing Santa Anna's
demand for surrender at Battle of Buena Vista

by, priests in large shovel hats—twenty-eight inches in diameter, a statistical American ascertained—saunter slowly along from church to café, from sacristy to market place.

Like a dark, a murky sediment beneath all these graceful evidences of civilization lies the *lepero,* that strange brother to the *lazzarone,* half beggar, half criminal, with all the disagreeable aspects of both. A cut-throat by night, a grovelling alms-chanter by day, dirty, half-naked, covered with sores and all the accumulated evil of centuries on his villainous countenance ; likely to appear suddenly in front of a ground-floor window terrifying the women occupants by his horrible apparition, or ready to stand in the gutter and shout a lusty "viva" for whatever *politico* desires to grease his palm.

How they scatter, this *canaille,* like the other occupants of the gutter, the mangy dogs when the noise of horses' hoofs approaches. A platoon of lancers clatters down the narrow and none-too-well-paved *calle,* smartly clad in red and blue, flashing their lances in the eternal sun of the Mexican plateau and escorting a gold-fringed coach wherein sits a Minister enjoying his all too brief honors of office ; or perhaps they precede at a slow pace the *viaticum* cart with its priest and oils of Extreme Unction. The street loiterers cross themselves devoutly and after the awesome cortège has passed, the cutpurse resumes his furtive travail, the pleasure-loving ecclesiastics their cigarettes and the *leperos* and dogs their snouting and snarling.

But let us enter one of the numerous churches which pullulate in the midst of the city and let it be at night and secretly for the stranger must have a "pull" to gain admittance. High in a pulpit stands a monk, his cowl thrown back revealing his expressive and agonized countenance, and exhorts a congregation almost exclusively composed of men to penitence. To the sound of the *Miserere* descending from the organ loft there is added another and more sinister rhythm — the regular sound of lashes on bare flesh. At first a monotonous cracking, it is varied by a splashing as the blood flows profusely on the floor. For a full half hour the members of the congregation flagellate themselves until they are almost prostrate from exhaustion. They are members of a sodality — fanatical relatives of those awesome Penitente Brothers who still survive in our own modern state of New Mexico. A dark, murky, mediaeval scene full of terror and gloom.

But religion in Mexico is not entirely of this severe nature. In the gold-heavy Cathedral the candles blaze joyously, a mighty orchestra plays, society women kneel serenely beside blanket-clad Indians — a democracy that even the new statutes have not been able to enforce. The gorgeous chasubles of the priests vie in brilliance with the uniforms of the genuflecting officers, the precious metal and jewels of the service contrast with the bare, crude stone of the floor. And above all sits bolt upright like a gem-becrusted statue himself, the old Archbishop.

More terrestrial exercises follow in the afternoon. Out on the Paseo along the Viga canal, "all Mexico" gathers carriages, on horse-back, on foot; a genuine parade, the ladies displaying the ample folds of their new Paris gowns — for the crinoline age is upon us, the gentlemen in frock coats and gold-headed canes or in brass-buttoned tunics and efflorescent epaulettes nodding and genially snubbing each other just as effectively as in the Bois or St. James Park. A more indigenous note among the equestrians : young men in Mexican *charro* costume, in richly-adorned leggings and jackets, ornamental sombreros, bridling their splendid mounts as they reveal the intricate embroidery of their sad-dlery—some accoutrements, it is said, are worth as much as $5,000. Beneath the legs of their chargers, barefoot sarape-clad Indians reach up with bunches of orchids, gar-denias, calla lilies, sweet peas to sell. If we follow the Viga far enough out we come to the canals of Xochimilco with their Venetian atmosphere, lazy gondolas against the background of profuse tropical foliage. Happy, colorful, languorous, frivolous Mexico !

But devout, as well. In Holy Week the city can sober down to the complicated daily services. The Sunday be-fore Easter the Cathedral nave is a perfect forest of palm leaves, the people bowing and kneeling beneath the branches. The streets, barred to wheel traffic, are filled with the pious who beat their breasts contritely as gaudy processions pass, long retinues of monks bearing sacred pic-ures, bishops with mitres and staffs and little carts bearing statues of favorite saints.

On Holy Thursday, according to custom, the devout pay visits to as many of the city's 200 churches as possible. The Temple of San Francisco is a favorite for it ranks with the Cathedral in sumptuous decoration and floral offerings ; another popular shrine is the Virgin de los Remedios, fa-mous for her cures, but suspect among chauvinists for her *achupin* associations. A marvel of costly ugliness—a plain, noseless countenance loaded with precious stones and attended by the priest without a nose. More popular, espe-

cially among the Indians is the Virgin of Guadalupe. On
Good Friday the populace to the number of forty thousand
crowd the Plaza Mayor while the Archbishop passes in
solemn procession to the High Altar of the Cathedral, and
on Saturday the city rejoices again, igniting the horrible
effigies of Judas, exploding them with pious fire-crackers.
All to end in the glory of Easter Sunday itself.

Afterwards an Elysian time of relaxation for these strenuous Catholics. A place called San Agustin de las Cuevas,
situated a fashionably few miles outside the city, gathers
the dollars that the clergy's collection boxes have missed
Booths of all manner of description appear overnight and
provide an extensive repertoire of games of chance. Here
a humble stall where the peons may risk their coppers, o
more substantial counter groaning with silver for the pett
bourgeoisie ; there a stately marquee where the croupier
gather in the gold of the mining grandees. For the sport
ing there is the cock-pit, or the bull-ring where the jade
appetites of the *aficionados* are stimulated a bit by opposin
the *torero* with a bear or a tiger. Military bands discours
airs from "Semiramis" while ladies and gentlemen danc
on the greensward, the former with the third change c
four toilettes necessary for a truly *de rigueur* day : one fc
the morning stroll in the Alameda or the Paseo, the nex
for display in the cock-pit or *correo,* then the dancing an
finally the more formal array for evening dinners and r
ceptions in the Palace or one of the legations.

In one of the latter functions this *haut monde* with
its gauche ostentation, its too facile courtesy, its variety
personality and monotony of ambition may be best o
served. The civilians making up for their austere eveni

attire with a conspicuous display of diamond studs and emerald rings, look enviously at the predominant military with their colorful jackets blazing with epaulettes, stars, ribands and other decorations, a symphony of scarlet, green and blue.   In their midst one may observe Paredes comparing a bit hungrily this resplendent spectacle to the awkward *tertulias* of his own provincial court in Guadalajara. Or listen to Tornel's dry, cynical cackle contrasting oddly with Sierra y Rosso's full-throated, idealistic tenor ; or note Valencia the polished ruffian, or Alamán smiling urbanely behind his scholarly spectacles ; and dozens of other celebrities, military, politico-military and capitalistic. They all greet each other with too ready a warmth, a much too profuse insistence that "my house is yours," or "I am your obedient servant" to make one incredulously surprised the next day when they imprison, exile or kill each other in the somewhat less polished atmosphere of *pronunciamientos.*

But how sumptuously they do it all—these parvenus of crinoline culture ! What a superb, rich, massive and homely opera house they have contrived to build to keep up with Louis-Philippe's and Victoria's world ! And what a throng—more tumultuous than at the Comique, less demonstrative than at the Rome Opera, but flashing with more jewels and gold than either two capitals combined could place on display ! As they applaud, a trifle too enthusiastically, to the saccharine strains of *Norma* or decade-old opus of Rossini, they marvel naïvely that *their* boxes actually have boudoirs behind them, and that *their* singers so fashionably Italian in nationality boast a ballet, laced with Continental propriety between the second and third acts.   Galli, Pellegrini, Belli, they take to their hearts, and when a blasé French attaché exercises his wit on a favorite, he receives the card of one of the more impetuous members of the gilded youth of the capital.

Across this highly prismatic stage strutted, or perhaps to be more accurate, limped proudly like a gaudy cockatoo, President General Antonio Lopez de Santa Anna. Proudly, yes, and insolently did he take up his reign with a virtual coronation in the Cathedral.   The Archbishop staggering under full canonicals and a huge crucifix marched down the nave to the door of the edifice, scarred and shattered by the shells of the new Sovereign.   But there the minister of Christ had to render unto Caesar a long ten minutes until he chose to appear.   Finally in the midst of a throng of generals tediously over-dressed, he did enter clad negligently—how exquisitely he understood the dramatic effects of contrast—in a simple field uniform.   The prelate escorted him to the front of the assemblage, where he stood during the Te Deum.   Thus did the Church perform "in that place all the honors which customarily are due to God alone," as a local journalist put it.

As if to show the Republic and the Church with their numerous feast days that he could invade the calendar too, he declared solemn holidays the anniversaries of his victories.   Thus the shouts that on September 11th hailed the Victor of Tampico nearly dimmed the rejoicing in honor of the curate Hidalgo four days later and the crowds that attended the Virgin's fiesta in Guadalupe on the 12th of December had little fervor left over after the celebration a week before of the loss of the famous leg.   But Tampico and Vera Cruz—not however, the Alamo or San Jacinto

—were forgotten in the uproar which he set up on his patron Saint's day in June. It was Santa Anna, Santa Anna all the year round.

Indeed it was on the sacrosanct 5th of December 1841 that he held a monster reception in the National Palace. Five adjutants, to each of whom he had given 1500 pesos for uniforms, arrayed themselves with agreeable extravagance and grouped themselves around his own effulgent figure while the lesser paladins stood out with the magnificence of chandeliers, in superb shakos, glittering epaulettes, flaming scarfs and boots *à la Napoleon*—with the heels the prescribed four inches in height. The Archbishop congratulated him with a speech which took on the uncomfortable quality of a sermon—a Jeremiah-like discourse—which reminded the figure on the precipice that if he failed in his duties he would be abominated as much as he would be praised if he succeeded.

A perhaps unnecessary admonition, for it is apparent that he realized that all eyes were on him, and that if not hostile neither were they altogether indulgent, only hopeful with a broad measure of skepticism in view of his past escapades. When he appeared that night in the tinsel playhouse now named *El Teatro Santa Anna,* the mummers were giving "El Gran Capitan" in his honor and he mounted through the foyer between a line of footmen, liveried in scarlet and gold, to a box decorated in the same hues where he was presented with a libretto bound in the same regal colors. The generals, as an observer who was present remarked, "in their scarlet and gold uniforms sat like peacocks around Santa Anna." But the latter maintained a quiet, unobtrusive manner as if deprecating all

this show and unaccustomed to public gaze. A wise rôle
to play for stories of his ostentations were going around.
On dit, and only in Mexico could it be said so often and
from so many lips, that he had just come from a banquet
at which, behind his chair during a long series of courses,
stood at strict attention, six colonels in full uniform—also
of scarlet and gold.

Meanwhile he had to turn his attention to the administration of this novel sort of republic. Copper coins had
deteriorated rapidly in the past few years through bad
coining and counterfeiting, and to meet this situation, Santa
Anna issued an order to turn in all these coins to the mint
which would later on repay the depositors in genuine coins.
This simply aroused more disorder and lack of confidence
and copper dropped from 80% to 60% in a few days. The
Government found that it had not sufficient funds to make
new currency and the scheme foundered. While the President morosely pondered his debacle, the *leperos* outside his
windows yelled their latest shibboleth "Death to Copper
Long live Silver !" But where was he to get the silver ?

Inasmuch as he had sworn to suppress the Federalists
with their impious designs on Church property, he had become the darling of sacristies and *obispados.* Convents
remembered him in all their prayers but he craved something more material. He found in the old Archbishop
sleepy with genial senility and charitable to an excess, an
excellent source of revenue. The old man was prevailed
on to let him have several substantial "loans" and allowed
him to take over and sell some abandoned Church buildings. Thus an hacienda formerly the property of the
Jesuits went over the counter to a profiteer named Escandón

for $200,000 ; a convent was sold to Valencia, but he was obliged to make no down payment for Santa Anna desired a financial hold over the accomplished betrayer of Presidents. Becoming more greedy he seized the wealth of the California diocese principally on the ground that it was too remote to be truly Mexican and overruled the Archbishop's feeble protests. It became a good joke among his janissaries how well he was defrauding the Prince of the Church.

He discovered in himself an enormous capacity—innate in all Latin-American dictators—at once to fawn on and revile foreign business men and capitalists. In response to the latter emotion he forbade all retail trade to foreigners. The American Minister, Waddy Thompson, had the pleasure of watching him strut just after the French Minister had delivered a sharp and perhaps unnecessarily technical protest against this law. "I know nothing about these questions of international law," he stormed, "I am only a soldier and have spent my life in the camp ; but eminent Mexican lawyers tell me that we have a right to enforce such an order and if we have to I know that it will be beneficial to Mexico. These foreigners come here and make fortunes and go away"—age-old complaint. "Let them marry here, or become Mexican citizens and they may enjoy this and all other privileges."

He added that he would cut his own throat before he would yield anything to menaces or insults—for so he regarded the suave scolding of the French diplomat. He worked himself up to a fine pitch of excitement, his eyes flashing and for the benefit of the astonished *Yanqui* discharged a heavy cargo of Latin eloquence, "What has Mex-

ico gained by her revolution if she is thus to be dictated to
by every despot in Europe; before we had but one master
—but if this is permitted we shall have twenty. We cannot fight on the water, but let them land and I will drive
them to their boats a little faster than I did in 1838," and
then casting his eye on his truncated leg—"with the expression of a tiger," Mr. Thompson observed—went on;
"They have taken one of my legs, they shall have the other
and every limb of my body before I will submit to their
bullying and menaces. Let them come, let them come as
soon as they please and in every defile of these mountains
they will find a Thermopylae."

A few days later we find this Alcibiades avidly seeking
out the hated Persians in a deal with an English company
for control of the silver mines of Zacatecas for a heavy payment of pounds sterling, of course, although Zacatecans
vehemently opposed this arrangement. He could not resist foreign capitalists for he was in constant need of money
and thus he started the concession mill a-turning—the
policy which reached its height a half-century later under
Don Porfirio Diaz.

His wars and his pageantry had to be supported. Yucatan was aflame with revolt clinging to a demand for home
rule with all the tenacity of its native *chicle* and while an
expedition for its subjugation was being fitted out, the troublesome Texans sent a vessel with aid to Campeche. The
latter, nourished on the memory of the never-to-be-forgot
ten battle of San Jacinto and on the florid eloquence of
Mirabeau Lamar, now were filibustering all over the South
west. One raid on Santa Fe and another on Mier across
the Rio Grande, at both of which places they were soundl

spanked and lost many prisoners, served to diminish their ardor a bit. The prisoners — their number reduced by some artistic executions — were brought to Mexico City where the American Minister performed his weary and none too easy task of mitigating their punishment.

Doña Garcia Santa Anna herself — kind-hearted lady — urged her husband to release them or at least to treat them humanely. With a less uncompromising feeling now toward Texans, he readily acceded. He discovered amongst them a son of Dr. Phelps, his kindly host at Orozimba, and he not only pardoned him but paid his way back to Texas. Another Texan youth, an orphan, he took in his household and raised as his son. Finally on his patron Saint's day, in June 1842, after the review of some ten thousand troops, he formally released all these prisoners. If he had not learned statesmanship, he had at least acquired some mercy. Yet he had other sides too.

It was Bishop Portugal of Michoacan who caused the rumpus. Why did the Minister of Ecclesiastical Affairs have to pay a visit to the President at such a critical time ? Did he not notice the abstract manner with which Santa Anna received him and the lack of attention which the First Magistrate gave to his discourse ? And why should he have been surprised when his laconic interlocutor arose abruptly and left the room ? The Bishop waited — waited but the President did not return. Impatiently he asked a lackey when the President might be expected back. "I hardly know, your Grace, for he has gone to visit Cola de Plata." "And who may Cola de Plata be, my son ?" "Ah, your Grace, Cola de Plata is the favorite game-cock of His Excellency and he is personally attending to its wounds for

it has just won an important fight this morning." The
Bishop shortly after sent in his resignation and precipitated
a minor Cabinet row.

For when the trials of affairs of state and administration
weighed too heavily on his begilded shoulders, he would
discover some malady — his leg was now a good excuse —
and would retire to Manga de Clavo or better still Encero,
his new and prettier hacienda, where he was free to absorb
himself in his large collection of game-cocks. From one
fowl to another he would go, examining them minutely
and prescribing the amount of feed each should have, this
one more, this other fat fellow less, the big roosters to be
definitely stinted.

Then he would watch their crowing triumph in the cock-
pit, for it was said that out of every fifteen, only one failed
to win victories for him. Perhaps he took a vicarious pleasure in this quick, impulsive slashing of the cruel spurs — in
these curious struggles it is possible he found a similarity to
his own love of undeliberate combat — quick unpremedi-
tated battle with strutting victory or total, humiliating defeat. A relaxation, a pleasure only second to his penchant
for public ceremony.

For the show went on in spite of depleted treasury and
weary taxpayers. He had inherited from the Viceroys a
ceremony most harmonious with his tastes — the *Besamano*
or "Handkissing," without of course in these democratic
decades any actual osculation of the Presidential fist. At
one end of the reception room of the Palace where the
diplomatic corps gathered, there stood a throne which Iturbide had ordered from Paris, but which had somewhat un-
tactfully been unloaded in Vera Cruz just as that monarch

was hastily leaving ; before it were aligned two long rows of chairs for the assembled diplomats.

Through this human alley the President, ushered by the Secretary of State and clad in the full uniform of the Chief of the army — a blue and red affair embroidered with gold leaf — limped painfully with the aid of a cane up to his Imperial seat. The *Besamano* then was completed with speeches and handshaking. But to leave His Excellency's presence, each Minister had to advance to a position in front of the President, bow, walk to the other end of the room, bow again, with each salute duly returned by the President himself. As an American envoy, with democratic disapproval exclaimed, "Such a scene has occurred in a Republic, before the President of the Republic, surrounded with soldiery, amid the beating of drums, the braying of trumpets and all the paraphernalia of a court !"

His leg doubtless handicapped him at such functions, but its disabilities were more cerebral than physical. It was a perfect King Charles' head in his conversation. He loved to dwell on it with histrionic melancholy. Madame de la Barca wrote, "It is only now and then that the expression of his eye was startling, especially when he spoke of his leg, which is cut off below the knee. He speaks of it frequently like Sir John Ramorny of his bloody hand and when he gives an account of his wound and alludes to the French on that day his countenance assumes that air of bitterness which Ramorny's may have exhibited when speaking of 'Harry the Smith.'"

It is perhaps not surprising, then, to find a most singular ceremony taking place on the 26th of September, 1843. In the cemetery of Santa Paula a large crowd had gathered

in spite of a broiling sun and between two files of gren
diers a procession of officials and military bore a small u
of crystal. It contained Santa Anna's leg dug up from
resting place in Manga de Clavo and brought hither fo
formal interment. A gilded column ornamented with t
inevitable inscriptions and *fasces* awaited it and after pl:
ing the urn on the capital, a small stone cannon topped
a Mexican eagle was superimposed.

This masterpiece of a stone-mason's art was dutifu
censed with florid oratory by Sierra y Rosso, one of Sar
Anna's most assiduous toadies. "Sweet, sweet and pro
is it not only to die for the Fatherland but to consecrate
it a certain kind of sacrifice which today we celebrate, et
etc." Thrasibilis, Timoleon, Leonidas all were dragged
to illustrate the glory of the Hero of the 5th of Decemb
Young soldiers were exhorted to come here and draw i
spiration so that "when the bugle calls you can cut simil
laurels."

He turned to the General himself as he compared him
the leader of the band at Thermopylae that held at bay t
Persian host, but Santa Anna was silent with down-cast ey
and that expression which so many had noticed, "of mi
gled pain and anxiety" as one observer put it. "You wou
think him looking on a dying friend with whose sufferin
he was deeply but helplessly sympathizing." And then f
Sierra y Rosso's peroration. "Although the voracio
scythe of time destroying this and a thousand other sple
did monuments which the Patria will consecrate to t
memory, thy name will last until the day in which t
sun will go out and the stars and all the planets return
the chaos where formerly they slept." But this rare bei

retired into the laconic fastness of men of action, looked even more solemn, said a few brief words in reply and the ceremony broke up.

Nor was Cæsar's wife above the privileges of the demi-gods. In 1843 Doña Inez became dangerously ill. The viaticum was brought to her as if she were a Byzantine princess, the Archbishop himself in the *carro del muerto* and a stupendous procession of friars, priests and soldiers numbering in the thousands. At least the candle-makers rubbed their hands in satisfaction at the purchase of 6000 candles for this procession. Even the precious Virgin of the Remedies was conveyed to the sick-chamber. Alas, she died shortly after and her widower after following her in an equally sumptuous funeral, waited only a month ere he selected another mate.

But the capital which took an almost family interest in the private doings of their semi-royal public entertainers maintained a rather high standard of post-mortem rectitude and was sincerely shocked when Santa Anna announced his engagement to a Señorita Tosta, a 15 year old girl of surpassing beauty. He might deceive Doña Inez flagrantly, he might have five acknowledged bastards, but he should not violate the Mexican canons of mourning.

Their reprobation, however, changed to somewhat more complex feelings at his next move. The disturbing news of his engagement came during one of His Excellency's periodic vacations at his Mount Vernon in the tropics; Señorita Tosta with her unrespectable pulchritude was in the capital, and the painful stump of the Leg could not make the journey to Mexico City. These important circumstances together with the young lady's laudable desire to celebrate her wedding in the magnificence of the National Cathedral produced a novel solution. The Archbishop, obliging in matrimony or finance, stood at the High Altar, the bells rang out dutifully, the cannon boomed and the handsome bride marched up the crowded nave on the arm of Señor Canedo, a prominent sycophant who acted as a proxy for His Absent Excellency in the strangest hymeneal ceremony the Mexicans had yet witnessed.

This coup, like an exploit of a rascally hero in one of the picaresque novels this Hispanic people liked to read, was, if anything slightly admirable in its audacity. Other actions had more critical responses. Yielding to the inevitable weakness of Dictators for horrible statuary, he had erected, naturally through the initiative of obliging toadies a particularly atrocious example of the sculptor's art in the Plaza Volador. It represented the late expeditionary of Texas in full regalia with one arm extended pointing to the north — to that erring province, it was sedulously circulated, which Santa Anna regarded as Mexico Irredenta But the irreverent alleged that with more forceful symbolism it pointed to the mint. As James Russell Lowell put it

"Hey, it's a parfect sin
To think wut Mexico hez paid for Santy Anny's pin.

Stories of his picturesque operations on the nation's purse mingled with other tales about the vast herds which roamed his estates near Vera Cruz, and which were sold at high prices to the army's commissary. A whole literature of satire leaped into print.

Venomous wags were happy to play a nasal and stert

rous obligato to his fustian pageantry. Such was the famous "Santa Anna's Dictionary" :

Army — a collection of automatons which are moved like pieces on a chess board at the will of the player. When they lack bread give them false finery and they are contented. When they become uneasy, discipline them and they are silent.

Patriotism — the art of deceiving the public by giving it false facts.

Oath — a ridiculous formula which I am accustomed to go through with and which I break daily.

Patria — a large area of land which I am able to dispose of at pleasure as of my own house.

Mexicans — poor devils whom I have deceived whenever it suits me and whom I control by kicks.

Yet Waddy Thompson found that he was not wholly the dupe of his entourage, nor unaware of the defects of his situation. He relates how a Mr. Hargous, a powerful American merchant in Vera Cruz, advanced money to Santa Anna when the treasury was low and funds were needed for the war with Yucatan. Santa Anna gave his personal pledge for the loan and stipulated a time for payment. Hargous went to Santa Anna and protested. Santa Anna said he had given orders not to pay, for the treasury had no money to pay the army, and that he must wait until more convenient time.

The American, much angered, shouted, "You know, sir, that I would not have advanced this money except upon the pledge of your word of honor, which I have not known violated before ; I have been your friend, sir, in more trials than one and have respected and confided in you ; henceforth these feelings are changed ; good evening, sir." The President called him back and said to the military friends by whom he was surrounded, "Gentlemen, have you heard the language which this man has uttered to me ?" The American fired up, "I come from a country where no station prevents a man from being told the truth. Is not what I have said true ?" "It is, sir," said Santa Anna, "it is and I respect you for your firmness in saying what you have ; I have flatterers enough about me, but few who will tell me the truth !" The money was paid immediately.

A baffling character, a "riddle" many would have it, for they could hardly reconcile his deeds with his professions his actions with the charming, almost noble cast of feature and personality. Mayer, an attaché at the American Lega tion, said : "I have seen Santa Anna in his coach, sur rounded with guards and all the pomp of the military, a the review of eight thousand troops ; in church at prayer in the ball room ; in a cock-pit betting ; in the audienc room ; at the banquet ; and in private interviews of delicat diplomacy, when the political interests of the two natior were at stake. No one can easily forget him ; according t public opinion he is a riddle in character ; he surely is nc in appearance ; and if his person and his manners are nc as with others to be taken as a fair index of the man, he either an arch-hypocrite or a capital actor."

An actor, possibly, who believed his rôles were real lif He showed now his singular aptitude for believing th eloquence was statesmanship and that *leperos* who a plauded — at one *real* a day — were the people. The re *Populus Mexicanus* was, in fact, becoming rather restiv

Taxes were getting heavier, and were clumsily levied in a direct manner, such as on the wheels of carriages and carts. His press-gangs were dragging in hordes of Indians and peasants, and their wives and families hung disconsolately about the barracks setting up affecting ululations. The clergy were beginning to see that his method of "protecting" them was just about as costly as the schemes of the radicals; and even the picked Congress muttered rebelliously at his high-handed attitude toward them.

He had presumably got his military *jefes* under control by favor, debts, etc.; this general to govern that province, another given a heavily mortgaged hacienda, and so on; but cracks were discernible in that protecting wall. He could not understand how popular clamor and unrest could percolate through to the military upper crust. Even the faithful Tornel seemed to get out of hand, erecting a column to himself in Puebla, mimicking his own grandeur. As for Paredes he was fancying himself "Imperator Mexicanus" in Guadalajara and many suspicious rumors were abroad about him.

Santa Anna got his hands on some letters written by Paredes, direct and irrefutable evidence that he was ploting. Calling the traitor in, he asked him if he had ever read the life of Napoleon. "Have you ever read the story of an officer convicted of the crime of treason? The officer's wife went to Napoleon and begged for her husband's life. Napoleon, softened by her appeal, said, 'So you want me to put myself in a position where I cannot let him be shot? Hein? If so, throw these letters in the fire.' The woman did so. 'Well then, Madame, I am now disarmed and no more proofs exist against your husband.'

"So now, Paredes, take these letters and tear them up. They are proofs of your crime." The erring General tore them up and swore fidelity to Santa Anna.

But this bit of dramatics did not keep him faithful and in the latter part of October, 1844, he pronounced in Guadalajara, drawing with him many smaller chieftains. The gaudy litter was seen careering up the mountain passes from Manga de Clavo and His Excellency emerged from it in the Plaza Mayor to view a situation of rather undesirable confusion. The Congress was registering seismographically the unrest of the country and the scurrilous pamphleteers were busy with their wares. But on the other hand there were active friends, Tornel, Sierra y Rosso and a stout politician, Haro y Tamariz who seemed to promise well as a steering leader. Then there was his faithful tool the President *ad interim,* Canalizo, called the "Lion of Guadalupe" because he was the only chief who had remained faithful to Bustamente and actually fought it out with the *pronunciados* at Guadalupe. It seemed safe to leave the capital in these hands and depart with a large body of troops for the north to subjugate Paredes.

A puerile anger against all who opposed him and a sensitive feeling about the ceremonial tributes due him as head of the nation soon embroiled him in Querétaro, where he established his headquarters. Because the faintly hostile assembly of that State did not meet him in a body when he entered that capital, he demanded an abject apology and when it was not forthcoming he obtained it at the point of a bayonet. Meanwhile in Mexico, Congress, which saw in the proceedings at Querétaro a sample of what the might expect, grew distinctly jumpy and Canalizo's ministry dissolved it, on the 1st of December.

Within a few days the whole city was in revolt, incited by a Deputy Llaca from Querétaro and receiving benediction from the military in the person of General Herrera, while crowds ran through the streets yelling, "Down with the Cripple." This slogan gave a hint to some enterprising *leperos* who went out to Santa Paula, extracted the sacred Leg from its urn and dragged it through the streets to the jeers of the temperamental populace. The Minister of War rescued it and buried it in a "decent place." The orgy reached its height when members of the various *barrios* or wards drew lots for the privilege of demolishing the unæsthetic, digit-pointing statue in the Plaza Volador. The happy *barrio* crowd who pulled this down followed with a joyous destruction of a wax effigy of His Excellency which stood in the theater lobby ; this *Teatro Santa Anna,* it goes without saying, hastily changed its name.

While Santa Anna received news of these amenities and fixed his bayonets, the deputies passed their time in an enjoyable debate as to what they should do with the picture representing their late President on the battle-field of Tampico which hung in the legislative hall, and with patriotic subtlety voted that it should remain only because it depicted the triumph of the Nation. They were awakened from these congenial forensics by an intercepted letter from Santa Anna relating what vengeance he was going to take on them if he could get them in his clutches. Herrera allayed their alarm by putting the city in a good state of defense. Valencia, always ready in the wings, now marched out on the crowded stage and gave highly questionable comfort to the rebels through his past knowledge of city fighting.

The printing presses in the capital were almost as active as the drill-grounds with such specimens as this, "Genius of evil (Santa Anna) and covetousness ! you are like Atilla the scourge of God ! Your power has been like that of Satan, a power of corruption, of ruin and destruction ! You resemble a fury of hell, blind, devastating and bloody ! Amid the horrors of civil war, amid lakes of blood and mountains of dead bodies you always present yourself like a spectre, inciting all to devastation, slaughter and revenge, etc."

As if the God of Dictators was not altogether deaf, the Deputy Llaca was stricken in sudden but natural death at this time. Santa Anna seized this demise as subject for his own equally ornate rhetoric : "Shade of Deputy Llaca, I pardon thee. You launched against me an odious accusation. God launched Death at thee. I pardon thee ! etc." But apostrophes won no combats and he tried to join battle with Paredes who turned away and feinted south toward Michoacan. Santa Anna seized Guanajuato and piled $100,000 worth of its argentine product on his commissary mules ; he needed it, for this metal was all that kept many of his generals with him.

Haro y Tamariz was allowed by Herrera to escape from the mobs of the capital and bear news of events to Santa Anna and an offer of peace from the city. But His Excellency at the tales of his Minister about the disorders in the capital withdrew nervously to the more hospitable vicinity of the volcano Popocatepetl. There he dictated his terms the most important point of which was that the desecrating capital should restore his statues and leg to their former positions of eminence. But Mexico, which was soaring above art in the welkin of Liberty, did not respond, and he made a rapid forced march to Puebla, which he hoped would be more tractable.

"It was a great stretch of your wooden leg that took you to Puebla!" exclaimed an American at the time. But it did no material good, for his troops were running off into the forests of Popocatepetl and the cannon of Puebla spoke an ominous welcome at his approach. After a little street fighting in the suburbs, the Santa Anna generals complained to their chief that these incursions made them unpopular with the inhabitants, and after some rather quaint military counsels of war, His Excellency lifted the siege and retired toward Perote.

It was the obvious time for a nice proclamation, but Santa Anna was beyond the benefits of metaphor. Seeing his cause was lost, he filled his pouches with money, took only four domestics with him, left the army and tried to make for Vera Cruz.

But some unusually enterprising Indians at Jico in the mountainous section of the State of Vera Cruz captured him and with aboriginal cruelty placed him in jail in his native town of Jalapa. He bore this humiliating homecoming with an Olympian courage, reprimanding the sentinel at the door for rattling his side-arms unduly and shouting imprecations at Rincon, formerly his companion at arms and now his jailer. He demanded a passport to leave the country and when it was refused, sulked and declined to eat.

Outside in the streets the people were singing and shouting with joy at his overthrow — perhaps no more than the customary ebullience of Mexicans at the downfall of their most recent tyrant. Santa Anna asked the cause of all this uproar and, scornfully unconvinced at the reply, requested to know "how" they had been made to express this enthusiasm ; his mind still working in the world of subsidized *claques* and bribed military. Nodding incredulously, he turned his attention from the time-table of English packets to the state of his own health.

His concern about his bodily condition became most acute when word reached Jalapa from the capital to take him to the castle of Perote. He supported his self-diagnoses with sharp reminders that he was a General of Division of the Republic and had his "rights," and finally bullied his captors into allowing him to take his wife and servants with him. With this retinue he was more interned than imprisoned when he got to Perote and he settled down in the gloomy fortress writing a defense of his actions as President.

A congenial and just now a most necessary task, for the deputies had decided on impeachment after several sessions marked by a monotonous (by this time) recital of his crimes and violations of office. But his congenital aptitude for clothing the obvious in the terms of the lurid had not left him in these moments of trouble. "Object of the anger o those who tried to disrupt the public peace, surrounded b a cloud of calumnies, menaced by the fist of Brutus throug the revolutionary papers ; I sought to allay those hates an unite on the side of the government the wills of its enemie Vain attempt!" He defended himself against charges c peculation swearing that he had saved a fortune of 300,00 pesos from his salary as General and President. He i voked all the occasions when he had "drawn his sword against the Spanish, the Americans and the French . . . while the vandals destroyed statues erected in my honor, violated the sacred repose of the tomb and desecrated my leg, I advanced against the enemies of the Nation." And finally, "Happy I, if my blood will be the last which the civil war let flow on my innocent Patria.   Happy those who are going to decide my case if my words sound in their ears like the idiom of truth."

His words sounded like nothing of the sort to the word-weary solons, but his old associates and the conservatives still had power enough to prevent any drastic punishment of the members of the late government.   Besides, the new government was none too strong and the Santanistas, as they were coming to be called, were already concocting a nice, new plot.   Best to get the old pronouncer out of the country, the provisional leaders decided, and after decreeing an exile of ten years for him, they bundled him off to Vera Cruz port, careful to the point of a touching anxiety about his safety, surrounding his coach with several regiments of troops known to be loyal to the Government.

But to the last he struck dramatic attitudes and as he sailed from Vera Cruz for Havana with his family in June, he issued a heart-rending farewell to his late victims begging them to forgive him.   "Mexicans !   Crippled and in my last years"—he was 51—"surrounded by a wife and innocent children"—his legitimate ones—"I go to bury myself, seek among strangers an asylum.   Treat benignly the errors which I have committed unwillingly and unintentionally ; before God believe me that I have worked sincerely that you might be independent, free and prosperous."

CHAPTER IX

OLD PEG-LEG VERSUS OLD ZACK

IF HE had been able to delay his expulsion just another two weeks, it was not improbable that he would have been able to charge victoriously into the Plaza Mayor again and transfer his canonized limb to its proper *In valides*. But the Herrera government had been noting among the swirling currents of the factions which threat ened its stability the growing power of the Santanistas – and their astonishing success in winning back the military in spite of the late desecration of statuary and rhetorical invective against the Author of the Bases.

The Government's affecting solicitude for our hero hasty embarkation was not misplaced, for he had hardly left Vera Cruz, indeed had not yet reached Havana when a daring escapade of his partisans enlivened the atmosphere of the capital, stagnant without a revolution for almost three months. It was a palace revolution, in design, for the revolters seized the National Palace, but in execution it lacked the expert *gritos* of such past masters as Valencia or Zavala and foundered miserably, owing largely to its weak beginning and the quick resolution of Herrera. A loud, but belated cannon-cracker going off after the pyrotechnic display was finished.

"Crippled," "in old age" and "among strangers" is

faintly unjust description of the exiled Napoleon of the West nor was Havana an exact counterpart of barren St. Helena. For at the age of 51, even with a wooden leg one may enjoy the pleasures of San Cristobal, especially if one has a pouch as full of pesos as Santa Anna's. He had his family with him graced by the presence of the beautiful young step-mother whom his zealous press-agents had sought to make familiar to the Mexican public as "The Flower of Mexico" but whom that irreverent body called the "Tostada"—"The Toasted One," or in our argot, "Hard-Boiled."

Besides, the strangers were not inhospitable and His Britannic Majesty's consul maintained an amiable if somewhat curious friendliness which was only surpassed by the inquisitive cordiality of the representative of the U. S. A. Then there was an impressive roost of game-cocks for him, no insufficient ammunition to fight the ennuis of exile. And like a dope addict turning automatically to his drug, he eagerly read a huge mail from Mexico where his "Santanistas" were laboriously reconstructing the edifice so recently cast to the ground.

But the Mexican political spectacle was much more absorbing than any combat of Silver-Tail and a feathered opponent, for the international situation had given it a hardly unexpected, but really serious turn. The two imperialisms of Mexico and the United States had now converged, on a wavering line traced from the Rio Grande to the Golden Gate and the clash threatened to become a genuine fight; and as of old it looked as if Texas was to be once the principal pawn and the board itself.

While our hero was scribbling diligently in Perote, Presi-

dent James Knox Polk signed the bill for the annexation
of Texas and the Mexican Minister at Washington had immediately broken off relations and left his post, carrying
out his threat so often uttered that such a bill would be
considered by the Mexican Government as equivalent to a
declaration of war. Thus ended eight years of sparring
since San Jacinto ; the Mexican displaying his extraordinary
aptitude for striking theatrical attitudes of uncompromising
resistance and the Yankee with a greater appreciation of
realities placing one diplomatic arm around the Latin
American neighbor and rummaging calculatingly with the
other in his own dollar-filled pants pocket.

The amiable drug-store proprietor from Jalapa, Herrera
who had been struggling for months to hold together his
rickety coalition of conservatives and anti-Santanistas, was
not fundamentally averse to the bait held out by the Americans. His treasury balance was low and the acquisition c
40 million dollars for "the adjustment of boundaries," for
in thus wise did the Americans seek to salve their own
pride and apply balm to the Mexicans', would save his
government. He had been softening his tone all through
the second quarter of '45 and in August he intimated he
would discuss terms with an American commissioner.

But in those days before wireless, before internation
cables — the telegraph had not yet reached Mexico and was
in its infancy in the States — facilitated the exchange
human stupidity, and yes, human efforts to get along with
neighbors, it was months before Herrera's gracious intim
tion reached Washington, and caused an envoy, one Joh
Slidell, to be appointed and sent off to Mexico. By the
time Slidell reached Mexico it was late in November a

rrera was struggling hopelessly in a morass of politics
h no higher policy than to survive at all costs. The
nerican question in the public statements of Mexican
cials had a reaction almost as inevitably identical as the
ee-jerk of a healthy individual to the application of a
ysician's hand — Mexico would never give up her rights
Texas not even for huge sums of money. This attitude
s a public fetish and Herrera by this time saw that he
e not take a less uncompromising stand. He refused
treat with Slidell and turned back to his own pitiable
uation.

itiable indeed for him, but highly enjoyable for the old
k-fight fan in Havana. The Federalists, discontented
h Herrera, turned to the Santanistas ; the latter smiled
iably back, and over in Guadalajara, Paredes, his appe-
for thrones still unsatisfied, was wistfully tracing on bits
paper his unexpressed desire "Imperator Mexicanus :
edes y Arillaga." For a long time he had had the
perial obsession and to gain his ends had recently in-
ued with a large and growing body of Mexicans who
rned for a European monarch for their country or at
st an over-seas protectorate. These men had throughout
fall months converted many of the clergy and large
cks of Herrera's conservative supporters so that by the
l of the year the mild-mannered Herrera was permitted
pack his entire government in a hackney coach and drive
of the Plaza while Paredes moved in his more exotic
lition.

aredes, amply plied with the fire-water of the European
ty which hoped for British support against the Yankees,
ok his fist at the Colossus of the north and curtly dis-

missed Slidell.   Swelled by some mysterious assurance o
military superiority and confident that the Yankees wer
incapable of fighting save with a check-book, the Mexican
not only hoped to win easily but accused the conciliator
Polk of trying to rob them, by his treacherous ambassador:
of the imminent and magnificent victory.   With great cor
fidence they sent Arista with a small army to the Ri
Grande and when he met General Zachary Taylor at Mata
moros he lost no time in taking the initiative by capturin
a platoon of cavalry under an hereafter inglorious and o
scure Captain Thornton.   War had begun !

Our hero was in fine fettle now.   It was reported that h
had taught the inexpert *Cubanos* a thing or two in the p
and that his cocks had earned him some 30,000 pesos,
sum which he quickly transferred to his partisans in Mexic
In October he had foiled an attempt to assassinate hi
which fed the bile of vengeance and gave him a pleasurab
feeling that he must be most important if his enemies to
the trouble to send to Havana to have him killed.   Best
all the *rapprochement* between him and the Federalists w
getting on swimmingly.   Farias, whom he had contemp
ously called "Furias" now received letters from him in t
most affable vein ; the radical himself who a few mon
before was speaking of his correspondent as "so audacio
so immoral, so corrupt a man" waxed affectionate.   F
him anything to upset the hated monarchists and conser
tives and their puppet, Paredes ; for the illustrious e
the red flag of radicalism would do just as well as any ot
to drape his somewhat lop-sided figure until he could in:
his wooden peg in the door of the Palace.

Everything was grist for his mill now.   In the north

Mexicans were astonished to perceive that the despised Taylor could fight. Through the months, Palo Alto, Resaca de la Palma and finally Monterrey marked a miserable list of Mexican failures — Paredes' squibs which went off with a disappointing sizzle instead of a round report. The brummagem Imperator was unsteady now and his variegated opponents worked zealously to push him over. Gomez Farias saw the possibility of a return to an idyllic Federalism, Tornel the possibility of cleverly concealed quasi-Centralism and Santa Anna the possibility of more and heavier statuary and a quantity of loot. All was ready for Paredes' fall and the "call" for the exile to return and save the country.

Only one thing intervened, the American blockade which had tightened considerably and which could materially delay if not prevent Santa Anna's response to the "call." But events were shaping to remove this obstacle. One day in February, 1846, a swarthy gentleman of Mexican extraction and manners that were too polished to persuade a democrat from Tennessee, called on President Polk. He professed to be an agent of Santa Anna, spoke vaguely of American support of the exile of Havana and promised that if Santa Anna could once get back into power he would settle this war quickly to the satisfaction of the United States. Polk wrote in his diary how much he distrusted this Señor Atocha and how little faith he put in his proposals. However, the incident stuck in his mind, and as he was desirous of prolonging the struggle for his own political reasons, he determined to deal directly with Santa Anna.

Accordingly he sent a naval officer, Commander Mackenzie, to Havana. Arriving there on the 5th of July, the

officer was able to get an interview with the ex-President and
was closeted with him for three hours during which both
parties learned some interesting things.   Santa Anna heard
first of all that Polk had signed an order giving him a safe-
conduct through the blockade at Vera Cruz.   Furthermore
the American President expressed a hope that he would see
Santa Anna in power again and that once in the Presidentia
chair he would advance the cause of peace with the United
States on the basis of a boundary following the Rio Grand
and west to the Pacific with ample monetary compensatio
to the Mexicans for this territory.

Mackenzie for his part listened to some intriguing con
versation, and was able to carry back to his master a not
which Santa Anna drafted—he cautiously destroyed th
original after permitting Mackenzie to make a copy—ven
ing his hatred of European and monarchical schemes an
intimating that he would be favorable to Polk's term
More, he gave many practical hints, from his own gre:
store of knowledge of Mexican political convolutions c
how these terms might best be achieved.   He suggeste
that Taylor advance from the north, defeat Paredes d
cisively and take San Luis Potosi ; he also made practic
suggestions about projected American attacks on Tampi
and Vera Cruz ; and promised that all these movemer
would influence Mexicans to call him back to power.   F
discourse and frank discussion, not to mention his offe
seemed to spring from absolute sincerity and Mackenz
elated, departed to render his report.

There seems to have been no sordid bargain made at t
interview as the enemies of Santa Anna have so often st
gested.   Polk sincerely believed—he seems to have forg

ten the experience of Old Hickory a decade before—that if Santa Anna would regain power he would have sense and force enough to make such a treaty, and that if he did return and fail to mount the throne in the National Palace, he would stir up such a war that the Americans could win easily.

Santa Anna himself did not seek bribes of money for his return—why should he?—and he undoubtedly felt that if recalled he could maneuver matters so as to comply with the Yankee desires. If he failed in this, so much the worse for the hopeful Polk, and perhaps he might even be able to beat the Americans and thus hoist himself again to the height of national favor. For such an adventurer the American safe-conduct was simply a means to an end. It is just to acquit him of a base deal with monied America. Santa Anna naturally wanted money, but he already had plenty and what he desired more was victory—not too difficult or dangerous a victory—and above all power. Within these somewhat elaborate qualifications, he was a patriot untouched by foreign gold.

One day late in August the lookout of the *St. Mary,* a vessel of the blockading fleet, sighted with annoyance a strange steamer which was attempting to pass the cordon round the port. It was not one of the familiar English packets which by special arrangement were permitted to pass in without red tape, and according to instructions the commander of the *St. Mary* signalled it to heave to. After rowing over to her and boarding, the officer was a bit taken back to find himself treated like an admiral, ushered into a saloon and introduced to a group of gentlemen whose complexions and extravagant courtesy stamped them as Mexican. One of them was disinclined for obvious physical reasons to rise and was introduced as General Antonio Lopez de Santa Anna. He intimated that he would like to land in Vera Cruz.

The boarding officer, surprised and not a little incredulous at the nature of the whole proceeding, rowed as quickly as possible to the flagship to transmit this absurd request and emerged a few moments later from his commander's cabin wondering why President Polk had given orders to allow this enemy firebrand to disembark. That night, cannon roared in the city and rockets burst to inform the Americans that the General had been met by a warm reception. But the nature of the hospitality was a trifle unusual, certainly to Santa Anna with his long experience of welcoming committees.

The guns of San Juan de Ulloa did fire a proper salute and a be-chevroned group met him at the gang-plank. But as he stumped down between two files of soldiers, the insolent fellows did not even take the trouble to stand at attention, a few scattered individuals among them fired their muskets in the air, the rest gaping in disrespectful curiosity a most discordant band blared music whose brassy clamour seemed a calculated insult ; Doña Tosta pouted angrily at the undemonstrative, staring crowd, one member of which an Englishman, found that the General had "an old Bailey countenance" in its villainy. Worst of all there was complete and ominous absence of the customary "vivas."

In the Palace, he had to sit and listen to a fellow from the town rabble who told him that "for more than twenty years you have endeavoured to ruin our country," and the rest of the affair had more the air of a court-martial than welcome.   A cultured individual from the capital preached an admonishing sermon, listing with unnecessary circumstantiality his past misdeeds and expressing the hope that he had reformed his ways.   In his consternation he forgot that he had not had time to alter his speech composed on the vessel in anticipation of this occasion.

But it hardly mattered, and while the happy expressions of gratification on his welcome were a bit incongruous, the rest of the speech was composed in the tradition of the handsomely ambiguous, and no harm was done.   "Mexico, there was a day, and my heart expands with the recollection, when leading forward the popular masses and the army to demand the rights of the nation, I was hailed by you with the enviable title, Soldier of the People.   Allow me again to take it, nevermore to be given up and to devote myself until death to the defence of the liberty and independence of the republic."   His partisans stimulated a little artificial demonstration in his honor and with that he had to be content as he went inland to his hacienda Encero.

There he had time, under the pretense that his leg was hurting him and that he could not get to the capital yet, to reflect on how *tempora mutantur*.   Never in touch with the popular pulse and having always confined his solicitudes to the military, he did not know how widely he had become a proverb of evil among the masses.   "As if the Devil or Santa Anna has arrived" was a saying ejaculated by every *peon* on occasions of surprise or astonishment on some unexpected event.   The more intelligent feared and hated him and only sought his aid when no better was found. Unfortunately for them there was no better to be found at the present time and among the crowd of military satraps

Santa Anna was the only one whose energy and resolution coupled with his influence among the soldiers were useful. Therefore all combinations sooner or later gravitated to Santa Anna. It seemed that this man who both fascinated and horrified them was essential to their safety—an old man of the sea without whose painful weight on their shoulders they could never feel altogether comfortable.

Taking stock of his situation, he found that he had returned only by grace of a highly precarious coalition of forces which themselves were acting favorably towards him only in the face of public distrust and ill will. He would have to proceed cautiously, prove his worth to the people, and his first step was to avoid any pretense to political power, to proclaim himself a simple soldier responding to the call of his country in distress. It was a good line and most fitting for his melodramatic nature. After a period of probation, perhaps there would be a re-shuffle and his chance would come to vault into the Palace again. Delegations from the army visited him and he felt tolerably sure of his old companions in that body. But for the present— humility and caution.

The American merchant Hargous who had been such a friend to him in other trying times, dropped in to urge him to support a policy of peace with the United States. But Santa Anna replied with rare candor that he was getting old and did not want to risk another exile, with the chance that he might die far from home. He added that he had enough money—were there still interests seeking to bribe him?—desired no more wealth, and while he admitted that the course suggested would be the best for the country he could only—lapsing again into his proclamatory ling-

—take up the sword in defense of the country. Later if Congress wished it and a majority leaned in that direction, so much to the good ; but he would not take the risk. In other words, play safe was his motto now.

The grouping now had all the elements of a scene from a comic opera ; with Santa Anna sticking timorously to Encero, and the Government factions so suspicious of one another that they could not decide on a suitable emissary to send to the returned exile. The latter declined several invitations from the Government to report to Mexico and only stirred from his retreat when they issued a peremptory command to come. He was met by a most courteous committee at a most diplomatically proper distance from the city and he nodded in the most deprecating manner to the individuals handsomely paid by the government to cheer him, as he entered the Plaza beneath an ornamental arch— which some wit compared to a scaffold. Santa Anna's scaffold ! Not a most inviting jest and he retired with precipitation to Tacubaya where he stayed at a safe distance from the capital and Palace.

All he ventured to request was that the statue of himself, so disgracefully upset two years before should be set up again and crowned with the national arms. He hastened to assure the Government that he was but a soldier "now eager to take up arms for the country." Mexico was wooing Santa Anna now with blunt outspokenness and he replied with sentiments more serious than his usual rhetoric.

"We will say to Santa Anna," announced the leading republican organ of the city, "if you recognize your errors, promote the welfare of the country, pursue a course entirely different from your former policy and prove by acts—not words—that your misdeeds were not crimes but errors, then Mexico will forget the past and reward liberally the citizen conferring upon her so marked a benefit." He responded by urging the Government to gather troops and supplies. "Every day that passes without fighting at the north is a century of disgrace for Mexico." Never had these two extraordinary lovers—now grown old and temperamentally shrewish—spoken to each other with such candor and understanding.

Quite properly did he place the responsibility on the Government, for in order to raise an army funds were necessary, and in their hands lay the machinery for obtaining them. In that operation they had not shown prodigious success. In September they had a grand total of 1,839 pesos in the treasury and their appeals for aid from the States brought some remarkable responses. The great State of Oaxaca turned in the prodigal amount of 75 pesos. But in spite of the unwillingness of the clergy and the merchants, alarmed at the prominence of Farias, to contribute, about $90,000 were raised, and Santa Anna went to Guadalupe to receive the blessing of the national Virgin as he set out for the north, with San Luis Potosí as his objective.

Mindful of those days in '24 when he had had such uncongenial relations with the Potosians, he sent a deputation ahead from Querétaro to sound out sentiment and obtain a formal invitation to enter the city. But the inhabitants of the northern metropolis, fearing the unknown Anglo-Saxon more than the familiar Latin scourge, sent a welcoming deputation and on October 8th he was ushered in with as many *vivas* and municipal decorations as his vanity desired.

As October and November passed in San Luis Potosí, he

fingered uniform cloths, inspected ordnance and talked to contractors, and a stream of messengers flowed south carrying varying staccato appeals with one unvarying meaning : "The army continues to remain in the most miserable state" ; "Send me money" ; "We will have to live on the country hereabouts" ; etc., etc. Yes, he was gathering many thousands of human units, and he had his eyes fixed dutifully in the direction of Zachary Taylor, but he could not move these thousands until they were clothed, provided with guns, powder, ball and hard-tack ; and Farias sent him nothing to purchase these articles.

But it was in the otherwise gloomy month of November that Farias did send him something. A congress had been gotten together after a fashion and proceeded with the business of electing a new executive. *Puros, moderados,* conservatives, clericals and Santanistas milled about in the most feverish confusion. A political hack named Salas, a fire-eater named Rejon, Farias, Santa Anna himself and even Almonte were candidates. Finally a compromise was struck by making Santa Anna President — it was understood that he was to remain in the field, thus being disqualified from holding active office — and Farias Vice-President and active head of the Government.

Short consolation, for our hero developed troubles other than pecuniary. Americans were threatening Tampico and the obvious move was to send some prominent general with an army to oppose them. The man most mentioned for this command was Valencia, but Santa Anna, fearing that the empty braggart might by some chance achieve success and establish himself as a rival chief, vetoed this appointment. When there were protests, a Presidential pen wrote haughtily to a pair of bespectacled Vice-Presidential eyes, "I ask the satisfaction that I consider due me. I do not consider myself, nor should I be considered, by the gentlemen who compose the government of the country, as a mere General commanding a corps of the army, but as the sole *caudillo* of the Nation to whom the direction of its destinies has been entrusted." He had reason to be so sensitive for his annoyances were increasing.

His past intriguing had come home to roost. Through the indiscretions of the agent Mackenzie and several newspapers in the States, some intelligence of Polk's exchanges with Santa Anna arrived in Mexico and his enemies made the most of it. It was recalled that the Americans had been singularly obliging in allowing the President to go through the blockade and the public leaped to the not unplausible — seeing it was Santa Anna — conclusion that he had made a deal to betray his country to the Americans. His apparent inaction in San Luis Potosi added confirmation to this and the maliciously fabricated stories of how the General and his staff were living in Oriental luxury supported by drafts from James Knox Polk.

While the most elemental passions of the populace were being aroused their professional wits touched an equally rudimentary level, for commenting on the Presidential protests which were being diurnally wafted to Farias —"cannon, but no ball, muskets but no bullets, etc., etc."—they jested, "Santa Anna wants three things, money, money money." It was the most melancholy truth. The half-starving soldiers who had been arrayed in new and gorgeou uniforms were living now off the city of San Luis whicl strained its resources more out of pity for their state than out of patriotism.

It was ironical that Santa Anna should now be cast as Job just when he genuinely desired to play a heroic Daniel. For considering the defects of his character and past, his conduct now actually bore a faint resemblance to the demigods of classical and Biblical literature with whom his adulators so often and anomalously compared him. He was a mountain of energy in organizing the troops and inspiring them with his lurid oratory. He sincerely wanted to fight and defeat Taylor now, it cannot be doubted — to drive the enemy from the *Patria* at any cost, even at some cost to his private fortune.

To Farias he wrote : "In order to be able to move from here I have placed at the disposition of the Commissary all my fortune. Do you know and does the world know that I have obtained 180,000 pesos by mortgaging all my estates and drawing drafts against some of my friends who no doubt will honor my signature ? I have not hesitated in this sacrifice when I go to expose my life. Perhaps my innocent family will remain to perish, but such is the destiny which has fallen on my unhappy fatherland where I am insulted and where I am called traitor in moments when I am sacrificing all to save it."

Allowing for the inevitable exaggerations in this, allowing that it did not represent all his fortune as he alleged, yet withal it was indeed unusual for a *caudillo* of Santa Anna's type to make drains on his own fortune to support an expedition which the government should have supported. Of course it was to his interest to win and vault to the throne again, but some meed of praise and approbation should be awarded him for his actions in these days.

His preparations for war, as was natural with him, bore a character less practical than piratical. One of the principal incentives he held out to his men was the possibility of loot and the treasures which allegedly lay in Taylor's camp-wagons. As he directed the designs of medals which were also to reward the expeditionaries, he neglected to hold a school of staff officers for the study of maneuvers. Likewise, troops were strenuously drilled but were given no marksmanship lessons. But with these somewhat incom plete measures, with a few forced loans, the portion of his own fortune, and the seizure of a large quantity of silver bars, quickly minted into dollars, he was able to lick the army into some sort of shape.

Late in January, he had knowledge that Taylor's forces were reduced and although he could hardly say that his outfit was ready, it appeared as if conditions would never be any better for beginning the campaign. He had lost about 3,000 men in desertions since the first of the year and he was fearful that the political scramble, getting more heated in Mexico, might recall his army to take part in some *coup d'état*. To the strains of "Adios," a popular song of the day, the army clattered out of the town of San Luis Potosi on January 28th, 1847.

They made a variegated, but not unimpressive appear ance. Santa Anna was seated in a sort of chariot drawn by eight mules and surrounded by his staff, gorgeously clad. An observer noticed that "a bevy of wanton women" fol lowed behind the chariot, and an equally interesting cortège five mules loaded with crates of game-cocks, brought up the rear of the Presidential party. The army streamed along, some detachments well clad, others miserably uniformed in mere rags and tatters ; but all suffered from the extremes of heat and cold which marked the climatic conditions of the northern deserts. Hot sunny afternoons were frequently broken by whirling snow-storms or heavy downfalls of rain. Sickness made more acute the general distress, and many, worn out by the long march, threw away their precious bundles of provisions. The army pursued its northward course under the triple threat of starvation, illness and desertion.

Far north, near Saltillo, Taylor had established himself, against all orders from Washington. For Old Zack's political sensibilities were even more pleasurably acute than those of Santa Anna's. For a long time he had pampered the ambition to follow in the Presidential succession Generals Jackson, Tyler and Harrison, and to bring to Washington the valuable experience of a life of bush-whacking. His fellow-democrat, Polk, he considered a trimmer, a pusillanimous country lawyer — a despised civilian, and he lusted for his place.

He had long remained the coy near-candidate waiting for his party to summon him, but when the arrogant General Scott, a Whig, and unfortunately his superior officer, deprived him of most of his forces and ordered him to stay at Monterrey, he brimmed over with bitterness. He was sure he saw a plot, Polk to Scott, to bury him in prenomination oblivion by stationing him in a quiet sector where he would have to remain idle for lack of men. It was too much ; he notified Senator Crittenden, one of his boosters, that he was now openly a candidate for the Presidency and against orders, indeed against common sense, he took his little army from Monterrey to the perilous heights of Saltillo.

> *Old Zack's at Monterrey*
> *Bring on your Santa Anner*
> *For every time we lift a gun*
> *Down goes a Mexicanner.*

So had been singing his partisans at home, and in truth he was at his best as the home-spun hero of excited political supporters. He had never been anything else but a rough and ready Indian fighter in the Seminole wars; he had never commanded forces in a real battle before the advent of the war and even after Palo Alto and Resaca de la Palma he was totally unfit to maneuver large bodies of troops or to direct competent corps of artillery, cavalry and infantry. The West-Pointers under him frankly despised him and fortunately for the army, one of them, General Worth, was a skilled soldier. Thus, with less than 9,000 men and an indomitable desire to shine as a candidate, Old Zack went forth to battle.

He marched south from Saltillo to a place called Agua Nueva, a most inappropriate ground for defense as his staff protested. He knew that Santa Anna was somewhere south of him but such was his lack of good scouts that he did not know exactly where. A platoon of cavalry had gone to La Encarnacion for what was intended to be reconnaissance but what turned out to be potation, and after a night in the *cantinas* awoke to find themselves surrounded by Santa Anna's dragoons. More Spartan spies were sought when a curious group of men appeared.

Dressed with almost burlesque outlandishness, wearing every sort of head-gear from Panamas to slouch hats, and black, gray, brown jackets and breeches of equally miscellaneous design and color, they presented, even compared with the far from smart regulars, a picturesque lack of military appearance. Each armed as if for a boarding party, with two of the new Colt revolvers, two pistols of older models, a rifle and bowie knife, a squad of ten of these creatures were said to be able to fire 1000 shots in 2 minutes. Their motto was no quarter and no surrender. They were Texan Rangers and their chief was Ben McCulloch.

Taylor rejoiced for they had aided him in the Palo Alto campaign and he sent them forth to locate Santa Anna. Reaching the fatal Encarnacion by the expedient of avoiding roads and keeping to the chaparral, they found themselves within Mexican picket lines. McCulloch made observations of the number and size of the smoking encampments in the vicinity—most extensive he found—and sent most of his party back to Taylor with the news. He remained with one other scout to spy more carefully.

In the night they groped on further and watched for the dawn on the side of a hill. As gray streaks ran across the eastern sky, it seemed as if hundreds of trumpets broke the air. The two rangers watched a huge camp come to life, the soldiers stretching themselves and building fires for breakfast, fires built of green boughs which caused a thick and protective smoke to hang over the district. With the aid of this smoke screen, they escaped and made for Agua Nueva. Arriving there they found that Taylor had left with his entire force. When the first body of scouts brought back the intelligence of a dangerously large army of Mexicans, Taylor saw that the perilous position had to be abandoned ere the Mexicans came up. The rangers had saved him from certain defeat by their reconnaissance.*

When Santa Anna had roused his benumbed and half starved troops from behind their smoky bonfires and marched them forward he came upon the cold ashes of the American encampment at Agua Nueva. Enormously disappointed, for he had planned a surprise, he proceeded until that afternoon when he discovered Taylor strongly established on a long line of steep mesas called La Angostura, not far from the hamlet of Buena Vista. It looked like an impregnable position and our hero did not care for this Thermopylæ pass, as he called it. Resorting to his customary bluffing, he sent a messenger to Taylor telling him that he had 20,000 troops and demanding surrender. Taylor swore a great oath in reply, which was translated into a dignified refusal by Colonel Bliss.

The afternoon was spent in sharp fighting to turn the American left and its only issue was a slight advantage gained by the Mexicans. Both armies tried to compose themselves for the night's sleep to the accompaniment of a biting wind from the bare sierras. The reposing Americans, reduced to about 8,000 now because of desertion faced, not twenty thousand Mexicans—as our hero had informed them with his inevitable practise of representing his forces before the battle as 30% to 50% more than reality, and after the battle as an equal percentage below but more nearly 15,000, with 4,000 of these cavalry unfit for use on this terrain. His men were underfed, co

* This material was furnished through the courtesy of Professor W Webb whose forthcoming book on the Texas Rangers will include t ment of these episodes.

many ill and all badly prepared for the morrow's combat, while the Americans, numerically smaller, were fresh and ready for fighting. All things considered the two armies were not unevenly matched.

When the sun rose, Santa Anna, with his incorrigible instinct for the dramatic, made one great pageant of his army; the different corps in various brilliant uniforms, the lances of the cavalry tossing their gleaming reflections to the equally shining bands—now intoning the wild, melancholy strains of "Adios," and priests in vivid chasules walking back and forth administering absolution. It was a stupendous picture and the shabby Americans felt properly inferior.

The focal point of the Mexican attack was the American left, for the right was protected by a labyrinth of deeply eroded gullies. Maneuvering indefatigably up the sloping ravines which ran from the mesas of the American left, the Mexicans enjoyed only partial success. Some Arkansas regiments, green men, broke and ran in disorder back to Saltillo; one brigade of regulars, largely through Taylor's stupidity was cut to pieces. But among the staunch men who remained were names afterwards notable, Bragg, Capt. T. W. Sherman, Jefferson Davis. In truth it was Sherman's artillery which prevented total dissolution of the American forces with its constant and deadly fire. Meanwhile the Mexican officers fingered their field glasses and observed with dismay that reinforcements were coming up from Saltillo. Somehow, somewhere, Miñon and his cavalry had failed in their mission to cut off Taylor's rear. Santa Anna displayed commendable courage—he never did lose a chance to dash recklessly about under fire in battle. He wore only a simple officer's uniform, covered by a white duster and with an old straw hat bobbing about on his romantic brow. He rode from one position to another despite the pain such equitation gave his leg, and unmindful of Sherman's shells bursting around him. One horse was killed under him, but he mounted another, leaving his sword idle in its scabbard and flourishing a whip while an adjutant galloped beside him to take messages. The soldiers were inspired by his example and during these stirring hours, our hero perhaps reached the most honorable zenith of his career.

Equal but more stationary valor was showed by Taylor who sat on his famous horse, Old Whitey, one leg thrown over the pommel of the saddle, and remained unmoved by the shells that burst near him, some fragments tearing his clothes. While Worth accomplished the more cerebral part of the leadership, Old Zack by his statuesque example did much to embolden his men.

The day ended even all. The Americans had put up stubborn and intrepid defense and had for the most part held their key positions, although they had suffered severe losses in dead, wounded and deserters. Santa Anna, he had been assisted by Miñon's cavalry, might have won. His generalship had been in the main good and while he had not achieved a victory, the prospects for the morrow were none too bright for his enemies.

But as he lighted his camp-fires and took stock of his situation, he had reason to feel depressed. He had lost perhaps 4,000 men through desertion; roughly 1,800 had fallen in wounded and killed and 300 had been captured. The rest were hungry, cold and discontented because the promised loot had not fallen with the expected celerity into their hands ; they might mutiny and flee at any moment. Deadened by fatigue and the feelings of discouragement which any reverse left on his temperamental nature, he foresaw a disastrous morrow.

It was not unnatural then that his reflections were more political and Machiavellian than military. If he refused battle now and retreated, he might avoid a possible defeat, and the political downfall which would inevitably follow. Moreover he could claim a victory, showing as evidences three captured field pieces and two American flags—fit trophies for a theatrical entrance into Mexico. It was not surprising then that he should choose retreat as the lesser evil. Folding up his tents during the night, he retired to Agua Nueva.

Camp-fires, however, were kept burning and the Americans watched gloomily for the dawn to break on another and possibly fatal day for their chances. Their surprise changed to jubilation when they discovered the retreat, and Taylor and Wool fell into each others arms thankful for their salvation. Thus the Battle of Buena Vista, called so by the Americans, became a signal triumph, good fodder for Old Zack's nominating cannon. And La Angostura became a *hermoso triunfo* for the First Consul who was returning to his capital, while the Americans rhymed decisively—

> *"And so for fear my precious leg*
> *Might boil some Yankee pot,*
> *I did just as I always do*
> *I run—you know for what."*

But the return of the Napoleon of the West seemed more like his famous prototype's retreat from Moscow. The winter now fell on the straggling horde as they retraced their weary steps over the barren desert. The wounded were placed in litters, four men each to carry them, but during the awful journey many of these bearers ran away and the wake of the army was one long line of frozen corpses. Through the night they trudged — moonlight nights now and an eerie scene — a true *Noche Triste* for the sorry descendants of Cortez.

When Santa Anna reached San Luis Potosi, his army had shrunk to insignificance, but he had the trophies to display and he claimed that Taylor had been badly defeated. The gullible Potosians gave him all the applause he wanted. He wrote exultingly to Farias, "Señor Taylor remains in Angostura so frightened and destroyed that he cannot move in any direction. However I have left 3000 cavalry there to check him if he does." Then, apropos of disorders in the capital, "What curse has fallen on our unhappy country! With what reason Taylor said in Saltillo some time ago: 'I do not fear Santa Anna for in Mexico there will be a revolution very soon.'" As he hurried toward the capital now, Taylor's words were in his mind, but disappointment was not in his heart, for he was approaching a battle-field where his peculiar talents could be exercised better than on the mesas of Angostura.

CHAPTER X

A NEW CORTEZ

AS HIS carriage rolled on from San Luis to Mexico, he sat relishing the highly satisfactory but a trifle mystifying attitude of the people towards him. Although he did not bear with him the head of the conquered Taylor, at one place he enjoyed the experience of seeing girls strew flowers in his path and some strangely familiar individuals insisted on accompanying his vehicle for short distances in their own carriages. Did not these admirers bear a close resemblance to his late enemies, the opponents of Farias and himself? When he reached Mexico he found a most agreeable confusion and his perplexity was dispelled.

Whilst he had been making ready to attack Taylor, the radical wing of Farias' party under an unscrupulous firebrand, Rejón, had invoked the terminology of the French revolution, of Marat and Robespierre to frighten the rich and the clergy from their too tenacious hold on the money bags. "The scaffold must be raised and we must drink their hearts' blood" and similar genial sentiments only served to arouse an equally violent counter-revolutionary movement.

Volunteer battalions recruited from the various social orders and groups of the city which desired to wear highly ornamental uniforms and to prevent their homes from being looted were formed, and adopted the names of certain revolutionary leaders as titles. Thus the clerks had their organization under the ægis of Mina, the artisans under the sponsorship of the sainted Hidalgo, etc. And their adversaries, commenting on the rather social nature of these groups of minute men, dubbed them the *Polkos,* which carried in its syllables the connotation of the fashionable dance—the polka. But they survived the epithet, and more, forced Rejón to retire from the political field.

But the imperturbable Farias blandly insisted that the sicker Mexico became, the better his remedy of Federalism and anti-clericalism would taste. To dislodge him, the conservative elements utilized the victorious battalions to start another revolt which met such resistance that the city was threatened with the interesting urban destruction which annually marked the reigns of Bustamente. These events—dubbed the Polkos' revolution—took place during the Angostura campaign and Santa Anna rode in on the results of it. Most people were tired of the bellicose battalions and everybody was disgusted with Farias. Folk who had formerly writhed at the mention of Santa Anna now discovered an affectionate attachment for him and the whole city professed a pathetic desire to have him back as ruler.

What a pleasant surprise for our hero! A few days before he had pursued a crestfallen retreat in the midst of a shattered army after a battle which in effect represented a defeat. With no money nor fame, save a little American ordnance and a forlorn trio of banners he found not a suspicious and skeptical populace difficult to cajole into the belief that he was a victor, but an overwhelming union of factions which was less interested in his recent military ventures than in his capacity to patrol the streets of the capital. Success, however unexpected, did not prevent him from striking a noble, self-immolating attitude and talking about his relinquishment of the northern campaign as "just another sacrifice on the altar of my country." He acknowledged smilingly the votive wreaths.

Smelling faintly of the incense of the customary Te Deum he assumed the active Presidency and ordered all hostilities to cease. As the most practical gesture in conciliating the conservative and clerical elements, he abolished the office of Vice-President, thus definitely ousting Farias, and established instead the office of Substitute President as a convenient emergency when he had to go forth to battle again. The straining limits of the Spanish language could not contain the transports of the clergy and while they were in this agreeable frame of mind, Santa Anna obtained two million in cash from them ere he took the trouble to rescind Farias' confiscatory laws. Moreover the sly old fox in his touching desire to guard the holy pesos, slipped in a decree placing Church property under the "protection" of the State, which served to abate somewhat the enthusiasm of such clerics as could remember his activities a few years previously.

But there were other matters beside such administrative pastimes. Down at Vera Cruz, an American general with a sonorous voice and the demeanour of a successful evangelist, known to the irreverent as "Old Fuss and Feathers," had majestically received the capitulation of the most important port of the republic. By dropping a few well-aimed twelve-pound shot into the city, Winfield Scott had induced the quaking merchants of the city to prevail upon a none too resolute Mexican commandant to give him a base for his projected expedition into the heart of Mexico. Santa Anna fulminated against the pusillanimous garrison, but it was his duty now to see that Scott got no farther.

His first step was to expel, with all the attendant threatricality, Black, the American consul, who had lingered in the vain hope that he might further peace negotiations. After this important measure he asked the Governor of Vera Cruz to draft all men between the ages of fifteen and fifty and to shoot all deserters. Somewhat more technical preparations followed when he called for skilled engineers to descend to the lowland and assist in the fortifying of strategic points. Canalizo, the "Lion of Guadalupe," was named commander under Santa Anna, and National Guards and regulars were sent down the Vera Cruz road in detachments of two thousand each. Appointing a presumably manageable creature, General Anaya, as Substitute President, the President started out himself on April 2nd.

On arriving in Jalapa he found that with true Mexican deliberation the engineers had not yet started at the work of fortifying Puente Nacional where a stand had been agreed upon, and that about one thousand of the disgraceful garrison from Vera Cruz had come up spreading stories of a Munchausen extravagance about the insuperable prowess of the Americans. He himself found it necessary to compromise with the relaxing airs of the tropics and rest in his hacienda, Encero. Not far away from this place he discovered a point called Cerro Gordo which commanded the road from Vera Cruz and which he selected as the bulwark against the Yankees, on the somewhat more historical than practical ground that it had been considered impregnable by the guerrilla bands who had bushwhacked here during the Independence struggle. But it did have the advantage of being on the edge of that dread zone where the *vomito* was soon to take up its semi-annual reign and where the Yankees if checked would face that formidable spectre.

With prodigious energy he threw himself into the task of fortifying this place. Under his strenuous exhortations the soldiers cleared away bushes and cacti, dug trenches, built breastworks, and set up their artillery. A dominant hill called El Telegrafo with a slope on the Vera Cruz side precipitous enough to make the most valiant assaulters hesitate, was made to bristle with armament. It all looked most unassailable and it was felt that if the Yankees could be held back the accommodating mosquitoes would bore their *coups de grâce* into the expeditionary forces.

Yet all was not so well as it seemed. There were ten thousand troops here, it was true. But those who had been at Angostura revealed a disquieting lack of spirit and seemed to have developed a neurotic fear of the Anglo-Saxon invaders. The fugitives from Vera Cruz also muttered in awed accents and the body of the Mexican army manifestly felt that they were facing some diabolic power. Worse, their officers who tried to stifle this sort of talk and sternly shot all deserters were no more sanguine; they were frankly sceptical of Santa Anna's ability as a commander. He had shown a meritorious energy, yes. But why had he not fortified La Atalaya, a hill not far from El Telegrafo, an admirable vantage point which the Americans would surely try to take ? Besides, what could their rank and file do with their antique muskets — obsolete weapons rejected by the English and palmed off on the Mexicans ? Their chief, Canalizo, was distrustful and foreboding.

Santa Anna himself was none too comfortable. The Government had given him no signal assistance and were bothering him with reports of an insurrection in the capital. He reverted to the staccato epistolary style which had produced such remarkable lack of response when he was in San Luis Potosi. From Encero on April 7th : "Let the Government provide for the defence of the capital. I can attend only to this road. Unless the Government sends money with the velocity of a lightning ray all will be lost and in no way do I consider myself responsible for any bad results."

Departing from the white sand dunes of Vera Cruz, passing Manga de Clavo which Scott had used as a temporary headquarters, an army of eight thousand Yankees stepped blithely forth into the tropical wilderness in the footsteps of Hernando Cortez. They repeated to one another, "Old Peg Leg has been licked up like salt at Buena Vista by Old Zack." Why couldn't they do it too ? As they marched through a veritable Eden where the scarlet miracle of the bougainvillea ran riot over the towering mangroves, it seemed hardly possible Old Peg Leg could be lurking with his legions amid this sylvan loveliness. But about fifteen miles above the Puente Nacional, the birds sang less, the Indian *jacales* along the line were ominously deserted and their *vedettes* came upon the enemy entrenched in the Fat Mountain — *Cerro Gordo*.

But they did not hesitate long. Captain Robert E. Le

of the Engineers busied himself with a road leading around to the rear of the Mexican positions and with an alacrity which must have given melancholy satisfaction to the Mexican staff, a General with a shabby slouch hat and an extraordinary command of expectoration took possession of La Atalaya with only a weak show of opposition from Santa Anna's troops. As the Stars and Stripes floated over its crest Santa Anna made the best of the bad commencement by sending heavy reinforcements to El Telegrafo in the person of one of his most courageous young officers, Colonel Ciriaco Vasquez.

The twelve-pounders which he had set on this hill were now replying to perky four-pounders which tobacco-chewing Twiggs had brought up on his capture of La Atalaya, and Vasquez did his best to inspire his pessimistic followers who spoke with an unmartial respect of the Yankee marksmanship and referred to them as the "Cursed Riflemen."

Carelessly, impudently, the Americans formed to scale Vasquez' position and when a lieutenant asked Twiggs how far they should charge, he replied with his usual verdancy, "Charge 'em to hell." With this rough exhortation the Americans swept over the breast-works at the bottom and rushed up the slopes. The Mexicans, all too ready to believe these adversaries were inspired by Lucifer, licked their rickety muskets and exclaimed as the advancing ranks failed to waver, "They seem to despise death !" Santa Anna from his headquarters watched the Yankees approach, then lock in combat, then sweep back his best troops in full flight. The Mexicans would not, could not fight now and the "bloody gridiron" was hoisted from El Telegrafo.

It was a general rout now and when Shields' men made the circuit of Robert E. Lee's path to the rear and emerged from some bushes to find themselves facing Canalizo's two thousand infantry and horse, it did not matter that their slender forces hesitated to meet the Mexicans' greeting volley, for it was only the momentary ballistics of fear. The two thousand turned about and ran down the ravines in the rear of Cerro Gordo, scattering hopelessly in the chapparal. Santa Anna, perceiving that his battle was lost, tried to form the fugitives, failed and galloped off after Canalizo.

The Americans were jubilant over such an easy victory and Scott made a great impression on them as he went through their ranks with tears streaming down his fine old mummer's face—for he was as able an histrion as Santa Anna. But an English veteran of the Waterloo and Peninsular campaigns who had fought with the Americans was less uncritical and dismissed it as "this shabby battle." Shabby, yes and hardly a battle, for however much Santa Anna had sinned by not fortifying La Atalaya, his negligence was mainly technical. His troops were beaten before Twiggs first fouled the edges of that famous hill; their morale had been left on the blood-stained mesas near Saltillo.

A lark now for the Yankees as they picked their way through the Mexicans' deserted camp. Some important loot such as a chest containing fifty thousand pesos and some picturesque articles too, when they found a carriage with a luncheon set, the luncheon itself, and a wooden leg. Was it Old Peg Leg's famous artificial limb? They assumed so and twelve months later—many of them were twelve-month volunteers — in Maryland, Pennsylvania and many a mid-western state appeared wooden legs as alleged trophies of the battle of Cerro Gordo.   Spacious but hardly ephemeral objects, for in many a fresh-water museum they still gather dust under proud, triumphant placards.

On a hill nearby, Santa Anna met Generals Ampudia and Rangel and after giving them orders to salvage what was left of his divisions set out for Encero in company with a couple of officers.   His leg was hurting him and he hoped to obtain a rest and a litter at his hacienda.   But not far from Encero he was fired upon by American *vedettes* and he changed his course.   Meeting a curate on the road, he asked the holy man for a fresh horse to replace his jaded one, but the holy man "pertly" refused.   This wounded him deeply.

He was but a beaten, cowed fugitive like the rest of his troops.   At Tuzumpam Hacienda he revived a little when two soldiers brought him the money-chest of their colonel, and a little farther on he came to a little village where some peasants gave him a few huzzahs and assisted him in feeling again like a General and President.   At Orizaba he was his old self again when he found a litter, much encourage- ment from partisans, and some National Guards who seemed game for more fighting.

Learning that another brigade of one thousand men was not far away, he took hope and began to build anew.   The hospitable neighborhood had to furnish all its males be- tween fifteen and forty and surrender some substantial "loans" which diminished its chauvinism but swelled Santa Anna's returning confidence.   Fugitives from the battle came streaming in, and soon what only Santa Anna could hopefully call an army was gotten together. But the only counter-attack he dare to make as yet was a drive by secret agents on the loyalty of Catholic soldiers among the American ranks—with offers of land and gold, and appeals to their feeling of religious solidarity.

A week later Puebla, that strongly clerical city, tendered him a surprisingly lukewarm welcome when he marched in at the head of his rag-tag army, for Scott at Jalapa had just demonstrated to the astounded Mexicans, and especially the priests, that the word General is not necessarily synonymous with plunder. Santa Anna stormed against the Pueblans for their lack of patriotism, castigated the fugitives from Cerro Gordo who had gathered there, demoted a few officers and, when the Church seemed disinclined to support him financially, seized some of the golden liturgical object from the Cathedral. He made a great show of seeking Scott's advance guards, but when they did appear he did not seriously face them. Presidential elections were scheduled for May 15th in the capital and he could not tarry for merely corporal combats.

"Nothing is left us save vanity and dissension," said wise man of the capital, and that was not an inaccurate comment on the situation there when Santa Anna approached. The circumstances of that troublous city were orderly after Angostura compared with what they were now. Where there had been two cabals before, at present there were dozens. Furthermore Santa Anna's reputation as a military medicine-man dropped quite low as people found it possible to remember that Cerro Gordo had evoked no greater talents for defeat than San Jacinto.

Our hero was met by the usual deputation of friends or

le the capital and in view of the state of things within,
ey persuaded him to refrain from assuming the Presi-
ncy, thus leaving at least Anaya on his side. Once again
 took up the rôle—now a little trite and hardly per-
isive—of "only a soldier." But as he walked on the
newhat turbulent stage his chosen lines were so badly
:errupted that he proceeded to turn a series of the most
onishing somersaults of his long career.

The intriguing Tornel buttonholed him when he arrived
 the city and poured into his ears a constant stream of
iuendo and accusation which swayed his volatile mind
 the conviction that his enemies wanted him to take his
>st recent course in order to get him out of politics. Per-
ided of this, he announced that he would make a great
icrifice" for his people and assume the Presidency. This
>erb self-immolation pleased no one and in addition made
 enemy of Anaya.

Now the fury of the humiliated Mexicans broke over him
 the alleged source of all their troubles and defeats. In
in did he issue nobly worded proclamations defending
; actions, in vain did he have extended conferences with
: plotting Tornel, nobody would believe him, much less
:en to him. Finally he composed another studied pæan
 injured innocence, saying that the plots of his enemies
:vented him from doing what he could for his country,
d he handed in his resignation again.

Just then the skies began to clear for him. Valencia,
io had sought his place as commander-in-chief, suddenly
>se San Luis Potosi as his fief. Ampudia and Arista
nt into banishment, Almonte, another dark horse for
: Presidency, was put in jail, and Bravo, always a danger-

ous rival, retired to private life. Also a *bloc* of radicals
became persuaded—by fair means or foul—that they
ought to support the martyr of Cerro Gordo. Once again
he executed reverse acrobatics and, asserting that chaos
threatened the nation, withdrew his resignation.

A few kept their tempers and their sense of humor
"Mexicans, I shall be with you even to the consummation
of your ruin," blithely chirped a satirist in the papers
"What a life of sacrifice is the General's ; a sacrifice to tak
the power, to resign, to resume ; ultimate sacrifice ; ulti
mate final, ultimate more final ; ultimate most fina
ultimate the very finalest. But let him cheer up. He i
not alone in making sacrifices. For twenty-five yea
Mexicans have been sacrificing themselves, all of them i
the hope that a certain person would do good to th
country."

Thus he returned to power, inspiring no confidenc
hated and distrusted by all, but able to prevail because th
anarchic opposition could produce no one stronger
craftier. Most of the States openly refused to send hi
men. Some of the northern ones were talking of secedii
and making a new confederation of their own. But, wi
his usual resiliency in such dilemmas, he did not despa
Faced with the unenviable task of organizing a defense,
displayed a rather versatile energy in importing powc
from Guanajuato, ammunition from Honduras, and g
eral supplies from New Orleans. Forges were set up
the capital and manufacturing of arms was attempted the
By emptying the prisons, by patriotic appeals and wholes
impressments he was able to form a horde of about twen
five thousand men.

A series of fortifications, grandiose conception, to entirely encircle the city was planned. His confidence buttressed by advices from Englishmen and other foreigners who had seen service in Europe that Scott would not dare to enter the Valley of Mexico, and should he so presume, would be badly defeated, he proceeded to make ready for the attack. Certain negotiations added to this return of confidence, for when an enemy tries to parley, he should be despised, he had learned that from long experience in *pronunciamientos*.

Scott, the splendid old actor, bitten just as badly as Old Jack by the presidential bug, thought that with the laurels of Cerro Gordo — doubtless he was aware how easily they had been won and perhaps he had legitimate doubts of his own capacity — he could retire from the war with honors sufficient to make a popular candidate, if the Mexicans would settle terms of peace. He had been talking to Nicholas Trist, a clerk from the Department of State whom Polk had sent with plenary powers to negotiate peace, and discovered that Trist had the power to draw on several millions of dollars which were marked only "special funds" and which the nation need not know about.

> *They just want this Californy*
> *So's to lug the new slave states in,*
> *To abuse ye, an' to scorn ye*
> *And to plunder ye like sin.*

A scribe named James Russell Lowell looked out from handsome colonial windows on Brattle Street over the peaceful sweep of the Charles River as he composed this vernacular masterpiece, and voiced the feelings of Northern abolitionists who saw in the whole war a Southern "plot,"

while that sensitive instrument the Stock Exchange recorded the pessimism and disapproval of the capitalists.
Scott as a good Whig knew that these were the main props
of his party and that he would have to conciliate the preju-
dices of those New Englanders who now just as ten years
before were discovering great virtues and capacities in
Santa Anna.

> *O Santy Anny gained the day.*
> *Hoo-ray! for Santy Anny.*
> *He lost it once, he won it twice,*
> *All on the plains of Mexico.*
> *Hoo-ray! for Santy Anny.*

Several Britishers in the capital who had devoted lon
careers and brought much honor and riches to the Unio
Jack by arranging suitable bribes to the right politician
now intimated to the American general that if the way wa
lubricated by liberal "advances" the Mexicans might agre
to terms of peace. Scott conferred with several of his ge
erals about this proposal but they held the quaint idea th
victory should be attained by military prowess and not I
mysterious black bags filled with greenbacks.

Nevertheless Santa Anna was approached and seem
favorable. Scott paid out $10,000 as a preliminary ar
plunged into negotiations. There was a suggestion th
the Americans should advance up to the walls of Mexi
when the natives would be so frightened and depressed tl
an armistice could take place and terms settled. But
terms Santa Anna preferred to haggle. He discovered
invincible attachment for California and the territory w
of Texas. The secretive parleys dragged on and natura

became no secret at all. An annoying cartoonist depicted President Polk amputating Santa Anna's remaining leg while ether sponges labelled $3,000,000 lulled the hero of Angostura asleep.

He could not permit this sort of rumor to spread because he was suspect enough as a result of the disclosures about Mackenzie's mission. He had suffered from this sort of accusation when he was in San Luis Potosi and he did not desire to undergo it again. He struck a righteous attitude of uncompromising patriotism, announcing that he would die in the last ditch rather than capitulate, and secretly sent a message to Scott urging him to follow out the plan of investing Mexico, for only then would the people be in the humor to negotiate.

He now believed that he could beat Scott if the latter dared to get himself into the maze of lakes and streams, little towns and lava beds which filled the Valley of Mexico near the capital. He selected a hill called El Peñón which commanded the road from Puebla to Mexico and fortified it in the most intensive fashion. Piling thereon every sort of redoubt, breastwork, trench and stockade, he dug ditches around it and arranged to have water inundate them at the proper moment. The army marched out of the city with flags flying over their heterogeneous ranks to take up their position in the new fort. Wholly impregnable it seemed — perhaps it was — and Scott would be stopped once and for all.

Here they waited. American reconnaissance parties appeared, looked at the place and retired with agreeable precipitation. Yankee officers scanned its serried redoubts and engineers made detailed observations estimating how many men would be lost in storming it. With mounting confidence Santa Anna waited for a frontal attack. He was aware that the Americans need not come that way but could veer to the west. There was a road in that direction, but Alvarez, a bandit leader, with some ragged cavalry was relied upon to cut off that move. Finally it was discovered that the entire American army had simply turned at right angles to El Peñón and followed the road to the west, a bad road certainly but apparently not impassable. Alvarez had failed him. The great stronghold of El Peñón, representing weeks of effort and fortification, was rendered absolutely useless. But it was too late to do anything but try to meet Scott on the other side of the lakes of Xochimilco as he emerged into the valley.

No flags were out, no balconies were decorated, no cheering crowds congregated as the crestfallen El Peñón forces clattered back through the city. But Santa Anna displayed a great ability to recover from his disappointment without the assistance of comforting *vivas*. With no little resolution he gave Alvarez another chance by directing him to proceed to the west with his horse. Valencia's highly unreliable services were sent to San Angel and Lombardini, a general with a low order of intelligence and a high esteem for Santa Anna was allotted the task of fortifying the little convent hamlet of Churubusco about six miles from the city's gates. Dashing here and there, distributing orders his old Panama hat flopping and his white duster trailing in the wind, our hero seemed the personification of military zeal.

But he reckoned without Valencia. That egotistical villain had come back from San Luis Potosi desirous o supplanting Santa Anna in command and, when he got to San Angel with his troops, prepared to meet Scott alone, regardless of Santa Anna's dispositions. The latter perceiving that this wing was in danger of being cut off from his own, sent orders to Valencia to join forces with him and to bring all his artillery. Valencia responded with a frankly insubordinate note whose gist was that he intended to stay where he was regardless of orders ; and Santa Anna had to submit.

Meanwhile the Americans had been driving back Valencia's skirmishers and sending cavalry around his flanks to cut off his rear. But he stood his ground and the cavalry, finding themselves too far from their base, had to retire. This minor success so elated Valencia that he distributed promotions, wrote out citations and acted as if he had already superseded Santa Anna. But he had not noticed that a body of Americans under Generals Smith and Shields had driven a wedge between his forces and those of Santa Anna and were dangerously threatening his own rear.

Santa Anna recognized the danger and got a messenger through to Valencia ordering him to spike his guns and retreat as fast as possible. When Santa Anna's messenger appeared with his unwelcome dispatches, Valencia stormed about and insisted that he could and would stay where he was. But when his own aides who had been out to survey the situation returned to tell him of his untenable position, he lost control of himself with chagrin ; "The traitor, he has sold us," he yelled as he ran distracted through his troops, spreading disorder and panic. "It's Santa Anna's fault, the traitor," were the somewhat disorganizing syllables with which he directed the retreat. More than a retreat, a rout, with the Americans attacking and the gunners, cavalry, infantry and *soldaderas* running away in hopeless confusion. From a rout it became a massacre, 700 Mexicans falling, 800 surrendering and only 60 Americans dead or wounded. A crushing defeat.

But the nuisance Valencia was out of the way and our hero could salvage about 7,000 troops out of the disaster, rallying them along Lombardini's lines near Churubusco. There he centered his other corps, those of Perez, Rincon and Anaya and a strange little regiment called the San Patricio for the Irish who formed it. These men were allowed their own emblem, a green flag adorned with a harp, and thus inspired they fought with great courage.

Indeed the battle of Churubusco is largely the story of their desperate tenacity, clinging to the battle-scarred walls of the convent, refusing to allow their Mexican companions to hoist a white flag under the American assaults until, completely isolated and overrun by Yankees, they had to give up. The main body of Mexicans, after maintaining a surprising and, for the Americans, costly resistance, finally gave way and retreated.

But they were less military in retreat than in battle and they ran, a disorderly mob, toward the city. Santa Anna in a white duster and straw hat was seen riding amongst them striking at the fugitives with his whip, but in vain and very soon the straw hat was carried along in the flood of hurrying shakos towards the Peralvillo gate.

In both battles, Padierna (Valencia's debacle), called Contreras by Americans, and Churubusco, Santa Anna's loss numbered roughly 10,000 while the Americans' was approximately 1,000, mostly at Churubusco, a serious re

duction of their none too numerous forces.   They were
the victors but they realized that a few more triumphs
like Churubusco would be fatal, and Scott accepted Santa
Anna's request for an armistice with alacrity.

As Santa Anna sat down to the conference table with the
little clerk from the State Department he felt none too comfortable.   There was Valencia not far away in Toluca
repeating his bitter complaints of treachery and Mexico
would not have been Mexico if he did not find willing
auditors.   Then there was a keen little lawyer named
Gamboa who, with irritating circumstantiality, was subject-
ing his military operations to the acid test of common sense.
It was alleged that his nephew who administered Manga
de Clavo was selling large quantities of provisions to the
American army and making large profits.   And under all
there was the persistent rattle of a thousand tongues which
had not forgotten to repeat the old charges of collusion with
Polk.

At Mr. Trist's suave suggestions he agreed to cede California, New Mexico, all claims to Texas, but with unusual
stubbornness he stuck at the boundary line of Texas.   He
insisted that Mexico should retain the territory between the
Nueces and the Rio Grande, and even when Trist raised
the indemnity to a prodigious figure he balked.   In truth
he feared that the passing of such a large sum of money
would stamp him as the seller of his country's honor, and
besides, after the days of bargaining gave him a breathing
spell, his military courage revived.   Perhaps Scott was quite
shattered by that last day's fighting, perhaps intimidated by
the apparently unassailable height of Chapultepec.   Had
he not seen cock-fights where a rooster, almost defeated, by

one final effort killed its opponent? He had gambled
often before. Why not again? Fate, which he blamed or
praised for all his victories and defeats, might intervene in
his favor now. So he broke off negotiations.

Whatever he may have expected to receive from the temperamental Atropos, his destiny now as recently seemed to
be to provide victories to the already surfeited Americans.
At Molino del Rey on September 7th he gave the Americans
plenteous exercise and some rather sanguinary laurels. He
had gathered about 15,000 to the Americans 6,000, a ratio
in Mexican-American combats which historians have
learned to accept without comment, and his ragged
legions fought with an egregious lack of fear and
regard for organization. They did their poor best, but it
remained for the rough Alvarez to make a debacle of it all.
His rôle was to charge with his cavalry at the proper moment, and as he moved across the plain the American gunners poised their fuses. Crash! went the artillery and
Alvarez' forces turned their tails to the spurts of flame,
racing with contagious panic across the field. It was the
end of Mexican resistance that day, but not the end of
American surprise. Entering the "king's mill" they found
it not a munition factory as supposed, but a deserted, empty
ruin for which they had paid dearly in dead and wounded.

But they could not stop, and Scott having planted one
banderilla poised himself for another aim as the blood
spurted out of the first wound. Before him rose Chapultepec Heights a thousand feet above the plain and commanding a strategic view of the city. At its top was a
heavy old vice-regal castle on which fluttered the banner
of the Eagle and Serpent. If he could imbed the red, white

and blue dart in this muscular shoulder, the city could not long withstand him.

Santa Anna now displayed his old tendency of confusing rapid and promiscuous equitation for generalship. He galloped from one city gate to another, transferring regiments with a great show of canniness ; some, with a hardly commendable foresight, he took from Chapultepec itself. He spread the rumor — what other comforting intelligence could he give his exhausted countrymen ? — that the Americans had no food and could not keep up the fight. And while Scott was constructing scaling ladders, he reminded the natives that it was September 11th, the anniversary of his "defeat" of the Spaniards, with a stirring review and series of speeches.

It was all a little pointless and tardy, especially when Bravo in Chapultepec Castle, observing with disquiet the approaching lines of Americans, asked that his regiments be sent back. But the Yankees had cut off his retreat and prevented any reinforcements. As the blue lines crept up the steep slopes with their scaling ladders, Bravo lit the fuses of the mines with which he hoped to blow his assailants to pieces. But the mines did not go off and the Yankees clambered over the parapets and received the surrender of the septuagenarian patriot and his youthful cadets. The Stars and Stripes imparted to a panicky city the information that the Mexicans had lost again.

This second *banderilla* was well-placed but not mortal, and Scott prepared the *espada* now, confident that his quarry would back up and fall once and for all. Near San Cosme gate the Anglo-Saxon files skirmished eagerly between the arches of an old aqueduct and a young lieutenant

named U. S. Grant planted a cannon on top of a seventeenth-
century church to rake the disorderly Mexican regiments
below.   The battle now centered on rooftops, and Rangel,
who had been left in charge by Santa Anna, found his
highest and most commanding battery over-topped by a
body of Americans on an adjoining roof.   Santa Anna,
riding up with reckless daring at the head of reinforcements, found himself stopped, turned about and carried
back by the flood of retreating Rangel followers.   It was
the last and most successful thrust of the American matador
and with General Worth now inside the city limits, the
town council sent emissaries to arrange for a peaceful occupation.   Scott, like a triumphant toreador, rode into the
Plaza Mayor and mounted the steps of the National Palace,
the Halls of Montezuma, as Old Peg Leg joggled his weary
stump out of the city in the direction of Guadalupe.

Entrance of victorious American troops into Plaza of Mexico City. Cathedral (left) and National Palace (right) in background

CHAPTER XI

RANGER'S REVENGE

B UT Santa Anna had left behind him one last un-
ignited petard which was to impair slightly Scott's
dramatic assumption of the power of the city. Pre-
ious to his evacuation, and through the gentle ministrations
f Tornel, he had arranged that the inhabitants of the city
hould carry on the war with the invader. Plans had been
nade for releasing convicts, arming the *leperos*, placing
oulders on the rooftops, and general preparations for a
ouse-to-house struggle. It was the skeleton of this plan
hat came to life, as the American troops deserted their
pen-mouthed inspection of the main Plaza for billets.
hots were fired and the city was soon in the greatest dis-
rder. Only by severe measures on the part of the Ameri-
ns, assisted by the moderating efforts of the City Council,
as the uprising quelled.

Santa Anna had hovered near in the hope that he could
ter the mêlée and treat the city to the sort of pastime it
d enjoyed under the Presidency of Bustamente. But
rning of the collapse of his plans, he retired muttering
precations at the unpatriotic nature of the Council. He
v that he had better retreat.

But where? The Government and Congress were run-
g helter-skelter to the north — they might be in Toluca,

they might be in Querétaro. *Quien sabe?* He hurled
after it his resignation of the Presidency and the appointment of a provisional triumvirate composed of Peña, the
Chief Justice of the Supreme Court, Herrera and a Genera
Alcorte—to rule while he sought further victory in the
field. As a matter of fact he did not care to get caught in
the inevitable *imbroglio* of politics which he felt would
follow. His own plans were somewhat vague. His friend
were urging him to proclaim himself Dictator. Some sai
that His Excellency would seek exile in Guatemala and i
truth he turned his ragged followers toward the south
But somewhere along the road from Mexico he learned tha
Puebla's garrison of Americans was weak and was strug
gling desperately with Mexican guerrilla bands.

As Santa Anna clattered along in the inspiring shado
of Popo and its sister, The Sleeping Woman, he felt aga
that he was the story-book hero of Tampico and Vera Cru
Why should he not yet rescue victory from defeat, redee
himself by the capture of the City of the Angels which I
had just heard afforded such a convenient predicament f
capture? Why should he not rally the cowering politicia
around him as Dictator and force Scott to sue for peace
more liberal terms? All was not yet lost, he felt, and I
passionate temperament, again sanguine, magnified
scraggly forces with the title of an Army. He had 2,0
horse, 4 light guns; Alvarez was close by with 600 caval
He heard that 2,500 National Guard were eagerly awaiti
his advent a little further on and all these forces wo
supplement the several hundred bandits who were inv
ing Puebla. The defenders of the city were largely
capacitated by illness and Colonel Childs, the Ameri

commandant, probably could not muster more than 200 effectives. Forward for victory!

But when he came up to Puebla his spirits dropped again. The besiegers were a sorry lot and his guns were much too light for bombardment. Moreover the Pueblans displayed their customary dubious patriotism by assisting Childs who had made himself popular, and they had even furnished him with a Mexican uniform out of which he had fashioned a Stars and Stripes to flaunt defiantly over the ramparts. As a last coup to his failing plans, word came that a force of Americans under General Lane was advancing from Jalapa to Puebla.

The fight that followed was another example of Santa Anna's singularly defective generalship. He placed part of his force at the town of Huamantla and sent a strong detachment to El Pinal which he thought commanded the road coming from Jalapa. There he planned to fall upon the main body of Lane's troops by surprise and any that escaped would be dealt with in Huamantla. But when Lane's force approached, he found that the conditions of the terrain did not favor a surprise and that furthermore Lane's swift advance guards had entered Huamantla and routed his men there. The battle resolved itself into a race, Santa Anna galloping from El Pinal to cut down the Yankee advanced guards in Huamantla and Lane's infantry double-timing up to beat Santa Anna to his goal. The latter made a brilliant show with his lancers, pennons waving gaily in the wind as they raced for Huamantla. They reached there first, did much damage to the Yankee *vedettes* scampered ungallantly away as Lane's main body arrived.

He tried to rally his demoralized soldiers but in vain. His campaign against the Americans was definitely over and, sadly aware of the fact, he retired to Tehuacan, a small city about 75 miles south of Puebla where he established headquarters, an unwelcome guest whose presence the inhabitants feared would bring on American attacks. It seemed as if no one wanted to harbor him. He made a gesture of retreating south to Guatemala and exile, but to get there he would have to cross Oaxaca. Juarez, in command there, was an uncompromising enemy of His Excellency, and refused to let him pass.

So he had to reconcile himself to staying in the little town with his pretty wife and some of the trappings of his past splendor. Somewhat comfortable in temporary housekeeping, he was far from so in politics. In a moment of discouragement he relinquished his command of the army turning it over to General Reyes, but he sought to retain some title to power by informing the world that while he had resigned the Presidency he could always withdraw his resignation.

On this point he carried on an acrimonious controversy with the remains of the government which had gathered Querétaro. The government took the position that he could not, for some occult reason known only to the magicians who altered and interpreted Mexico's mercurial constitutional regulations, withdraw his resignation and that, further humiliation, he would have to stand trial for his sins as a defeated commander. It was a sentence of complete effacement and all that he could do was to parry it with all the vigor of his facile pen.

Sitting at his writing desk in Tehuacan he informed the

world that Congress had no power to try him and that he
was still *de jure* President. He intimated strongly that the
reason the solons were so obtuse toward him was that they
were engaged in the nefarious business of making a peace
favorable to the Yankee.

Indeed they were doing just that, for they could do no
other. Manuel Peña y Peña, the affable old Justice of the
Supreme Court, was characterized by such a great fund of
common sense and a corresponding incapacity—which
goes with it—to get ahead in the scramble of Mexican
politics that he was destined by nature to fill the ignoble
rôle of signing the necessary but unpopular peace with the
conquerors. As President *ad interim* he had an adversary
—or accomplice as the chauvinists would have it—who
met him more than a sympathetic half-way—Nicholas
Trist. This little bureaucrat exerted himself laboriously to
satisfy the appetites of the extreme annexationists in Washington and at the same time to protect the exquisite national sensibilities of the Mexicans. Polk's government
modestly wanted what they already had conquered, California, New Mexico and Texas to the Rio Grande ; Peña's
government needed some shreds of self-respect and a large
sum of money. It was Trist's congenial task to make a
peace out of these elements, but it was not accomplished
without the confusing diapason of Mexican internecine
life.

Peña had his hands full. First of all there were those
extraordinary individuals who after all the presumably decisive military rounds of the past two years, still preserved a
romantic belief that if the struggle was prolonged the
Yankees would be licked. Then the radical anti-clericals

desired to continue the war for their own Machiavelliar
reasons—to force the Yankees to take over the Mexicar
government and accommodate them with a Federalist sys
tem. The monarchists and imperialists with an eye cocke
on European intervention whooped it for war for equall
selfish purposes. Lastly the Santanistas argued for the
invariable nostrum—a Dictatorship under Don Antonic
One last bubbling over of these fermenting elements too
place in Querétaro but was crushed by a determined sho
of force from Peña's supporters. Peña concluded his e
tended conferences with Trist and a tentative treaty
peace was signed. The United States were to retain the
conquests, California and New Mexico; Texas was reco
nized as part of the United States; and the Mexicans 1
ceived the sum of $15,000,000. A few months later tl
treaty was confirmed by the Congresses of both nations a
by June 1848 the American forces were moving out
Mexico.

But meanwhile our hero had brought to a characteri
cally adventurous turn his dramatic rôle as Mexico's sav
from the Yankee peril. As he was sitting comfortably
his headquarters in Tehuacan contemplating his next
fiance of the traitorous Peña, only fifteen miles av
Colonel Jack Hays was whipping his mount with the f
of a hunter who is on top of his quarry, of a man v
hastens near the object of his vengeance—for the Te
Ranger leader with some six hundred men was at last
the point of catching a distinguished prize and wiping
the ancient score of the Alamo. He had travelled a l
road to reach this happy stage of his life work. First
appointment from President Polk to come to Mexico,

lowed by months of guerrilla fighting near Vera Cruz, then a hint as to the whereabouts of Old Peg Leg, permission rom Scott to make the raid and finally formation of the expeditionary force whose command he yielded to General Lane of the Regulars, assisted by Major Polk, brother of he President. But half the six hundred were his faithful, ncouth Texans and he was now near the goal. To various nembers of this party who afterwards wrote their memoirs ve owe the story of this expedition.

They had started from Puebla two days before, in the greatest secrecy, the object of their mission unknown to arrison and inhabitants alike, and they had proceeded with qual care, galloping by night over the barren mesas and ing artfully concealed in deserted haciendas by day with ders that not a man should show himself outside the cienda gates while the sun was up. It had rained and ormed during the first part of the journey, but on this ght the stars, seemingly so close in that high altitude, idly twinkled a Godspeed to them. They had hardly t their last place of hiding when hoof-beats and lights parently coming in their direction made them pause.

They cautiously surrounded the oncomer and found ight but a carriage drawn by four mules and containing Mexican gentleman and his servants. At the Rangers' uest he alighted and graciously consented to answer stions which General Lane and Colonel Hays put to 1. He was Miguel Mosso and yes, he had just seen ta Anna at the village of Tehuacan some fifteen miles y. And would the general have the kindness to allow to proceed, for see, here was a safe-conduct pass signed by the American General Persifier Smith, commandant of this district.

His papers were clearly genuine, but Hays, who wished nothing to intervene between him and the imminent capture, insisted that Señor Mosso be detained for a few hour at least as a precaution. He was seconded by most of the other officers but opposed by General Lane who objected on the ground that a safe-conduct pass should be scrupulously respected. "Don't you know that the penalty for violation of such a pass is death?" An argument that failed to move the fearless Hays and he only submitted when Lane used his authority as commander to order the release of the Mexican.

The two parties left in opposite directions, the cavalry so impatient now that in spite of the unfamiliar country they were soon cantering into the little hamlet of Tehuacan. The silent streets returned a rather ominous echo to the clatter and the principal house of the village had its gate open with a rather disquieting hospitality. Santa Anna's headquarters and not a soul in them! The bird had indeed flown. Little did they know—but strongly did they suspect—that Señor Mosso after leaving them, had detached one of his mules and sent a servant by a short cut to warn the General. With his staff, his personal family and an escort of cavalry Santa Anna was racing over the mountains to Tenotitlan where safety and a large body of troops awaited him.

But he left behind—albeit unwillingly—a house full of trophies whose splendor was enough to detain even the most eager pursuers. For the Americans, rushing from room to room, surrendered their disappointment to a feeling of overwhelming wonder. Hatred of the Mexican and chagrin for the thwarting of their hopes changed to astonishment at the furnishings of the house. From huge regal beds, to sumptuous draperies, from elegant escritoires to bejeweled knick-knacks the soldiers went gaping and exclaiming.

They noted with satisfaction a candle tipped over leaving a trail of wax on a green tablecloth — evidence of the confusion their approach had wrought. And a white satin cover fastidiously tied with pink ribbons was bisected by a long black stain, still wet, leading from an overturned crystal ink-stand. What a cumbrous and imposing bed this was, manifestly a State affair, with posts reaching to the ceiling, and what a lark the unpacking of seventeen large trunks provided !

An amusing scene, with a rough cavalry officer examining a pretty satin slipper doubtless meant for the tiny foot of Doña Santa Anna ; another holding up to view her full court toilette. Dresses they found in surprising numbers, certainly enough to stagger these rough creatures whose humble wives were never adorned with anything better than calico. A coat of Santa Anna's was discovered, a garment so heavily embroidered with gold braid that the soldiers were inspired to put it on the scales and found that it weighed fifteen pounds. Here was a sash almost as thickly gilded as the coat ; there a life-size portrait of the general himself frowning out from the ornamental frame at this desecrating scene ; and finally the most fascinating treasure of all in a long green velvet case.

It was a cane of wondrous beauty. The staff was of polished steel, a humble metal which served to set off the top of solid gold. This took the form of an eagle blazing

with diamonds, sapphires and emeralds, the beak containing one immense diamond, and other jewels in the claws,
etc.   The Texans gazed enraptured at the resplendent object ; then with one accord they cried out :
    "Give it to Colonel Jack."
    Trooping into the next room where General Lane was
reclining on a bed and the Ranger leader was sitting on a
cane chair, the Texans made the presentation and Hays
accepted it as befitted a citizen of that State which had
collected few spoils from Don Antonio and his country.
As the room was still ringing with words of admiration at
the beauty of the cane, Major Polk walked in and inno-
cently remarked with none of the tact which he should have
learned during his service as U. S. Minister to the Kingdom
of Naples : "I should like such a thing as this very much
to give to my brother."
    But Hays, rough frontiersman as he was, remarked with
diplomatic suavity : "I have no use for such an ornament
Take it, Major, and give it to the President and say it is
present from the Texans."
    Væ Victis and ere the Rangers left, these interesting spoil
were divided as recompense for their disappointment on no
encountering their proprietor.   The sash of gold was a
lotted to the State of Texas, the oil portrait to Indiana, th
crystal ink-stand to Governor Downey, and a moroc
bound volume artistically tooled with the inscription "Señ
General de Division Benemerito de la Patria, Don Anton
Lopez de Santa Anna," etc., to the expedition's surgeo
But the trunks full of feminine garments were sent
Señora Santa Anna with General Lane's expression of ho

that the next time he found her dresses he would find her in them.

But the Rangers found plenty to do to forget the miscarriage of their adventure. For a long time they had been the terror of the guerrillas, who formed the most troublesome part of Mexican resistance after the dispersal of Santa Anna's armies. The most picturesque and blood-thirsty leader of these desperadoes was one Jarauta, who had learned this sanguinary trade in Spain during the Carlist troubles. Quick, murderous raids on wagon trains or small squads of Americans followed by rapid retreats into the tropical jungle were his *forte*. Fantastic mutilation too, of unfortunate Yankees, but this only whetted the Rangers' thirst for revenge.

Some of them were in familiar territory, for the center of their activities was Perote where the dungeons of the huge, gloomy fortress had held many Texans captured during the ill-fated Santa Fe expedition in '42. There, during this period of imprisonment, one of their number, Captain Walker, had been made to dig a pit for a flag-pole. With a gesture of defiance he swore that the Americans would return one day and capture this place; and as an evidence of his assurance he placed a ten-cent piece at the base of the pole. When he did return in '47 the coin was there to corroborate his story.

Not only Jarauta and his bandit groups learned to fear the Texans. After the fall of the capital, many Texans were quartered in the City of Mexico whose inhabitants acquired a profound dread of them. The *leperos* had a habit of sneaking up on inebriated Yankees, stabbing them in the back and leaving them to expire in the dark. But the Texans took to simulating drunkenness, with one hand on their reliable Colts, and taught some salutary lessons to the murderers. Whenever a Texan was found dead, his fellows would shoot up the quarter thereabouts leaving dozens of Mexicans dead and wounded as a warning. "Texas Vengeance" indeed became proverbial and the Mexicans came to consider them devils incarnate.

After the provisional peace had been signed Santa Anna humbly applied to the Americans for a safe-conduct pass to leave the country. It was granted and a Colonel Hughes was named to take charge of an escort for Don Antonio. A Yankee poetaster's stanza seemed appropriate now —

> "At San Jacinto, long ago
> I gained my early fame.
> To Vera Cruz, I'm starting now
> Because, you know, I'm lame."

Colonel Hughes, a Maryland officer, with his aide, Major Kenly, gallantly invited him to a banquet near Perote. With no little curiosity then did the Americans await the appearance of this famous warrior and politician, so long depicted as a horrible monster of cruelty and treachery.

When the *videttes* announced that his carriage was approaching, the Marylanders formed to receive him, and as the cavalcade, consisting of a body of smartly uniformed lancers, came up followed by a carriage drawn by eight mules, Major Kenly gave the command "Present Sabers!" The carriage halted and the ex-President, his wife and daughter alighted. But instead of a ferocious ogre, griffon in human form, it was only a stout, middle-aged gentleman in an olive coat and brass buttons, and a s expression of countenance who acknowledged their salute as he teetered uncertainly on his cork leg. The Major could not contain his astonishment and exclaimed how much the General resembled his own father back in Maryland.

But their wonder extended to Doña Santa Anna and well did they approve the name given her by the Mexicans, "The Flower of Mexico." Her extreme youth — she seemed hardly more than eighteen — contrasted with her husband's aged appearance, and accustomed to the swarthy half-Indian squaws of the country, the Americans were ravished by her fair skin, hazel eyes, dark hair, sweet little mouth and teeth, "rivaling ivory in beauty." A perfect lady, too, courtly and gracious as if she were presiding in the National Palace in Mexico City.

Over the mangoes and the wine, Anglo-Saxon cordiality mingled with the polished courtesy of the Mexicans. American lieutenants exchanged compliments with Santa Anna's aides, the Doña chatted vivaciously with Colonel Hughes and the General passed the cigars, while all sympathized with Señorita Santa Anna, a thin, worried little girl of fifteen. She had endured months of hiding and pursuit with ill grace and complained that her education had been neglected for she was always on the march, "siempre caminando." The afternoon was wearing on, when Major Kenly noticed among the curious who were looking in the doorway at the gathering, a familiar face which struck terror in his heart.

It was none other than the stolid visage of Colonel Jack Hays, who with his Rangers was stationed not far from Perote. Kenly was well aware of how the Texans felt

about Santa Anna and doubted not that this appearance of
their former enemy would arouse talk of revenge.   Struck
by a sudden and audacious inspiration, he rose from the
table, went to the door and asked the Ranger leader to come
and meet General Santa Anna.   Jack Hays uttered a long
reluctant "Well" which was as good as an assent and followed the Major   "General, let me present to you"—he
paused as the General looked up from some fruit he was
eating—"Colonel Jack Hays."

The name came as a veritable bomb-shell to the whole
table.   The Mexican officers arose from their seats and
stood tense and motionless.   The Señora turned pale, but
she blanched even less than her husband whose whole appearance and demeanor, a minute before so gay and
gracious, changed.   But Colonel Hays with gentlemanly
unconcern as if nothing had happened, bowed politely and
retired.   By this time Kenly was thoroughly nervous
Rumors came to him of a projected Texan attack on the
General and he arranged that the Santa Anna carriage
should be surrounded by files of cavalry bearing the Ameri
can flag.

If he had known what was taking place in the Texan'
camp, however, he might have been even more upset.   Fo
when the Rangers first learned that Santa Anna was ap
proaching, revenge became the reigning topic.   All the
officers had gone off either to Perote or Jalapa—they wer
stationed along the road between the two towns—and th
rank and file were "at a white heat" as one of them put
Captain Ford by some chance learned of the uproar ar
returned.   But when he saw the frenzy of his men,

General Winfield Scott

Contemporary print of Santa Anna

knew that he could not hope to restrain them by the authority of his rank.

He commenced to argue with them and to attempt to dissuade them from their resolution to exact blood vengeance for their murdered comrades of the Alamo and Goliad. To Ford's assertions that the world had already punished the Mexican by its horror-stricken condemnation, and that Texas had won a victory by its magnanimous release of him in 1836, they only replied that he had murdered prisoners in cold blood. When their officer retorted that Santa Anna was a prisoner now, they replied that he was not technically a prisoner of war. Old arguments that twelve years before had impassioned Sam Houston, Stephen Austin, Colonel Rusk and Mirabeau Lamar were revived and thrown back and forth, until Ford warned them that the death of Santa Anna would be a "blemish on the fair name of Texas."

That indeed mollified them and at the prospect of dishonoring Texas, they relented, "Then we will not do it." Their humor changed now and they insisted on riding up to the banquet and having a friendly chat with their old enemy. But Ford vetoed this; "No, boys, not a word. We will align you on the road and enable you to see the General as he passes but you must observe profound silence while he is in hearing." The line was formed on each side of the road and the Texans stood in silence as they awaited the approach of the General's carriage.

Major Kenly meanwhile had communicated some of his apprehension to the Mexican coachmen who without any orders whipped their mules into a gallop, shouting "Upas, Upas" to the animals. Kenly rode in front with saber drawn as he approached the Texan camp and the cortège followed at a killing pace. The General sat bolt upright, stiff and silent, not a little pale, for he was undoubtedly aware of the circumstances. The daughter crouched down beside him and Doña Santa Anna, either unconscious of the situation or unusually game, smiled and bowed to their undemonstrative spectators. It was over in a minute, with the cavalcade dashing down toward Jalapa and the Texans watching the departure silently, their last leave-taking with this man who had once again escaped their vengeance.

Well might he show his gratitude to the Marylanders by a luncheon the next day at his pretty hacienda "El Encero" where he proposed to wait for the Havana packet. The place was set high on a spur of the mountains with the lofty peak of Orizaba in the background and far below the blue waters of the Gulf. After lunch he permitted his visitors to watch an interesting ceremony. Striding up and down, with passionate gesture and dramatic intonation, he dictated to several industrious secretaries his farewell proclamation to the Mexican people, one of those flowery documents whose elegant prevarications he knew so well how to compose. It was preceded by the customary "Fellow Citizens," and at the bottom, below the bold signature was the inscription which this superb rascal never omitted and which suggests perhaps that he was a subtle ironist—"For God and Liberty !"

When on April 9th he boarded the English packet a La Antigua, he doubtless entertained far from blithe reflec tions. It was from this port in 1823 that Iturbide ha departed from his overthrown Empire, and Santa Anna lef his native land, his power apparently as severely shattere as that of Agustín I. With the self-pity that was characte

istic of him he might well have felt bitterly against Mexico
for her repudiation of his efforts.   Had not Roa Gamboa,
various deputies, and the Capital press assailed not only his
military policies but also his patriotism and integrity?
Had he not left a pleasant, a comfortable exile in Havana
to perspire and harrow his soul on the plains of Mexico?
Had he not for such an ungrateful people mortgaged a considerable portion of his property in the defense of these
unsympathetic plebs, who now offered him no security that
he would ever get these sums back?

Yet he might well have felt the satisfaction, reviewing his
career of the past eighteen months with detachment—if,
that is, he was ever capable of detachment—of feeling that
he was well deserving this time surely of the title of Defender of the *Patria*.   For through the peculiarities of the
situation he had been able to exert his talents to the fullest,
to have served as the most capable instrument that the country could find, and to have attained the most genuine laurels
of his military record.

At Angostura he had transcended all his former efforts
in war and with one inspired lunge had attained the summit
of his career as a soldier.   His handling of his men was
well-nigh flawless, his disposition of forces, his courageous
inspiration of his troops and his indomitable energy brought
him within a hair-breadth of an overwhelming triumph.
That he did not follow through to a complete rout of
Taylor's men was due more to factors beyond his control
than anything.   He had reason to feel proud.

He had labored with commendable energy and zeal at
Cerro Gordo, he had made the best of a bad job at Padierna,
Contreras, salvaging the corps thrown into confusion

by another commander. He had rallied these men with
great resiliency and directed them in the bloody engagement of Churubusco, forcing Scott to pay most dearly for
his empty victory of that day. At Molino del Rey, at
Chapultepec, at San Cosme Gate he had displayed great
courage and indefatigable activity in trying to defend the
already doomed Capital. He clearly deserved the *Benemerito* for these embattled days.

Naturally his notable defects as a commander were most
obvious in these campaigns. He could evoke a splendid
conception, an attractive plan or coup, but he customarily
failed to take into account its possible failure and to make
provisions for miscarriage of his designs. Thus at the
bristling redoubt of El Peñon he suffered his most mortify-
ing disappointment by assuming that Scott would attack
there, and only there. Likewise at Cerro Gordo, he out-
lined a rather imperfect defense, and while the defeat was
only partly due to the fiasco of La Atalaya, he was respon
sible as a commander for the neglect of this important hill
An open ear to advice and counsel—of which he was repre
hensibly intolerant—would have saved him much troubl
in such situations.

But his long series of defeats and disappointments—i
the latter category, Angostura which was practically
drawn battle—were due to the "system" which he himse!
had a strong rôle in building up. National disunion in
crisis which might be traced back to his own high-hande
policy with the various States, a debauched treasury an
fiscal régime which could not furnish funds or supplies th
preventing a victory at Angostura, a corrupt and fantas
cally immoral military caste of which he was the most ou

standing example, and a ragged, undisciplined soldiery, the fruits of years of military abuses which he never attempted to remedy — all these factors, all these sins came back to him in these trying times and checked his every move.

Yet all these forces together with the extraordinary political conditions were the exigencies, the checks and balances on his power which held him in line, and enabled him to accomplish as much as he did. When he landed at Vera Cruz in September '46 and found a hostile country taking him on sufferance as a soldier only, he was placed in a groove where his peculiar talents were best served. The problems of ruling the nation, always too profound for his restricted intellect, were not of his concern, and he could concentrate his energies — which were formidable — on the military campaigns. Likewise, absence of political power prevented him from engaging in his puerile foolery with baubles of office, emoluments, fawning of sycophant politicians and all the other seductions to which he was all too ready to yield.

The logic of circumstances, too, served Mexico well by placing him at the head of her armies. She had a large stable to choose from, true, but what pitiful stallions. The braggart and traitorous Valencia, the bejewelled and empty-headed Lombardini, Alvarez the *guerrillero* of the Sierras, the amateur general-politician Herrera, Paredes the visionary *pronunciado,* Arista a lesser Santa Anna, and Ampudia, corrupt and willing to sell his country ; thus ran the rôle of her Pretorians, and while our hero combined all their defects, he was their superior in capacities and energy, and had the good sense to recognize and to follow the main chance. Well did the British Minister sum up his importance during the war : "Be his errors what they may, he is the only Mexican who could have created the forces he has managed to get together for the defense of his country." In other words, he was the best possible man for the job of repelling the Yankee.

That he landed in Vera Cruz by the courtesy of James K. Polk and surveyed the task before him through the narrowed eye-lids of an opportunist, of one who wishes to gain much personally from the situation, is true. Likewise, that he would have tried to carry out his agreements with Mackenzie, if they coincided with his ambitions and if they fitted into the circumstances—that too is to his discredit, or credit, for such a course might have saved Mexico all the horrors of the latter part of the war and obtained for her a better bargain in the peace. But in such a course Santa Anna would, just as he found he had to do, have made the best of matters for his own personal advantage. Advantage, yes, but not necessarily pecuniary aggrandizement. However imperfect a patriot he was, it is unfair to claim that he would have sold his country, in the baldest sense of the word. He did not care for money, except in so far as it nourished and fed his own steps to power. He would have accepted American gold, but only to further himself as the political and military head of the Santanist faction. Within those narrow limits, he was a patriot Mexican.

And as such he was eminently the product and most picturesque example of his time. For Mexico was filled with opportunists who were willing to "sell" their country either for their own personal advancement or the furthering of their own creeds and ideologies. The Imperialist doubtless convinced that a foreign prince and strong despotism would have best put order in the lamentable conditions of the country were, many of them, sincere. Among the Conservative leaders there were sincere men, like Lucas Alamán, who earnestly desired to promote the good of their country in this manner. Nor were the liberals free from this opportunism. It is undoubtedly true that many of them wanted Scott and his American troops to remain in Mexico and to support a liberal government. This would have meant a real American intervention beside which the French intervention a score of years later would seem like a minor matter. It would have meant that the liberals would bear the odium of intervention, the charge of being traitors, charges which they themselves hurled at the conservatives during the French intervention. It is not improbable, nay highly possible, from his policies and his actions, to indict the liberal Gomez Farias on the charge of "selling" his country. His "betrayal" might have turned out for the best, just as Santa Anna's or Paredes' schemes — that is simply one of the unproven hypotheses of the intricate mathematics of Mexican politics.

CHAPTER XII

GILDED ᴄАPOGEE

SANTA ANNA stayed in Kingston, Jamaica, for two years, at the end of which time he had little to show save a string of prize cocks and an inter minable pamphlet defending his military actions in the wa with the United States. It was published in Mexico bu it aroused little notice, for under Santa Anna's old frien and rival, Arista, the Mexicans had another military satra to watch, cheer and hiss. His show of revolts and counter revolts, half-measures and proscriptions occupied the cer ter of the stage for three years — a longevity of régime tribute in itself to his ability as a *jefe*. But in Jamaica San Anna chafed at the stiff English customs and people, an he sought the tropical, Hispanic environment of Cartagen in the Republic of Colombia.

"The Queen of the Indies," with its old walled parape where pirates and hidalgos had fought it out for centurie was now a quiet little fruit port. But not quiet enoug for our fatigued hero who moved to a little town a few mil from Cartagena called Turbaco. It had all the lowla atmosphere, all the miasmic vapors on which Santa An had always thrived and he came to like it. Particula because he chose, with his unerring flair for the histrion a house once occupied by none other than Bolivar hims

The *Libertador* of Mexico in the house of the *Libertador* of South America ! How he exploited this in his mail to Mexico.

But he did more than posture. He bought an extensive estate here and set himself up as a landed proprietor. He introduced the cultivation of sugar to the country, then followed with tobacco, and taught the natives how to raise herds similar to those which roamed his vast estates between Jalapa and Vera Cruz. He was apparently so enamoured of Turbaco that he had a tomb built for himself in the local cemetery. The natives, overwhelmed by such a novel idea, and moved by local pride in the agricultural innovations of their guest, issued proclamations of thanks and gratitude to him. To all appearances he was settled here for life.

Perhaps the unusually long reign of Arista lulled him into a sort of desuetude, but he was not forgotten in Mexico by any means. His old friend Lombardini was forging to the front and, after Arista descended from the chair, was one of the obvious candidates for President. Tornel was lurking about and the Santanista party was a recognized part of any combination. After Arista's retirement — which was caused by his failure to hold some of the rising chieftains down and by an unruly Congress — the Chief Justice Ceballos took charge. He was a weak politician and was soon supplanted by Lombardini.

This extraordinary looking man was the best example *absurdis* of the military type. Tall and heavy, with a voice whose resonancy made audible his commands if it did not make them respected, he boasted that his *bigotes,*—as he called the strange Kaiser Wilhelm type of mustachios which the military caste in Mexico affects — were so stiffly waxed that not the strongest wind could move them. He had an infantile love of medals and military decorations, his breast being so thoroughly covered with such trinkets that he was often called "The Jewelry Shop." With this array of finery augmented by extra borders of gold and glittering epaulettes he made a striking figure. But he had the good sense to realize that he was not strong enough to hold power long, for he regarded his term of provisional President as but a preparation for Santa Anna's return.

He lavished over a thousand commissions on the army within a few months, a reminder, as it were, of what they might expect to follow ; he dipped his hand liberally in the public treasury, squandering some funds allocated for Indian relief, and he granted some very lucrative concessions to foreign capitalists who had a way of showing their gratitude in a pecuniary manner. Finally he had a decree put through Congress declaring that a dictator should be elected for a short period until public order was restored with a special provision that a citizen living outside Mexico could be eligible. Everyone knew for whom this was meant ; Lombardini was an excellent prelude for the return of our hero.

Indeed the people seemed to want him back — in one of those charitable phases of the Mexican temperament which alternated between hate and admiration for their most gorgeous soldier-cock. It was recalled that after all he was the most patriotic and energetic defender against the Americans in the late war, and his defeats at the Yankees' hands were forgiven. Also his voluntary return to exile was made to appear a great act of self-immolation although he had

taken three months of vain plotting to make up his mind.
The soldiery recalled his concern for their pay, promotions
and adequate costuming, and their influence was far from
negligible. Finally, the old cry for a dictator was heard,
and even highly intelligent men such as Lucas Alamán, the
minister and historian, felt that if properly coached and restrained, Santa Anna could place the country under effective
order and control.

As soon as the tide turned, there was a scramble to mount
the band wagon such as always occurred when his return to
power was heralded. All sorts of inhabitants of the capital
who hailed originally from the *tierra caliente* maintained
that they were related to him, legitimately or illegitimately
—which considering his notorious sexual promiscuity was
not altogether improbable. Various words of *jaracho* argot
became the fad, and even the most cultured people affected
the accent indigenous to Vera Cruz and environs. Por-
raits of him that had remained dust-covered since that fatal
December 6th, 1844, were gotten out, and there was talk
of hunting up the leg and placing it in its regal urn in the
principal cemetery ; the theatre reverted to the old name of
Teatro Santa Anna. All was ready for the Grand Old
Prestidigitator to return.

But he lived up to his last farewell word—he waited not
only until he was called, but until a delegation called on
him in Turbaco. The scheming occupants of the band
wagon were so jealous of one another and even distrusted
their idol so much, that they sent three members ; each one
spy on the other and to prevent Santa Anna from con-
versing privately with any one of their colleagues.

They found him in the old house in Turbaco, a bit the

worse for the ravages of age and campaigns. His visage had perceptibly hardened, doubtless by the bitter memories of his defeats and the assaults of his enemies, military and literary. His white teeth still shone intact but the mouth had drooped, the lower lip now pendant and the nose fat and vulgar instead of as formerly statuesquely heroic. His eyes were still attractive with a formidable steely glint, brow as formerly that of an old tragedian, hair now lusterless and thin, the upper lip still shaven—alone among his caste without the *bigotes*—and the same Vera Cruzan pronunciation. Moreover, the famous leg was as of yore of cork, for he still disdained the mechanical limbs which so many artisans had designed for him. And he retained that pristine note of command in his musical voice, so admirably modulated to condescend with conciliatory compliments when necessary.

As one of the envoys wrote: "Many times did I ask myself on what did he base this power of suggestion—this singular man who confessed that he had never read but one book in his life, that he had pronounced for the constitution and the republic because these vocables had seemed more euphonious than those of Empire and Monarchy; that he had oppressed and pillaged without fear or hesitation; and I came to believe that all his prestige arose perhaps from knowing how to utter phrases which sounded well in the ears of this people who were formed to esteem words more than their content and to devour the brilliant and attractive skin of the fruit, leaving aside the pulp which was soapy in taste and of ugly aspect."

The envoys tried to draw the conversation around their business but the sly old man put them off, asking

about his friends in Mexico, the faithful puppy Sierra y
Rosso, Alamán the conservative Seneca, the arch-intriguer
Tornel, the clever Haro y Tamariz and Miguel Mosso who
had rescued him from the Americans' expedition.   On the
latter subject he was profuse with hatred—"Our natural
enemies"—and he dwelt bitterly on the loss of his clothes
and ornaments.   From that he got around to the leg—
the inevitable focal point of his plaints and self-pity—speak-
ingly solemnly of his sacrifice of the limb and the ingrati-
tude of his compatriots.   Then with the gesture of an
hidalgo he swept his arm to draw attention to the country
and his estate, painting its beauties in his mellifluous
phrases, emphasizing how happy he was to remain here in
peace, far from mad and muddled Mexico.

The envoys were somewhat disheartened at this expression of content, but their hopes rose when he started to
assail the late President Arista and contrasted him—glittering hint—to a "man who loves virtue and morals,"
asking rhetorically why the people preferred such a monster to their natural benefactor.   A good lead and they
plunged into their mission, taking heart as the old hunter
listened keenly with avid interest.   After some hours of
talk, he rolled out the following : "My heart is nothing if
it is not Mexican ; in spite of all the past I desire that my
compatriots know how dear they are to me.   I do not want
History to say some day that when I was called to make
the happiness of the people, I saw with indifference their
fate.   You can return on the next packet and say to those
who sent you that in the month of March I shall set out
from here for the shores of Mexico."

It was on April 1st—whose risible associations were not

unrecalled—that the guns of Ulloa boomed and the exile descended from the English packet *Avon* and walked in triumph to the thunder of "vivas" under an arch erected to resemble Napoleon's Étoile arch in Paris. He went through the routine of *besamanos* and Te Deums in the church and he read the proclamation which was a composite of the work of Alamán, Sierra y Rosso and other anxious advisers but which he alleged he had "dashed off" on ship-board. It was packed with "your friend" and "your fellow citizen" and was a mass of hollow oratory. He received hosts of friends at his hacienda Encero.

There on the verandahs overlooking the Vera Cruzan Eden and the blue waters of the bay of Campeche, the most curious *olla podrida* of various political parties gathered. The clergy were heavily represented and their spokesman talked of Santa Anna in terms of the Fathers of the Church; "This new Gideon, this well-beloved of the people, this unconquerable hero, this defender of religion, this star of the Occident—the illustrious exile of Kingston (sic)."

The *agiotistas*—profiteers—were there, headed by the crafty Escandón, eager for concessions and pecuniary favors. They wanted our hero to recognize some four million worth of debts which the recent government had contracted from them; they wanted to obtain the custom concession, the tobacco monopoly, and the much talked about projected railway from Vera Cruz to the capital. Gravely and receptively he listened to these men. Then there were the old militarists who nodded their heads as they had long predicted his return—"One can't have sermon without St. Augustine nor a revolution without Santa Anna."

There was Haro y Tamariz, who hated Escandón, and Suárez y Navarro, an ally who detested both of these. Then there was Sierra y Rosso dashing off sonnets in honor of his return, Lombardini shining like a Christmas tree and smiling to his military clique with triumph at his success in getting back their champion. Only one dissenting voice. A deputy from Puebla who warned him about his past errors and expressed the hope that he had reformed—an awkward and unfortunate speech for which his last landing at Vera Cruz had set the precedent.

A pretty bit of by-play took place now as the new Dictator approached the capital. Haro who had returned there several days previously from Vera Cruz satisfied with Santa Anna's equivocations that he held the reins of power, went forth to the gates of the city to witness the grand arrival and was greatly upset to see Santa Anna riding in Escandón's coach with his bitter enemy beside him—an ominous association. Little did he know that the enterprising business man had in his pocket a receipt for eight hundred thousand pesos in payment for the tobacco monopoly. The *leperos* in their enthusiasm unhitched the mules and drew the carriage themselves to the Sagrario where a Te Deum was heard, following which ceremony the Archbishop escorted him across the Plaza to the National Palace.

He closed himself in his chambers, but one man had a key to a secret door giving him access to the new Dictator. That was the aged and cultured Conservative Alamán. He was perhaps the most intelligent and learned man in public politics, a Mexican Thiers, and he believed in a rule of iron, with order restored, the Church respected, industry encouraged and the country developed. He believed in building up the country, but not along the lines of self-government; and he was not inclined to remedy the abuses in the army and the Church. Thus a sincere, but reactionary statesman was the first to guide Santa Anna on his return.

Yet for one Alamán there were many others less altruistic who struggled for his confidence and favor. Haro y Tamariz, big, bluff, a man of the lower bourgeoisie speaking in the slang of the capital, a parvenu who sought higher ranks and dominance, yet not without ability. A good man if watched. Then there was the literary Suarez y Navarro who composed a biography of the Dictator, one long paean of praise for the successes of Tampico and Vera Cruz; he wanted to be Minister of War. And weaving his subtle way among all was Lorenzo the Magnificent, for so they called Tornel for his patronage of arts and letters — his act of contrition for numerous cold-blooded plots.

However, the constructive ideas of Alamán and Haro seemed to prevail at first. The military methods of the army were reformed, with Prussian and French instructor teaching the men how to maneuver and better than that the generals how to handle large bodies of men. Education — albeit only among the bourgeoisie — was fostered and the Jesuits who had done so much in this direction in the eighteenth century were recalled. But the most material achievement was the creation of the Department of Fomento or Public Works, which started a road building program, took steps for the encouragement of infant indu tries, built telegraphs, then just coming into Mexico, and made surveys for the construction of a railroad. Lastly a corps of able lawyers renovated the sadly dilapidated judicial system.

The country was well policed and disorder was severely put down, the first in many years. Colonization of great areas in the provinces was arranged for, and mining received an impetus. In the finances Haro put some order, and although the expenditure increased greatly, only a small deficit resulted, which Haro proposed to raise by a loan on Church property. A dangerous suggestion, for the clergy arose in wrath and Haro had to resign ; another of Santa Anna's supports removed, for Alamán died two months after the new government went into power.

With such able advisers gone, our hero commenced to move from one extravagance to another. He suppressed all the state legislatures, even city councils, and completed the most thorough centralization that the Republic had ever seen. All folk had to come to Mexico City for favors, and even petty legal matters had to be handled in this way. Lawyers in order to get their licenses had to journey to Mexico City and pay tribute ere they could practice in Sonora or Yucatan. To carry this out a huge bureaucracy, with prefects, sub-prefects, head clerks and petty clerks was formed, holding office by their fidelity to Santa Anna rather than by their ability. Santa Anna gave jobs as prefects to various military men whom he knew how to handle.

A Secret Police was organized, a veritable *Cheka* which pursued all suspected of opposing our hero. Old Federalists, Conservatives who became critical when rebuffed, military enemies were all under surveillance and sooner or later found their way to the dungeons, or to an outgoing packet from Vera Cruz. A score of prominent heterodox papers were suppressed within the month of May, 1853. "Democracy has caused more damage than the *matlazahuatl*," the ancient black death of the Aztecs which recurred at intervals in colonial times—thus droned the Conservatives in approval of the censorship. Santa Anna preached a crusade against his military enemies by decreeing that all those who surrendered to the Americans during the late war should be prosecuted.

Thus did he start a thorough purging and re-organization of the army along personal lines. All his old adversaries were eliminated and his friends elevated. Commissions were distributed liberally. Often for money, for it was said that Doña Santa Anna established a sort of court, obtaining higher ranks for innumerable of her courtiers and at times virtually auctioning off colonelcies and generals' grades. The progressive degeneration of officers naturally followed. They became lazy and untrained, not taking the trouble to go through maneuvers in winter, alleging the cold as an excuse, and in summer the heat. When they did consent to study tactics, they were followed by *cargadores* who carried their guns or accoutrements. "Three-quarter soldiers" and "Ay Mamma's," they were called. Little could the Prussian drillmasters do with this material.

An army of ninety thousand was raised, mostly regulars for the National Guard was suppressed. They were easier to manage; the favoritism, peculation and spy system insured almost perfect loyalty, so that—one advance—there were no pronouncements disturbing the corps. Santa Anna even had his men hunt down the peasants in Jic who in 1844 had captured and delivered him to the Herrera forces.   Vindictive and terrible was the hand of iron now and well did a pamphlet which managed to get published somehow shriek : "Neither Nero, nor Caligula, nor Dionysius of Syracuse are comparable to Santa Anna.   He eclipses all these, putting Mexico under a black tyranny."

Nero in one respect certainly, for he was prodigal with the *panem et circenses*.   However much the plebs might be "oppressed" they had plenteous entertainment to divert their stifled spirits.   Santa Anna now transcended that tawdry épopée of 1842-44 and gave to Mexico the gaudiest show since Bucareli, Vice-roy and Captain General of New Spain, mounted the resplendent throne in the National Palace.   In the fall of 1853 he became a bit apprehensive about the stability of his title of Dictator — a provisional office only.   Soon after some hot young officers declared a Plan at Guadalajara demanding that this title should be made perpetual for the good of the country.

But these ambitious and rising young fellows were to be outdone by others eager also to rise in the esteem of this god-head of promotion and pecuniary favor.   Therefore when they suggested that Dictator, a blunt brutal word, should be replaced with "His Serene Highness," it followed immediately that this was made superlative, "His Most Serene Highness," thus surpassing Iturbide's title which was but the modest "Serene Highness."   Others vied with these and suggested, in quick succession, "Marshal," "Grand Admiral," in view of his decree that the Mexican Navy be increased to all of twelve vessels.   Others wanted "Grand Elector" and the army, slow of wits but feeling that it should outdistance all, pronounced for "The Savior of

Mexico." Curiously enough, the strongest suggestions came from little hamlets where a few peons hoed *frijoles ;* they wanted, so it was said, an "Emperor." But Santa Anna, mindful of the failure associated with Emperor Iturbide, did not share these peons' enthusiasm. However, it served to make the others sound less ridiculous.

So in one form or another the Plan of Guadalajara was warmly supported. Santa Anna inclined his head graciously. He was moved by all this splendid devotion and enthusiasm, he intimated, but he knew where his path lay, through duty and sound principles which he could not desert for any title, or unconstitutional proposal. Then followed more expostulations, more remonstrances, appealing to the Savior of Mexico to keep the country from anarchy by the only means possible. Finally our hero reluctantly acceded to the request to save the country. He would make the supreme sacrifice for the Patria. On December 16th he was proclaimed His Most Serene Highness and his dictatorship was declared to be indefinitely prolonged. He modestly declined the offer of captain general at this time. He had to draw a limit, it seemed.

Santa Anna now became less a man than a ritual, a highly colored and complicated rite demanding of its worshippers homage unfailingly accorded. How hieratic, how resplendent, in his gorgeous uniform he looked on that fine winter morning in 1853 seated in his carriage with the Commandant of his army riding near him like postilion ! For he had just revived the Order of Guadalupe which Iturbide had founded, with its brummagem nobles and castes, its ceremonies and services, and was now riding in the first Grand Procession. Over his blue unform he wore a cape of the same color with borders of gold in intricate patterns of circles, palms and caracols. From the collar hung a cross of gold, two arms of which bore the colors of the national flag and the center an image of the Virgin. On the top of the upper arm was an eagle and on the lower a palm and an olive branch. The center bore the legend "For Heroic Patriotism." It was the High Grand Cross of the Order of Our Lady of Guadalupe.

His carriage was in the center of the glittering parade. At the head of the procession pranced four mounted guards, flawlessly dressed and followed by a quartet of adjutants. Then the Scribe of the Order carrying stylus and scroll with two assistants in his wake. Behind these the Caballeros —Cavaliers—whose robes of blue were bordered with white taffeta and whose boots were adorned with the national coat of arms, a non-military group of the order. Then came the Grand Crosses, the cream of this overnight hierarchy, the aristocracy of this parvenu Empire, for our hero had given the accolade to various powerful generals and *agiotistas* who had risen from their knees as Count of Santiago, Marquis of Salvatierra, Marquis of Aycinena, Marquis of Guadalupe, etc. Their insignia was similar but smaller than that of His Most Serene Highness and in addition these nobles were permitted a plaque of gold garnished with diamonds to be worn on the left side ; and these too were discreetly smaller than the President's. Bringing up the rear were the city officials, the congressmen, the cabinet secretaries and companies of soldiers.

As they approached the shrine of Guadalupe, cannon roared a salute. Santa Anna stiffly emerged from his coach and entered the holy place where Archbishop Lazaro de la Garza y Ballestros escorted him to a dais near the altar. His wife and offspring, as befitted members of a royal family, sat near behind him and listened to the hymn, "Veni Creator," — a title that suggests further adulation of His Most Serene Highness. Before the clergy could mount the pulpit, our hero made a dignified speech urging on the members of the Order to practice honor, fraternity and patriotism.

But one may imagine him dreaming a bit during the sermon that followed, recalling the occasion when he heard the harsh order : "Sir, in the Emperor's presence, everyone stands," and his rage and ambition which these words aroused. An ambition which had raised him finally, now, to a position that even Emperor Agustín I might have envied. For here was his apogee — his gilded apogee Was he not acclaimed by plebs, by bourgeoisie, by military ? Nay by God Himself, for had not the Pope issued a bull *Ne Dum Tituli* especially for this occasion ? But as he sa in his chair of honor and listened to the preacher cens him with florid compliments, his still handsome visag wore that melancholy brooding expression so often note by observers — a picture of regal dissatisfaction. Yet n one could divine what thoughts revolved beneath tha clouded brow, what greater honors he desired, what mor exalted heights he contemplated. For had he not onc said : "Were I God Himself, I should still want somethin more" ?

In truth only a few weeks later he did establish a foo hold in the infinite when he climbed to an almost pr latical rank, for it became the custom of bishops-elect pass before him in the ceremony of their investiture. Th we find him again in the shrine of Guadalupe before a crowd of notables lay and clerical, in the rich uniform of a general of division surrounded by kneeling aides-de-camp and flanked by the Papal Nuncio and the Primate of Mexico. As the newly made bishop knelt before this trio, the deacons handed to Santa Anna each badge and stole of episcopal rank which he kissed and handed back ere it was placed on the recipient. A gaping American present termed him "the most imposing in appearance of any person in that assemblage."

This passion for orders, ranks and uniforms became infectious; other orders and insignia were created until even the schoolmasters wore gold medals with inscriptions dignifying their position. It came to pass that all public officials had to wear uniforms suitable to their rank, from ministers, prefects, sub-prefects down to petty clerks. By special favor the Ministers were allowed yellow suits and even their lackeys were permitted to include this holy hue in their liveries. In the afternoon parade on the Viga the coachmen of these various castes disputed the right of way for their equipages and in Mass in the cathedral these bureaucrats elbowed each other for precedence before the altar.

To dissolve this confusion an official proclamation in one hundred and two articles regulated, among other affairs, the attire of members of the bureaucracy specifying everything down to the number and size of buttons, the width of the belts, the thickness of the gold borders of the uniforms of all classes from the Ministers down to the porters in the buildings. It was settled once and for all that Ministers should have the right to carry batons and be addressed as Excel-

lency. Augustinian fathers and Dominicans thereafter had
to wear white cords on their hats, and light green cords
worn over the left arm were obligatory for coachmen. If
the latter class were fortunate enough to drive the carriage
of a Minister they could leave the line in the Paseo, and
lo ! in the temple of God these cabinet worthies led all
the rest.

Culture and learning too were to be domesticated into
the official family and thus we may enjoy the picture of
Santa Anna, who boasted that he had only read one book,
and whose malapropisms and pronunciation of polysyllables
were comparable to Negro comedians', sitting in solemn conference for one whole evening with his Cabinet over the
matter of dress for the ceremony in which they were to
receive Doctors' degrees from the University. What length
the robes should be, whether the mortar boards should
have little tassels or big, whether they should be colored or
black, etc.: of such were affairs of state.

But after such labors there were relaxations. Observe
Santa Anna as he leaves the Capital for his retreat in Tacubaya, for the immense Bishop's palace where far from pious
orgies are now held to divert His Most Serene Highness.
He goes to the suburb to inspect the new Blue Room which
has just been decorated with appropriate sumptuousness at
the cost of twenty-five thousand pesos. The cortège was
headed by the Lancers of the Supreme Power, a newly
created body which rejoiced in red and white uniforms and
white-plumed helmets. Then comes white-faced Manuel
Escandón, the skinflint profiteer in a coach, and is followed
— fitting precedence — by the President in his carriage
proudly displaying the golden Cross of Angostura which

he had recently ordained to perpetuate the memory of his "victory" over Zachary Taylor; a regiment of dragoons bring up the rear. At the entrance of Tacubaya the parade passes under floral arcs, erected by the townspeople — dare they do any less? — and fifteen hundred *leperos* who have been paid a *real* apiece shout "Viva Santa Anna."

His Saint's day was solemnly celebrated. In the morning a Military band serenaded him before the Palace and at eleven, at two and at sunset salvos of artillery paid tribute. After the diplomatic corps presented their felicitations *en masse,* the plebs were given banquets and games. The *agiotistas* loaded him with presents; one gave him a collection of coins from the various nations of the world; another some fine-bred horses; another a ring; in all gifts amounting to more than a million pesos in value. Softened by these demonstrations, His Most Serene Highness pardoned a few criminals and made some promotions in the army and bureaucracy.

But while he fingered these trinkets, cholera was raging, the crops suffered a drouth, trade languished and the treasury showed a huge deficit. For with the increase in expenses to keep up this pageantry, hardly a cart wheel in the republic moved without paying a tax, not a downspout carried water from the roof of an adobe hut that did not pay for the privilege; the *alcabala,* that troublesome poll tax at city gates was renewed and many other annoying impositions. The bourgeoisie grumbled at these and the plebs specially protested against the wholesale impressments to fill the huge army quotas.

In the luxurious Italian villa of his friend Escandón in Tacubaya he had dinner one night with the American minister, Charles Gadsen, a blustering, crafty railroad promoter. As if in answer to our hero's predominant desire, the Yankee proposed that Mexico sell the United States a large tract of barren desert called the Mesilla district. The States could use it for a transcontinental railroad, while it served no purpose in Mexico. Thus began the negotiations which later resulted in the acquisition by the United States of the territory which is now southern Arizona. Santa Anna demanded $20,000,000 but under the haggling of Gadsen lowered his price to $15,000,000 without being able to close the deal. Gadsen wanted a bargain for the United States and was willing to wait, while our hero, although fidgety for money, was apprehensive about alienating any national territory, always an unpopular move in Mexico.

Meanwhile he did not hear the rumbling of discontent and went ahead with his ceremonial entertainments. On March 4th, 1854, Count Cortina gave a ball in his honor. There were floral decorations, long mirrors on the walls, gas-light chandeliers—the last word in illumination,—lancers in green uniforms forming long files in the hall and everywhere the magic letters "SS.AA.SS." signifying *Su Alteza Serenissima,* "His Most Serene Highness." Generals, officers, diplomats, ministers, mingled in well-dressed crowds while the President was attired in full military uniform. His wife, *Flor de Mexico,* in a black tunic covered with pearls was dancing with Mr. Doyle, the British minister at two A.M. when her spouse disappeared. A dusty adjutant had come to tell him that his old companion Alvarez had pronounced in the province of Guerrero.

He was greatly surprised for he had rested tranquil in the belief that all the generals were taken care of. The more dangerous *jefes* with posts abroad — Almonte at Washington, Uraga in Berlin, etc.— the less formidable ones with fat assignments in the provinces. But wretched little Alvarez, who could not conduct a cavalry charge, discontented with his position in Guerrero! It seemed incredible. However the situation looked dangerous, for however despicable Alvarez had shown himself in the war with the States, he was a formidable guerrilla fighter and besides, the liberals were reported to be concentrating in the south with their heady democratic propaganda. In view of all this he decided to leave the capital, to conduct the army himself and to crush the rebellion.

Down through the lowlands to the south he marched with ten thousand men, many gaudy uniforms, too many useless officers. At Chilpanzingo he held a review and everybody marvelled, so said the reports, at a curious incident. While His Most Serene Highness sat on his horse watching the troops, an eagle soared over the troops, circled above Santa Anna's head as if seeking to alight on his helmet, and then flew away. Dispatches of this were solemnly discussed in Mexico with appropriate superstitious comments.

But the metal eagles of his standards were to be less propitious. At Acapulco, that jewel-like port on the Pacific, where caravans to the Indies weighed anchor, Alvarez had been joined by Comonfort, the liberal who brought funds from New Orleans and New York, those nests of reported Federalists and anti-clericals. Up the slopes of San Diego Castle, swept the legions of our modern Caesar and they faltered and fell before the fire of the revolters. But the dictator had no stamina or fight in him, so after

executing a few rebel officers he retreated, his line of march
resembling the return from Buena Vista with Alvarez the
guerrillero now harassing his rear guard and flanks.
More disastrous skirmishes and a reassembling of his troops
at Chilpanzingo.

But his dispatches to the Capital were all of the most
victorious nature with announcements of captures, holo-
causts of rebels, etc., and when he reached Mexico City the
triumphal arcs were all waiting for him.   Sierra y Rosso,
now a most lyrical Minister of the Treasury, who proclaimed himself Santa Anna's "Homer," compared his chief
to Xenophon and his badly trounced followers to the Ten
Thousand.   A wind storm destroyed the arcs the day after
the arrival and the superstitious gossiped that evil was in
store for the new Xenophon.   Cynics said there was no
victory.   But they were wrong.   His Most Serene Highness was celebrating a different but genuine kind of triumph, for his commissioners had just arrived from
Washington with the news that Congress had ratified the
Gadsen Purchase and the consideration was to be $10,000,-
000.   His last, his only triumph, over his old enemies, for
the crafty Yankees did not know that His Impoverished
Highness was willing to go down as low as $5,000,000, in
his desperate need of money.

But he did not boast.   In the Cathedral listening to the
Te Deum with the Cavaliers of the Order of Guadalupe
about him, he seemed older, and actually nervous.   Hardly
Serene, this Highness.   Was it for this the Archbishop ordered masses said, or was it for more "victories," or was
to modify the orgies which our hero was revelling in in
Tacubaya?   One of his prostitutes he had raised to the

virtual rank of a Maintenon, and she had the power of distributing commissions and favors. This Louisa, a woman of the lowest class, evidently fearing the downfall of Santa Anna in his campaign, left the Palace in Tacubaya with all his medals from his coat and sold them to the denizens of the slums. So *leperos* were soon adorned with the Angostura cross, beggars with the Cross of Tampico, the Order of Charles the III, and the Grand Master of Guadalupe, etc.

He became touchy about his dignity and position and displayed the most puerile jealousy of any other heroes of the moment. Herrera died and was buried with ceremony and many glowing obituaries in the papers. This excited His Serene Highness' ire and he had articles inserted in the papers attacking the record of the dead President. Colonel Yañez returned to the Capital after the successful capture of a French freebooter, Raousset, who had been operating in Sonora. He resented even this victory and the fame of Yañez who was sent away unrewarded as if he had done harm by defending the country. A Spanish poet, Zorilla, whose verses had enchanted the intelligentsia, came and was made much of in the salons, many parties being given for him. When Santa Anna noticed this he flew in a rage and sent orders through his subordinates that such parties were exciting his displeasure. So all the salons were darkened and Zorilla slunk away into oblivion.

The year 1854 passed with revolts kindled from the successful uprising in Guerrero now flaming in Michoacan, Vera Cruz and several Eastern states. Down in Oaxaca General Benito Juarez was tapping a flood of surging Indian feeling which was soon to challenge the mestizo dom-

ination so long exploited by Santa Anna. And in the same
state a young student named Porfirio Diaz joined the rebels
—an ironic beginning to a career so similar to Santa Anna's. To put down these revolts, His Serene Highness had
to draw liberally on his funds. He had need of all the
pesos he could get, for not only were the liberals threatening his power, but also Willie Walker and his filibusters
were attacking Baja California. Nevertheless he was able
to repay himself for the money he had expended in his
'47 campaign against Taylor ; he had purchased three more
haciendas, his personal fortune was well prepared if . . .

But he refused to recognize the imminence of defeat and
another exile. At first he had given savage orders to exterminate the inhabitants and burn the fields and dwellings
of all districts where revolt appeared, but this only aroused
fiercer resentment and rebellion. Still believing that the
unrest could be allayed by chicanery, he shifted his tactics.
He announced that he would allow the people to vote on
the question of the permanency of his dictatorship. But
it was a plebiscite in which the balloting was public, subject
to the interference and supervision of his partisans ; few
dared to vote against him and he was returned by a large
majority. He employed all sorts of stratagems to regain
popular favor. He consorted with the balloonist Acosta
—the Lindbergh of that day—and tried to get some re
flected popularity from him. With much ceremony he laid
a few rails of track of the first railroad in Mexico to demon
strate how readily he was supporting public and industrial
development.

But while he was making these democratic gestures he
was taking frantic steps in other directions. He commit

sioned Gutierrez Estrada, the most consistent exponent of a monarchy among Mexicans, to negotiate in foreign capitals for the naming of a European prince to the throne of the Montezumas. Distrustful as he was of the stability of his own rickety throne, he was even more so of his army, for he arranged for the raising of regiments of Swiss mercenaries.

The spring of 1854 and early summer were filled with abortive, hopeless expeditions to Michoacan and to the south and after each his forces and treasury funds dwindled. But the most significant sign of approaching dissolution appeared when Escandón began lending money to the Comonfort liberal armies at the same time as he was advancing money to Santa Anna. Heads he wins, tails he wins; the stock exchange was now betting on his defeat. Realizing now his predicament he put on a brave front, swearing that he would fight to the last, while he made secret preparations to leave the country. On August 9th he made a clever get-away without anyone suspecting where he was going and when he was well on his way to Vera Cruz, his Ministers opened a sealed envelope appointing a triumvirate as his successor. He now took that descending Calvary to the Gulf of Mexico which he had suffered so often before— but now for the last time. Before setting sail for Havana on August 16th, he issued a farewell proclamation that was almost feeble in its inanity and lack of color. He announced that he was leaving Mexico "until order which seemed to have suffered in some way should be restored."

There is a weariness in these last words as of an admission of failure, as if this, his eleventh sojourn in the Presidential chair (counting all his pro-tem terms) had finally dis-

couraged him. Politically, indeed, this last régime of his
was a striking failure. To topple from the exalted throne
of His Most Serene Highness to the level of a fugitive, fleeing like a felon to an outgoing vessel, has a marked dramatic quality. For he had commenced eighteen months
before with the support of all the strongest cliques and
parties, had drawn to his train the most able administrators
in the country, had filled his treasury with the revitalizing
American dollar, had all the chances to wave his scepter not
histrionically, but in earnest, to anticipate Porfirio Diaz by
thirty years — yet here we find him hobbling off in a panic
from a debacle which was largely of his own making.

For in spite of the few positive reforms which he had
sponsored, he had genuinely failed in his rôle as Dictator ;
he had been unable to keep the country in peace, by the
iron hand or by conciliation, by fair means or foul, in short
to stifle thoroughly the chronic chaos which had been the
blight of all well-meaning reforms. Unlike General Rosas
of Argentina who had with bloodthirsty fervor beaten down
all the *caudillos* who threatened to reduce the southern republic to a state of shameful disintegration, he had not
made himself, for all his gaudy titles, the master of the
army. His Pretorians, faithful while the money flowed
and while sternly watched, were inherently treacherous,
and were ready to respond recklessly to the same Caesarian
ambitions which had moved himself. Santa Anna could
admirably form conspiracies, engineer *pronunciamientos*
"reach" this general, persuade that, but he could not inspire
respect, loyalty, or what was of prime importance in his
métier — fear.

Nor were the roots of his transitory power strongly im

bedded in the soil of the people. Rosas of the La Plata republic had the enthusiastic support of his *gauchos,* who felt that he was one of them, who recognized in his utterances the accents of the cowboys of the *pampas,* who respected him as the virile ideal of their own wild life. But Santa Anna was notorious for his temperamental courage, and his posturing and strutting made of him more of a freak than a bold bad hero. Hence his shifting poses, at one time fawning on the plebs with the idiom of democracy, at another drooping autocratically on his ornate dais. Neither was convincing, and while for the mass of the people he figured mainly as a fantastic hobgoblin, for the more affluent classes he existed as no more than a highly suspected instrument for their own particular ends. Americans have considered him the most unmitigated villain in their history, but they forget that he was hated even more in his own country. Indeed his figure is so odious south of the Rio Grande that in a republic indiscriminately devoted to memorial statuary no work in bronze or clay rises in his honor.

But historians have been constrained to elevate a rather high pedestal for Santa Anna. Across the lurid background of the thirties and forties he was undeniably the foremost actor. No other man so fundamentally influenced, so thoroughly dominated the first decades of the Mexican Republic. He was at once the product and symbol of his times, the most able opportunist of all the adventurers of those days who strove for power, but just as incapable as any of the rest of sluicing the wild flood of unrest and disorder into some straight channel.

CHAPTER XIII

LAST AVATARS

BUT he did not tarry long in San Cristobal de la Habana. He turned his course to Turbaco again. There among the tobacco and sugar plantations which he had started, he devoted himself to good works. Never an ardent son of the Church, he made some restitution now for his former thefts by rebuilding the local Parroquia, furnishing it with altars and precious furnishings and constructing a parish house for the *cura*. He seemed content to desert the sword now not only for the plough-share but also for the pen. For it was at this time that he commenced his vain-glorious and highly unreliable memoirs. "From my earliest years, inclined to the career of arms for which I felt a true vocation—" thus he commenced with striking veracity a manuscript of interesting prevarications.

But while he reviewed his long intervention in the affairs of his unfortunate Patria, he was not unmindful of current events in Mexico. A bit bewildering the picture now, with the resolute Juarez inveighing bitterly against the Church, and really doing something about it ; the fiery-eyed Comonfort taking and attempting to carry through anti-clerical measures as if he meant them, and on the other side generals and war-lords flourishing their sabers against the godless

Contemporary Mexican cartoon of Santa Anna, his game-cock on his back, returning for the last time from exile

nsistently without de-pronouncements or backsliding.
ronouncers now knew their fate if captured was death,
ad there was no amiable bargaining between adversaries
hile their cannon blew holes in the National Palace and
ie Cathedral. Not the sort of field for a man like our
ero, yet he still had hopes.

Early in 1858, Comonfort's power was shattered and
anta Anna felt that perhaps he had a chance among the
aifting currents which would follow the Liberal leader's
ollapse. He had not many satellites left in the capital,
ith Tornel and Alamán dead, but these few urged him to
eturn and try a re-shufflle. In February of this year he
ft the villagers of Turbaco, who drew up a petition of
aanks for benefits done and a memorial asking him to
emain, and went to the Island of St. Thomas in the West
adies.

But when he arrived there he received word of Comon-
ort's fall and the accession to power of General Zuloaga,
ae of his old lieutenants, who had so far forgotten his
aaster that he won the trumped-up election by a vote of
venty-six against one for Santa Anna. Making the best
E it, the latter issued a proclamation. "Fellow citizens, I
arned with satisfaction that the execrable and perjuring
rant (Comonfort) had been ousted from his post, which
e should never have occupied. I learned also with
easure that they have created an administration which is
ader the influence of citizens distinguished in their
apacity and true patriotism. I have thanked heaven for
ae good accorded to the Mexican people and as I did not
oubt that so many illustrious citizens knew how to provide

for the necessities of the Patria I stopped here to continue my peaceable life."

He found it more interesting in St. Thomas, which was an important port of call, where innumerable nations and republics had consuls—the kind of a cosmopolitan atmosphere that an old Pretender would like. The red and white crossed ensign of the King of Denmark had flown over it for centuries of far from prosaic history. The pirate Blackbeard had made this his rendezvous and still on its headland stood the castellated walls of buildings said to have been his strongholds, for the division and preservation of his loot. But for all its Danish Governor and its mulatto and half-caste population, it was an environment far from alien to our Mexican hero. Spanish was the common tongue, and the very houses were of Hispanic design, with patios, grilled windows fronting on narrow cobblestoned streets. He might have been in old Vera Cruz so far as the climate was concerned. The flowers bloomed all year long and people fanned themselves through long siesta hours.

There has been some evidence advanced that however peaceful this retreat was, there was little tranquillity in the mind of the former Dictator of Mexico. An Englishman, Edward Gibbon Swann, who was in the Antilles at that time wrote a book called "Santa Anna's Ghost." In it he describes the General as beset by remorse for a crime of passion. According to Swann's story, Santa Anna had been very much enamoured of a Doña Juanita de Islas y Bustamente at the time of his defense of the Mexican capital against the Americans. The lady, in turn, was loved by and returned the love of a dashing young officer Don Baldomero Valdespina ; the latter's credentials as a aide to the enemy Valencia made him especially odious to Santa Anna. In a garden in Guadalupe Hidalgo, after the evacuation of the capital, Santa Anna was pressing his suit with the reluctant girl, when Don Baldomero appeared, knelt before the damsel and kissed her hand. Santa Anna, overcome by rage, drew his pistol and shot both girl and cavalier.

As this tale goes, he brooded over the deed and intelligence of his mental torment spread through the island. A Doña Manuela, in love with Santa Anna's rascally secretary, Don Sebastian, was induced to join a plot against the former President and to impersonate the shade of Doña Juanita. Several times she appeared in the night before Santa Anna and uttered ominous words which terrified the superstitious man. Finally she was unmasked by Mr. Swann and the Danish authorities. She then removed some of the fright she had caused by confessing the plot and revealing the fact that Doña Juanita had not expired from Santa Anna's bullet, but had recovered and was happily married in Mexico. Mr. Swann's book has no documentary support and is written in the lurid style of Hoffman and Eugene Sue ; little credence can be placed in it. It must remain, therefore, as but another piece of the legendary lore which surrounds the figure of Santa Anna.

According to more reliable reports, he settled back into a languorous life, writing his memoirs and watching the post from Vera Cruz. But it brought little to him. Haro was the only prominent one of his old retainers who still survived and his most interesting exploit seemed more a mimicry of, than an action in behalf of his old *jefe*. He raised the standard of revolt against the Government with a plan demanding Iturbide's son as Emperor and specifying that, if he declined the honor, Haro himself was to assume it. But Haro was defeated and left the country. New names, or names only faintly familiar to the former President, as subalterns and colonels among his armies, now loomed up as Generals and Governors. He was getting old, he sadly realized.

But the Destiny which he both praised and blamed so often was working in his behalf, but far from the plains of Anahuac. In a romantic castle on the Adriatic sea, jutting out into those blue waters with a view of neighboring Trieste — romantic enough to inspire the brush of an Arnold Boecklin — an Austrian noble was boring himself with a handsome wife and the acquisitions of years of travel. He had voyaged far,—but he still could ask "What is this Mexico they are talking about?" For in the capital of the crinoline Empire of Napoleon the III, there was much discussion of that distant and turbulent republic.

Napoleon III too was a victim of ennui — ennui with his mistresses, with his court, his unsatisfactory sparring with such statesmen as Palmerston and Bismarck, and he desired some crusade for his talents and prestige. A planting of French influence in some part of the world where the ubiquitous Union Jack had not entered, and where easy victories by French arms would stifle the unrest which the Victor Hugos and Gambettas of his country were agitating. Empress Eugenie kept a cosmopolitan court at beautiful St. Cloud and among her foreign courtiers was a young Mexican Hidalgo, charming, gracious and filled with suggestions about the need of Mexico for a foreign Prince. She liked him.

She liked less an older son of the Eagle and Serpent, called Gutierrez Estrada, but deferred to his years and experience with Mexico. He too urged that a European monarchy placed in Mexico would be its only salvation. He mentioned often the name of Santa Anna—for had he not served several times in his ministries and had ample occasion to note that the old warrior's name was a potent one when a change of régime was wanted? What was the joy of our hero when he was admitted to this intriguing, how he hastened to reply from St. Thomas whenever a letter came from France, or the beautiful Castle of Miramar where our romantic and bewhiskered prince, Archduke Ferdinand Maximilian, was priding himself that Napoleon would select him as the man to occupy the throne of the Montezumas.

It looked like another opportunity for Santa Anna, but wait. Hidalgo did not agree with Estrada and when he had the ear of Eugenie alone, he would tell her how perfidious and unreliable this Santa Anna was, and how little Estrada really knew about Mexico. He introduced to his patroness another Mexican, sleek, handsome, and of exquisite courtesy. We have seen him before, in irons with Santa Anna in Columbia, Texas, riding up the Mississippi with the defeated leader of San Jacinto on the way to see Andrew Jackson, and languishing in a jail in Mexico City while our hero rode dejectedly back from Cerro Gordo. General Almonte now, the bitter enemy of the reigning jefe of Mexico, Juarez, and a rather contemptuous adversary of our hero. Had not Santa Anna remarked condescendingly of him : "A good lad"? And would he not naturally have a scornful idea of Santa Anna's courage after the latter's conduct following the battle of San Jacinto? Besides, he wanted to play the rôle of Dictator himself and he sought this new enterprise as a stepladder for his own fortunes. Accordingly, his remarks to Eugenie were suavely damning of Santa Anna.

Thus through the years '59, '60 and '61, the letters flew thickly between St. Thomas and European capitals and watering-places. Gutierrez Estrada was loyal to his old patron and had a legitimate argument for Santa Anna's adhesion to the Monarchy, for the latter had commissioned Estrada in 1854 to make tentative discussions with royal houses about such an enterprise. Estrada's plan was to have the dilettante Maximilian declared Emperor of Mexico, after a provisional regency should be set up in the country, composed of some bishop to represent the clerical elements, of Estrada himself and of Santa Anna. Our hero was to receive a large salary and be honored with the title of Duke of Vera Cruz and Tampico, surely a tempting bauble, this last. Estrada thought a few thousand French zouaves would do this trick for the regency, but Santa Anna who knew the state of the country, urged large forces. When he received such propositions, the old chameleon found himself believing that a Republic was a pernicious thing for the Mexicans and a Monarchy the only salvation. He wrote to the Archduke Maximilian offering his service and declaring that "the overwhelming majority of the nation is longing for the restoration of the Empire of Montezuma."

By 1862 the affair was in full swing. The American Secretary of State was now far from exacting about the Monroe Doctrine since the armies were locked in struggle in Dixie, and Napoleon and Maximilian thought the time ripe to start the adventure. But Santa Anna, more cautious now with declining years, exclaimed against a mere eight thousand French troops; he insisted on more and declined to go to Vera Cruz to pave the way, on the ground of illness. Almonte leaped into the breach—promising the anxious Estrada that he would call for Santa Anna when he got the affair going in Mexico. Thus we find Almonte with French soldiers battering down the liberal defences in 1862 and having himself declared provisional head of the nation.

Santa Anna suspected the worst and corresponded furiously with Estrada, sending appeals to Maximilian protesting his loyalty. So impressed was the Archduke and new Emperor, who was on the point of going to his new Empire, that he insisted that Almonte have Santa Anna meet him when he arrived in Vera Cruz to take up his scepter. But Almonte again found a handy excuse and ere long Santa Anna felt that he would soon have no finger in the pie at all unless he went to the scene of operations himself.

Late in February he hastened from St. Thomas to Vera Cruz where he was welcomed by a polite but exacting French officer at the port who requested him to sign a statement promising to make no proclamations or political manifestations while in Mexico without consent of the government. The statement was in French and perhaps our hero did not understand it—nor perceive in this procedure a snare of Almonte's. But he had no sooner landed than he sent off to his friends in Orizaba a proclamation which he had not been able to resist writing, a perfectly loyal document, friendly and supporting the Imperial régime, but naturally parading his personality and career throughout its length. He remained a few days in Vera Cruz with his son and Gimenez, an old adjutant of his who had come from Mexico to greet him.

But on March 12th, while he was sitting in his chamber in the house of a friend recovering from an attack of dysentery and discussing plans for his trip to Mexico, two French officers appeared and placed him under arrest for violating his promise. The proclamation had been published by his zealous friends in Orizaba, and had come to the notice of Almonte. Almonte who was chief adviser to the French marshal Bazaine, saw an opportunity for ridding himself of Santa Anna and had inspired the arrest. No amount of protests from Santa Anna that he had not understood the French statement he signed, nor furious telegraphing to Almonte in the capital achieved any good. So he sadly steamed away from the shores of Vera Cruz for the fourth time an exile.

When he returned to St. Thomas he wrote a letter of fierce protest to Napoleon III whose soldiers had treated him so churlishly, but the latter, who saw the finest set of whiskers on two continents installed in the Halls of Monte- zuma without the aid of Santa Anna, ignored his squeaky remonstrances. All Santa Anna could do now was to watch the progress of the new Empire and discover reasons for hating it. In the following year, his affection for the Republic had returned with so much warmth that he issued another proclamation, assailing the monarchy and calling for the Republic. But nobody heeded. Juarez was now the leader of the anti-Imperialists and he had no use or re spect for Santa Anna. Sadly then, the old plotter returne to his autobiography and threw himself in remembrance of things past, of more glorious days, while he bided his time.

A curious encounter, a visit from a famous man, revived his hopes. In the winter of 1865-66 William H. Seward, Secretary of State in Lincoln's and then in Johnson's Cabinet, took a vacation and toured the West Indies. He stopped at the island of St. Thomas and looked it over as a prospective purchaser, for the United States was already looking with imperialist eyes at the Caribbean. But he found time for sight-seeing as well as affairs of state. He viewed the town as "a German toy village" as he somewhat clumsily put it. He found it "quaint, bizarre," gaped at the mulatto women with burdens on their heads, the profusion of fruits in the market place and at "Blackbeard's Castle." Another sight his cicerone pointed out as they walked through the town was a pleasant airy little residence overlooking the bay which he said belonged to and was occupied by ex-President Santa Anna of Mexico. Another curiosity like the "castle" and he recalled that the ex-President had sent congratulations to him on his arrival.

Accordingly, he presented himself at the door of the house and made a call on the man who had stirred the United States and Texas so deeply when the Secretary was a young politician. Our hero limped up from his table of books and manuscripts to meet the famous American with more than his usual courtesy. Seward was astonished to see this seventy-two year old veteran whose appearance suggested a man in his late fifties, and who monopolized the conversation with a description of Mexican politics, damning Maximilian for a failure, Juarez as a mere "hostler" who had forced himself ahead in politics, asseverating that

when Mexicans would unite he would be ready to sacrifice
his remaining leg for the cause.   He added craftily that he
hoped for American aid, and gave to the Secretary a copy
of his latest proclamation.   Mr. Seward graciously withdrew saying that if ever General Santa Anna was in Washington he would be pleased to see him, etc.   And he
promptly dismissed the old curio from his mind.

Not until one morning in the following May did he have
occasion to remember him, when he received a letter from
Elizabethport, N. J., from his late host recalling the recent
visit in St. Thomas and saying that he, Santa Anna, was
sending a special emissary to Washington to arrange details of a conference.   The emissary arrived and Seward
had the severe duty of telling him that he could not deal
with Santa Anna.   The emissary mentioned with surprise
and Mr. Seward heard with surprise that the General had
received a letter signed "Secretary Seward" asking him to
come to Washington to organize an expedition against
Maximilian.   Seward closed the interview assuring his
visitor that he had not written nor signed any such letter.

When the emissary returned to our hero, this denial of
Seward's came as a sad confirmation of many suspicions.
He, the old trickster, the crafty plotter, had lost a large
part of his fortune and here he was in the midst of foreigners, knowing no English and stopping in one of the
culprits' homes.   And, he ruefully reflected, it all led back
to that polite visit of Mr. Seward in St. Thomas.

Shortly after this call, the nature of which soon spread
through the international settlement's gossip clearing house
a young Colombian, a revolutionary himself in exile, came
to see our hero.   He told him about his unfortunate revo

lutionary enterprises in South America and drew from Santa Anna his plans to get help from the United States to oust Maximilian. The young man volunteered the information that he was going to the States and he offered to carry a message to Seward from Santa Anna. Santa Anna was not backward in accepting this intermediary and smiled with satisfaction some time later when this man, Mazuera, wrote him from Washington saying he had a satisfactory interview with Seward and that he was returning with an important offer from the American.

A month later he appeared in St. Thomas harbor with a ship and several other Spanish-Americans, among them an impressive and plausible gentleman named Baez who was introduced as a political refugee from Venezuela. They all spoke the same language of Santa Anna, which consisted of filibustering plans, ships, guns, and landings on the coast of Mexico. Baez offered to sell the ship which would take Santa Anna to New York where he could obtain supplies for the expedition with the aid of Seward.

Seward? Well, Mazuera promptly produced a letter purporting to be from the latter with a nicely forged signature, saying that the Congress had appropriated forty millions of dollars for the use of an expedition in Mexico, and that thirty of this sum could be used by Santa Anna. In order to get to New York our poor hero in his eagerness consented to make a down payment of 40,000 pesos on the ship. When he arrived in New York, Baez took him to his home in Elizabethport, and then leased him a house in New York for several months for the huge sum of $2000.

He was soon involved in a series of wrangles with the

owners of the ship *Georgia* who demanded further pay-
ments, and with Mazuera who claimed that he had ordered
the manufacture of rifles on Santa Anna's request. Litiga-
tion followed and ere long Santa Anna was stripped of the
greater part of his fortune, his lawyers themselves
having taken 30,000 pesos as honorarium. Still pursued
by adventurers and swindlers, he took a house on Staten
Island.

Stumping about the then very rural suburb, he found the
need of an English interpreter and secretary, and he engaged a youth named James Adams who lived nearby.
This enterprising young man observed that the General
had a peculiar habit of slicing a piece off a tropical looking
vegetable and chewing it. He found the stuff while not
exactly palatable yet elastic enough to tire the most persistent jaws. "Chicle" the General informed him was the
name of the substance, and months later when Santa Anna
departed, he bequeathed the remainder of the chicle to
young Mr. Adams. The latter experimented with it, contrived to blend it with sweetening elements and placed the
product on the market. Within a few years, he was able
to found a flourishing factory which became the famous
Adams Chewing Gum Company. Our hero had thus succeeded in making a more lasting impression on American
life by this fortuitous circumstance than by any of his campaigns in the Southwest.

When he had first landed, he had sent a handsome offer
to Romero, the Juarez representative in Washington, to
join forces with the Juarez republicans against the Empire
Romero replied rather curtly, that if Santa Anna had been
a thorough-going Imperialist he would have welcomed hi

change of opinion, but since he had been allied with the odious Clericals and Conservatives, he could not trust him. Soon the various Mexican republican clubs throughout the country were fulminating against the late Serene Highness in terms that recalled the violent pamphlets of former days in Mexico. "Resolved that we see in Santa Anna the odious tyrant, whose inclination has always been to oppress, ruin and betray us," etc.

But Santa Anna, who seems now to have relapsed into senile delusions, kept insisting to his friends that he had a treaty with Seward to facilitate a revolution against the Mexican Empire. He wrote to Seward in August saying that "while Juarez, Ortega and other republican leaders dispute among themselves" Maximilian's throne is tottering and that when it falls "the country will fall into an abysm of anarchy." He added that he was sending another emissary to Washington to see him. But Seward still refused to treat with Santa Anna.

No wonder, for Santa Anna's son had written asking if, as his father had insisted, Seward had signed a treaty with him. Seward replied in the negative, and then the young man wrote later asking him to intervene in Santa Anna's affairs as he was squandering his fortune with adventurers who played on his credulity. He mentioned a Hungarian, Naphegi, who, he asserted, tried to poison his father. Seward with charity asked Romero to go to New York and straighten the matter out. Romero declined and pointed out the moral of all this — that Santa Anna was senile and partly crazy and should be completely disregarded.

Through the winter rumors arose that Santa Anna was fitting out a filibustering expedition by sea, that he was planning to invade Mexico on the Rio Grande, that he was under control of Naphegi, and that he was trying to issue bonds on his estates in Vera Cruz State, which property Juarez had declared confiscated and which the Maximilian government had sequestered.   In December another appeal from our hero to Seward, praising the Monroe Doctrine, asking for support and proclaiming "I the founder of the Mexican Republic am ready to shed my blood to the last drop to avenge its affronts". . . "Do the inheritors of Washington wish that these desires of my heart remain without any result ?   I do not believe it."

But on June 3, 1868, just as Maximilian was being condemned to death in Querétaro by the victorious Juarez forces, Santa Anna arrived in Vera Cruz harbor surrounded by a crowd of German adventurers and filibusters announcing that he came under the protection of the United States, and that he wished to confer with the officers of the Vera Cruz garrison about forming a republic.   The garrison courteously consented to listen to his project on board Santa Anna's ship the *Virginia.*   A dozen *caudillos* sat in his cabin and silently listened while he read a flamboyant proclamation, urging them to throw off the yoke of Maximilian and form a republic.   Then one by one the officers stated quietly their refusal.   Most insisted that they were still loyal to the Empire.   Others who were not so friendly to Maximilian, said they were disgusted with Santa Anna's abrupt departure from Mexico in 1855, etc.   They finally filed out leaving our hero with neither an audience nor an army.

But he was in for more trouble.   Commander Roe of the American squadron anchored in the roads came on board the filibustering *Virginia* and insisted that the man who claimed he had the protection of the United States should pass over to the American flag-ship for questioning. Santa Anna protested vehemently but yielded. Then followed a night of virtual captivity in a cabin on the American vessel, hours of florid Latin expostulations, threats of legal action, much loose bandying of Seward's name and an hysterical refusal to eat the meal which the American courteously offered. Finally when Roe had ascertained that his troublesome guest had no credentials to support his claims, he released the captive with the warning that he could not make a landing in Vera Cruz from the ship *Virginia* which flew the American flag.

But the filibustering party had not ended their efforts yet. Apparently setting sail for another port, they turned about after dark and returned to the harbor. It was on the early morning of the 8th that they stood near the castle flashing signal lights. In vain ; no response came from their fellow conspirators on land who were evidently expected to deliver the fortress. Again at the same hour on the 9th they made another attempt, also fruitless, and not having sighted another ship which was expected from New York to aid them, they sailed away from Vera Cruz.

Still flourishing his rejected proclamation Santa Anna anchored a few days later in the harbor of Sisal near Campeche, state of Yucatan. Transposing a few terms he launched it on the somnolent little port. "Yucatecans ! Finding myself so near to you on my way to the paternal soil, I hasten to salute you, profoundly moved on contemplating the immense contrast between what we were and what we are today. You remember that in the years 1824

and 1825 I had the honor of exercising in this Peninsula
the highest military and political authority and that I received friendly demonstrations from you which I could not
forget. . . My mission among you is purely of peace and
concord. In critical times I come to offer my helpful mediation, among the disharmonious members of the family."
But the inhabitants of Sisal could not remember the years
1824 and 1825 and were only vaguely aware of the national
"disharmony" with the result that all the enlivening syllables fell flat.

But a few days later, as Santa Anna was preparing to
sail back to Havana for a new start, the drowsy commandant came to life when he read an intercepted letter
which Santa Anna had incautiously posted in the local post-
office. It was an indignant and reproachful epistle addressed to his secret agents in Vera Cruz, betraying the
details of the plot, his failure to make connections at the
castle and his plan to make a new attempt after visiting
Havana. Hastily boarding the *Virginia* with a body of
soldiers, the commandant sternly "invited" Santa Anna to
come ashore with him. The old General, invoking the
protection of the American flag and protesting loudly,
found that he had to yield before the bayonets of the soldiers ; he disembarked accompanied by his faithful secretary and adulating Boswell, Luis Vidal y Rivas. After a
few days of incarceration in Sisal, the captives were sent to
Campeche where Santa Anna complained bitterly on being
driven like a felon through the streets of this city which he
had ruled as Governor some forty years before.

But he was placed in prison and stayed there for two
months. Little did he know that his forcible extraction

from an American vessel had stirred up a storm in the
United States, that this affair had brought to his aid Congressmen and Senators indignant that the American flag
had thus been flaunted.   Protests rained in on Seward who
insisted that he awaited definite information from Yucatan.
But now that Mexico was again in revolution, authentic
information was hard to get.

New York papers published scare-heads that Santa Anna
had been executed and this report, together with Maximilian's late execution in Querétaro, inspired editorial
writers to moralize liberally.   The austere *Times* and
Herald deplored it all but took the view that Santa Anna
had met the inevitable fate of adventurers.   But the *Express*
of the same city, intent on proving its independence of out-
look, and incidentally betraying the proverbial tenderness
of American democrats toward European royalty, wept
tears over both Santa Anna and the martyr of Querétaro.
"The worst fears of the friends of Santa Anna have finally
been realized.   The same fate which befell the unfortunate
Prince Maximilian a few weeks ago has also overtaken the
ex-dictator.   In truth it appears that the mestizo, creole (sic)
Indian Benito Juarez is of the same mould as those who do
not hold the least sample in 'dirtying themselves to gain a
throne,' closing the doors of mercy to humanity.   He could
have done better to pardon Santa Anna, letting the poor old
man return as a proof that even a Mexican President is not
a monster of cruelty as has generally been believed in view
of the assassination of Prince Maximilian."   It should be
noticed that ultra republican America with its notorious
weakness for European nobility, was profoundly moved
over the Emperor's execution.

A hot summer the old man spent in the prison of Campeche and in the fall when Juarez got around to it, he had Santa Anna transferred to the dungeon of San Juan Ulloa at Vera Cruz where he waited a few more months. Finally in October 1867, he was remanded for trial and had to stand before a military court and answer for his plottings with Estrada and Maximilian. He stoutly denied writing any incriminating letters to these personages and defiantly stated that "my zealous works of the past epoch will be better known and esteemed when those of these defamers will be depreciated." The tribunal sentenced him to eight years more of exile. On the 1st of November, for the fifth time, he boarded an English packet leaving Vera Cruz, for exile.

He stopped off at Havana, but was requested to leave that city by the commandant, Gen. Lizurdi ; on the instance of Seward and Juarez, the old man in his bewildered senility claimed. And he took vessel for the Bahamas where he settled down in Nassau to continue to write the later and most inglorious chapters of his autobiography. With the resentment and rancors of an aging man, he vented his hatred on Juarez, and wrote and had printed a pamphlet attacking the "aborigine." Its furious accents were prefaced by a pitiful exordium — the old man showing his "medals." "PROTEST. Antonio Lopez de Santa Anna, General of division : Benemerito of the Patria, Ex President of the Mexican Republic, Grand Master of the national and distinguished order of Guadalupe ; Grand Cross of Charles II of Spain and of the Red Eagle of Prussia. Decorated with crosses and honorary plaques for actions in war, etc etc. . . In the sad but tranquil isle of 'New Providence here where the infuriated passions of an oppressive party, etc."

In 1874 the ban of exile was removed and he returned to Mexico. But no guns boomed from San Juan Ulloa as he landed ; a few friends met and escorted him not to a fine coach bound for Manga de Clavo, but to a railroad "Car" which rolled him past his old hacienda where, alas, a stranger now slept. He was met by his family and some old soldiers, among them the faithful adjutant Gimenez, at the station in Mexico City, and went to his home in the Calle de Vergara. There he held a sorry court with octogenarians and broken-down generals coming to pay him visits.

As befitted a former President of the Republic, he wrote to the incumbent of that office, one whom he had never known, Sebastian Lerdo, asking for an appointment. The President subtly put him off by insisting that to climb the National Palace steps would be too much of a task for the ex-President because of his mutilated leg, and suggested that Santa Anna should wait until he, Lerdo, should pay a call at the house in the Calle Vergara. But Santa Anna waited and waited ; Lerdo did not come.

The rest of the government and the press were not so kind. On the curious basis that national defeats are an occasion for anniversaries, the government celebrated the battle of Churubusco on the site itself with speeches and reviews of troops. But it issued no invitation to attend to the ex-President who had commanded the Mexican forces so creditably there. Aggrieved, he wrote his reminiscences of the battle for a newspaper, but the Republican organs ridiculed it and others with even less charity reprinted our

hero's correspondence with Estrada regarding Maximilian's
projected Empire—which hurt still more. He talked
about leaving ungrateful and spiteful Mexico. But he had
no money, living on the bounty of his son-in-law, for the
Government steadfastly refused him a pension. Finally
Escandón, the famous profiteer, died and left him fourteen
thousand pesos. But even with this windfall, he stayed on
in Mexico, perhaps from sheer fatigue of age.

What a touching picture his friend Gimenez paints, of
the former President visiting the shrine of Guadalupe.
After all he had been faithful to this, the patron Virgin of
Mexico, in his fashion, for had he not favored her above the
gachupin Virgin of the Remedies? And had he not
named one of his illegitimate daughters Guadalupe? An
abbé led him up to the high altar, opened the glass door
and allowed him to kiss the sacred picture. Turning he
surveyed this famous nave where in former days he had so
often walked in splendor, with no less than a mitred Archbishop escorting him—on the occasion of a victory imagined or real, on his Saint's day, on the anniversary of the
loss of his leg, on the parade of the Order of Guadalupe—
that time when he had sat so regally on a dais; he had
countless gaudy memories of this shrine. Finally, laboriously toiling down the steps, he hobbled out the door—just
an old man with a wooden leg.

His ills increased, his eyesight failed and complete senility
set in. The Flower of Mexico, now a shrewish middle
aged woman, gave him just enough attention to see that the
Escandón legacy was conjugally disposed of, and he died
penniless on June the 21st, 1876. Forty coaches followed
him to a modest tomb in Guadalupe cemetery.

BIBLIOGRAPHY BY CHAPTER

PROLOGUE

Bancroft, *Works,* vol. XVI; *Gazeta de Mexico* (1813); Documentos
. . . *Santa Anna*; Yoakum, *History of Texas.*

CHAPTER I

Alamán, *Historia de Mejico,* vol. IV; Alvarez, *Santa Anna hasta* 1822;
Bancroft, *Works,* vol. XII; Bustamente, *Cuadro Historico;* Lerdo de
Tejada, *Apuntes . . . Vera Cruz;* Poinsett, *Notes on Mexico;* Rivera
Cambas, *Gobernantes, Historia de Jalapa;* Robertson, *Rise of the Spanish-
American Republics;* Santa Anna, *Mi Historia.*

CHAPTER II

Ancona, *Historia de Yucatan;* Bancroft, *Works,* vol. XII; Bazancourt,
Le Mexique Contemporain; Beltrami, *Le Mexique;* Löwenstern, *Le
Mexique;* Muro, *Miscelanea Potosina;* Fayette Robinson, *Mexico and Her
Military Chieftains;* Santa Anna, *Mi Historia;* J. H. Smith, *Poinsett's
Career in Mexico,* American Antiquarian Society *Proceedings,* vol. XXIV;
Suarez y Novarro, *Historia . . . Santa Anna.*

CHAPTER III

Bancroft, *Works,* vol. XIII; Bulnes, *Grandes Mentiras;* Bustamente,
Voz de la Patria; Callcott, *Church and State in Mexico;* Mirabeau Lamar,
Biography of Santa Anna; Lerdo de Tejada, *Apuntes;* Prieto, *Memorias;*
Rivera Cambas, *Historia de Jalapa;* Santa Anna, *Mi Historia, Cor-
respondencia;* Tudor, *Tour;* Zamacois, *Historia de Mejico.*

CHAPTER IV

Castañeda, *Mexican Side of Texas Revolution;* Chabot, *Alamo;* Ford's Memoirs; *N. Y. Herald,* June 22-30, 1836; Villa-Amor, *Biografia de Santa Anna;* Williams, *Alamo.*

CHAPTER V

Bulnes, *Grandes Mentiras;* Castañeda, *Mexican Side of Texas Revolution;* James, *The Raven; N. Y. Herald,* June 22-30, 1836; Raines, *Life of Santa Anna;* Santa Anna, *Manifiesto; Southwest Historical Quarterly,* vols. VI, XXVI; Texas Folk-lore Society, vol. VI; Wharton, *San Jacinto.*

CHAPTER VI

American Historical Association, *Report,* vol. II, part 1, 1907; Bustamente, *Gabinete;* Castañeda, *Mexican Side of Texas Revolution;* James, *The Raven;* Raines, *Life of Santa Anna;* Santa Anna, *Manifiesto.*

CHAPTER VII

Blanchard, *San Juan de Ulua;* Bustamente, *Gabinete, Apuntes;* Calderón de la Barca, *Life in Mexico;* Farragut, *Farragut;* Fossey, *Le Mexique;* Gilliam, *Travels;* Gomez Farías, Correspondencia; Löwenstern, *Le Mexique;* Mason, *Life in Mexico;* Mayer, *Mexico As It Was and Is;* Paredes, Correspondencia; Prieto, *Memorias;* Riva Palacio, Correspondencia; Santa Anna, Documentos.

CHAPTER VIII

Bancroft, *Works,* vol. XIII; Bustamente, *Apuntes;* Calderón de la Barca, *Life in Mexico;* Callcott, *Church and State in Mexico;* Fossey *Le Mexique;* Gilliam, *Travels;* Lowell, *Bigelow Papers;* Mayer, *Mexic As It Was and Is;* Prieto, *Memorias;* Rivera Cambas, *Historia de Jalapa* Sierra y Rosso, *Discurso.*

CHAPTER IX

Balbontin, *Invasion;* Bancroft, *Works,* vol. XIII; *Brother Jonatha Great Pictorial Battle Sheet;* Bustamente, *Nuevo Bernal Diaz;* Gimene *Memorias;* Gomez Farías, Correspondencia; Kenly, *Maryland Volu teer;* Lerdo de Tejada, *Apuntes;* Monitor Republicano; Muro, *Miscelanea;* Negrete, *Invasion;* "Prisoner A," *Encarnacion Prisoners;* Ramirez, *Memorias;* Rivera Cambas, *Jalapa, Gobernantes;* Roa Bárcena, *Recuerdos;* Santa Anna, Documentos; Semmes, *Afloat and Ashore;* Smith, *War with Mexico;* Taylor, *Broad Pennant;* Truxton, *Adventures;* Stevens, *Stevens;* Webb, *Texas Rangers;* Polk Papers.

CHAPTER X

Balbontin, *Invasion;* Ballentine, *English Soldier;* Bustamente, *Nuevo Bernal Diaz;* Carreño, *Jefes;* Colcord, *Roll and Go;* Cuevas, *Historia de la Iglesia;* Gamboa, *Impugnacion;* Latrobe, *Rambler;* Negrete, *Invasion;* Prieto, *Memorias;* Tudor, *Tour;* Rivera Cambas, *Jalapa;* Rives, *United States and Mexico;* Ruxton, *Adventures;* Roa Bárcena, *Recuerdos;* Semmes, *Afloat and Ashore;* Smith, *War with Mexico.*

CHAPTER XI

Brother Jonathan . . . Battle Sheet; Cuevas, *Historia de la Iglesia;* Ford's Memoirs; Kenly, *Maryland Volunteer;* Riva Palacio, *Mexico á Traves de Los Siglos;* Rives, *U. S. and Mexico;* Smith, *War with Mexico.*

CHAPTER XII

Portilla, *Historia de la Revolucion Contra . . . Santa Anna;* Prieto, *Memorias;* Rippy, *United States and Mexico;* Salado Alvarez, *De Santa Anna a la Reforma;* Sierra, *Mexico;* Vidal y Rivas, *Biographie;* Wilson, *Mexico and Its Religion;* Zamacois, *Historia.*

CHAPTER XIII

Secretaria de Relaciones Exteriores, *Correspondencia;* Bancroft, *Works,* vol. XIV; Corti, *Maximilian and Charlotte; Fortune,* May, 1931; Gimenez, *Memorias;* Santa Anna, *Mi Historia;* Seward, *Autobiography.*

BIBLIOGRAPHY

SOURCES: DOCUMENTS, LETTERS, MANUSCRIPTS, ETC.

Alamán, Lucas. *Archivo de Don Lucas Alaman.*

American Historical Association. *Annual Report,* vol. II, part 1. Washington, 1907.

American Antiquarian Society. *Proceedings,* vol. XXIV. Worcester, Mass., 1914.

Ford, John S. *Memoirs of John S. Ford* (transcript, Univ. of Texas papers).

Gomez Farías, Valentin. *Correspondencia.* 1821-1855.

Lamar, Mirabeau. *Life of Santa Anna* (transcript, Univ. of Texas papers).

Paredes y Arrillaga, Mariano. *Correspondencia.* 1825-1846.

Polk, James K. *Papers.* Library of Congress.

Riva Palacio, Mariano. *Correspondencia.* 1830-1880.
Miscellanea. 1716-1867.

Riva Palacio, Vicente. *Correspondencia.* 1858-1896.

Santa Anna, Antonio Lopez de. *Documentos relativos a Don Antonio Lopez de Santa Anna.* 1825-1876.
Mi Historia Militar y Politica. 1810-1874, Memorias Ineditas. (Manuscript in Genero Garcia Collection, University of Texas.)

Secretaria de Relaciones Exteriores. *Correspondencia de la legación mexicana en Washington durante la intervencion extranjera,* 1860-1868. *Coleccion de documentos para formar la historia de la intervencion.* 10 vols. Mexico, 1870-1892.

United States Department of State. Archives. Correspondence with consular agents in Mexico.

NEWSPAPERS, PERIODICALS, ETC.

Brother Jonathan Great Pictorial Battle Sheet. New York, 1847.

El Cosmopolita. Mexico, 1838-1841.

Fortune. New York. May 1932.

Gazeta de Mexico. Mexico, 1810-1815.

La Lima de Vulcano. Mexico, 1838-1840.
El Monitor Republicano. Mexico, 1843-1845.
El Mosquito Mexicano. Mexico, 1834-1843.
New York Herald. 1836-1837.
New York Post. 1836-1837.
Southwestern Historical Quarterly. Austin, Texas, 1923.
Texas Magazine. Vols. I-IV. 1896-1897.

SECONDARY WORKS, CONTEMPORARY ACCOUNTS, PAMPHLETS, ETC.

Alamán, Lucas. *Historia de Mejico.* 5 vols. Mexico, 1849-1852.
Alvarez, Francisco de Paula. *Santa Anna hasta 1822.* Guadalajara, 1844.
Ancona, Eligio. *Historia de Yucatan.* 5 vols. Merida, Mexico, 1878-1905.
Balbontín, Manuel. *La Invasion Americana.* Mexico, 1883.
Ballentine, George. *Autobiography of an English Soldier in the United States Army.* London, 1853.
Bancroft, Hubert Howe. *Works.* San Francisco, 1882-90.
Bazancourt, César Lecat. *Le Mexique Contemporain.* Paris, 1862.
Beltrami, G. C. *Le Mexique.* 2 vols. Paris, 1830.
Blanchard, P. *San Juan de Ulua.* Paris, 1839.
Bulnes, Francisco. *Las Grandes Mentiras de Nuestra Historia.* Mexico, 1804.
Bustamente, C. M. de. *Apuntes para la Historia de . . . Santa Anna.* Mexico, 1845.
   Cuadro Historico de la Revolución Mexicana. 5 vols. Mexico, 1843-1846.
   Gabinete Mexicano, etc. 2 vols. in one. Mexico, 1842.
   Nuevo Bernal Diaz del Castillo, etc. Mexico, 1847.
   Voz de la Patria (editor). Mexico, 1828-1831.
Calderón de la Barca, F. E. *Life in Mexico.* New York, n.d.
Callcott, Wilfrid Hardy. *Church and State in Mexico.* 1822-1857. Durham, N. C. 1926.
Carreño, Alberto Maria. *Jefes del Ejercito Mexicano en 1847.* Mexico, 1914.
Castañeda, Carlos E. (Editor). *The Mexican Side of Texas Revolution by the chief Mexican participants: General Antonio Lopez de Santa Anna, D. Ramon Martinez Caro, General Vicente Filisola, General Jose Urrea, General Jose Maria Tornel . . .* translated by Carlos E. Castenada. Dallas, Texas, 1928.

Chabot, Frederick C. *Alamo, Altar of Texas Liberty.* San Antonio, Texas, 1931.

Colcord, J. C. Comp. *Roll and Go.* Indianapolis, 1924.

Corti, Egon C. *Maximilian and Charlotte of Mexico.* 2 vols. New York, 1928.

Cuevas, Mariano. *Historia de la Iglesia en Mexico.* 4 vols. El Paso, Texas.

Escudero, J. A. *Memorias.* Mexico, 1848.

Farragut, Loyall. *D. A. Farragut.* New York, 1879.

Ferry, G. *Revolutions du Mexique.* Paris, 1864.

Fossey, M. de. *Le Mexique.* Paris, 1857.

Gamboa, Ramon. *Impugnacion al Informa del Señor Gen. Santa Anna.* Mexico, 1849.

Gilliam, Albert M. *Travels in . . . Mexico.* Philadelphia, 1846.

Gimenez, M. M. *Memorias.* Mexico, 1911.

Gruening, Ernest H. *Mexico and Its Heritage.* New York, 1928.

James, Marquis. *The Raven, a Biography of Sam Houston.* Indianapolis, 1929.

Kenly, G. F. *Memoirs of a Maryland Volunteer.* Philadelphia, 1873.

Latrobe, C. J. *The Rambler in Mexico.* London, 1836.

Lerdo de Tejada, M. M. *Apuntes historicos de . . . Vera Cruz.* 3 vols. Mexico, 1850-1858.

Lowell, J. R. *Biglow Papers.* Boston, 1886.

Löwenstern, I. *Le Mexique.* Paris, 1843.

Mason, R. H. *Life in Mexico.* London, 1852.

Mayer, Brantz. *Mexico As It Was and Is.* New York, 1844.

Muro, Manuel. *Miscelánea Potosina.* San Luis Potosi, Mexico, 1903.

Negrete, E. del Castillo. *Invasion de los Norte-Americanos, etc.* 6 vols. Mexico, 1890-1891.

Poinsett, J. R. *Notes on Mexico.* London, 1825.

Portilla, A. de la. *Historia de la Revolución . . . contra . . . Santa Anna 1853-1855.* Mexico, 1856.

Powell, Willis S. *Brief Sketch of the Life of Santa Anna.* St. Louis, 1844.

Prieto, Guillermo. *Memorias.* Mexico, 1906.

"Prisoner A." *Encarnacion Prisoners.* Louisville, 1848.

Priestley, Herbert I. *The Mexican Nation.* New York, 1923.

Raines, C. W. *Life of Antonio Lopez de Santa Anna.* (In *Texas Magazine,* Vols. 1-4.)

Ramirez, J. F. *Memorias, etc.* Mexico, 1853.

Rippy, J. Fred. *The United States and Mexico.* New York, 1926.

Riva Palacio, Vicente. *Mexico, a Traves de Los Siglos.* 5 vols. Barcelona, 1889.

Rivera Cambas, Manuel. *Gobernantes de Mexico.* 2 vols. Mexico, 1873. *Historia . . . de Jalapa, etc.* 5 vols. Mexico, 1869-1871.

Rives, G. L. *The United States and Mexico.* 2 vols. New York, 1913.

Roa Bárcena, J. M. *Recuerdos.* 2 vols. Mexico, 1901.

Robertson, W. S. *Rise of the Spanish-American Republics.* New York, 1918.

Robinson, Fayette. *Mexico and Her Military Chieftains.* Hartford, 1851.

Salado Alvarez, V. *De Santa Anna a la Reforma.* Mexico, 1902-1903.

Santa Anna, Antonio Lopez de. *Mi Historia Militar y Politica.* Mexico, 1905.

Sedgwick, John. *Correspondence.* [N. Y.] 1902-1903.

Semmes, Raphael. *Service Afloat and Ashore.* Cincinnati, 1851.

Seward, W. R. *Autobiography.* New York, 1877.

Sierra, Justo, Editor. *Mexico: Its Social Evolution.* Mexico, 1900-1904.

Sierra y Rosso, Ignacio. *Discurso que pronuncio . . . Sierra y Rosso, en la Colocacion en Sta. Paula del Pie que Perdio en Vera Cruz . . . Santa Anna.* Mexico, 1851.

Smith, Justin Harvey. *The War with Mexico.* New York, 1919.

Stapp, W. P. *Prisoners of Perote.* Philadelphia, 1845.

Stevens, H. *I. I. Stevens.* 2 vols. Boston, 1900.

Suarez y Novarro, Juan. *Historia de Mexico y del General . . . Santa Anna.* Mexico, 1851.

Swann, Edward Gibbon. *Santa Anna's Ghost.* Sussex Hall, England, 1894.

Taylor, F. W. *The Broad Pennant.* New York, 1848.

Thompson, Waddy. *Recollections.* New York, 1846.

Truxton, G. F. *Adventures in Mexico.* New York, 1915.

Tudor, Henry. *Tour in North America.* London, 1834.

Vidal y Rivas, Luis G. de. *Biographie du . . . Santa Anna.* Paris, 1863.

Villa-Amor, M. *Biografia del General Santa Anna.* Mexico, 1857.

Webb, Walter Prescott. "The Texas Rangers in the Mexican War." M.A. Thesis, University of Texas, 1920.

Wharton, Clarence. *El Presidente.* Austin, Texas [1926]. *San Jacinto.* Houston, Texas, 1930.

Williams, Amelia. "A Critical Study of the Siege of the Alamo." Ph.D. Thesis, University of Texas, 1931.

Wilson, Robert A. *Mexico and Its Religions.* New York, 1855.

Yoakum, H. K. *History of Texas.* Redfield, N. Y., 1856.

Zamacois, Niceto de. *Historia de Mejico.* 23 vols. Mexico, 1878-1903.

MEXICAN PRESIDENTS FROM THE ESTABLISHMENT OF THE REPUBLIC TO THE LAST TERM OF SANTA ANNA

Oct. 10, 1824–Apr. 1, 1829, Guadalupe Victoria.

Apr. 1, 1829–Dec. 18, 1829, Vicente Guerrero.

Dec. 18, 1829–Dec. 23, 1829, José Maria Bocanegra, ad interim.

Dec. 23, 1829–Dec. 31, 1829, Pedro Velez, Luis Quintana, Lucas Alamán, Provisional Government.

Dec. 31, 1829–Aug. 14, 1832, A. Bustamente.

Aug. 14, 1832–Dec. 24, 1832, Melchor Musquiz, ad interim.

Dec. 24, 1832–Apr. 1, 1833, M. Gomez Pedraza.

Apr. 1, 1833–May 16, 1833, Valentín Gomez Farias, acting.

May 16, 1833–June 3, 1833, A. Lopez de Santa Anna.

June 3, 1833–June 18, 1833, V. Gomez Farias, acting.

June 18, 1833–July 5, 1833, A. Lopez de Santa Anna.

July 5, 1833–Oct. 27, 1833, V. Gomez Farias, acting.

Oct. 27, 1833–Dec. 15, 1833, A. Lopez de Santa Anna.

Dec. 16, 1833–Apr. 24, 1834, V. Gomez Farias, acting.

Apr. 24, 1834–Jan. 28, 1835, A. Lopez de Santa Anna.

Jan. 28, 1835–Feb. 27, 1836, M. Barragán.

Feb. 27, 1836–Apr. 19, 1837, José Justo Corro.

Apr. 19, 1837–Mar. 18, 1839, A. Bustamente.

Mar. 18, 1839–July 10, 1839, A. Lopez de Santa Anna.

July 10, 1839–July 17, 1839, N. Bravo.

July 17, 1839–Sept. 22, 1841, A. Bustamente.

Sept. 22, 1841–Oct. 10, 1841, J. Echeverria.

Oct. 10, 1841–Oct. 26, 1842, A. Lopez de Santa Anna.

Oct. 26, 1842–Mar. 5, 1843, N. Bravo, substitute.

Mar. 5, 1843–Oct. 4, 1843, A. Lopez de Santa Anna.

Oct. 4, 1843–June 4, 1844, V. Canalizo.

June 4, 1844–Sept. 20, 1844, A. Lopez de Santa Anna.

Sept. 20, 1844–Dec. 6, 1844, V. Canalizo.

Dec. 6, 1844–Dec. 30, 1845, José Joaquín de Herrera.

Jan. 4, 1846–July 28, 1846, M. Paredes y Arrillaga.

July 29, 1846–Aug. 4, 1846, N. Bravo.

Aug. 5, 1846–Dec. 23, 1846, Mariano Salas.

Dec. 23, 1846–Mar. 21, 1847, V. Gomez Farias, acting.

Mar. 21, 1847–Apr. 2, 1847, A. Lopez de Santa Anna.

Apr. 2, 1847–May 20, 1847, Pedro Maria Anaya, substitute.

May 20, 1847–Sept. 16, 1847, A. Lopez de Santa Anna.

Sept. 20, 1847–Nov. 13, 1847, M. de la Peña y Peña.

Nov. 13, 1847–Jan. 8, 1848, Pedro Maria Anaya.

Jan. 8, 1848–June 3, 1848, M. de la Peña y Peña.

June 3, 1848–Jan. 15, 1851, J. de Herrera.

Jan. 15, 1851–Jan. 6, 1853, Mariano Arista.

Jan. 6, 1853-Feb. 7, 1853, Juan de Ceballos.

Feb. 7, 1853–Apr. 20, 1853, Manuel de Lombardini.

Apr. 20, 1853–Aug. 12, 1855, A. Lopez de Santa Anna.

INDEX